The Spectator and the Topographical City

A John D. S. and Aida C. Truxall Book

THE SPECTATOR AND THE TOPOGRAPHICAL CITY

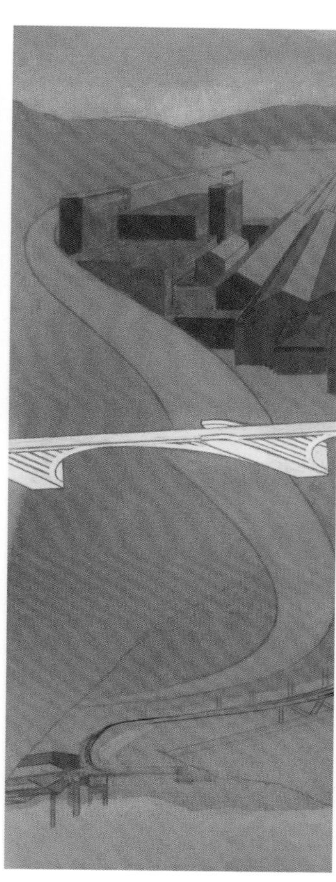
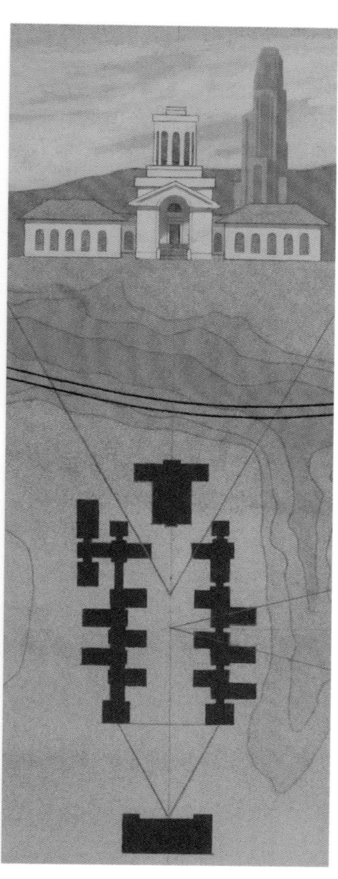

Martin Aurand

UNIVERSITY OF PITTSBURGH PRESS

This publication is supported by a grant from The Graham Foundation for Advanced Studies in the Fine Arts.

Published by the University of Pittsburgh Press, Pittsburgh PA 15260

Manufactured in Canada
Printed on acid-free paper
10 9 8 7 6 5 4 3 2 1

LIBRARY OF CONGRESS CATALOGING-IN-PUBLICATION DATA
Aurand, Martin.
The spectator and the topographical city / Martin Aurand.
p. cm.
Includes bibliographical references and index.
ISBN 0-8229-4288-7 (cloth : alk. paper)
1. Human ecology—Pennsylvania—Pittsburgh. 2. Urban ecology—Pennsylvania—Pittsburgh. I. Title.
GF504.P46A87 2006
304.2'30974886--dc22

2006015779

The first fact of architecture
is the topography of a place and the
way that human beings respond to it
with their own constructed forms.

Vincent Scully, *Architecture:
The Natural and the Manmade*

Contents

Preface

The most provocative urban studies are those that address the physical environment of a city in unconventional and uncompromising ways; studies in which the author establishes a point of view and parameters for analysis that are rooted in his or her experience of a city and its inherent qualities. Such studies have different agendas, assume various conceptual forms, and display multiple modes of expression. Their common aspiration, however, is to get inside the physical city and explore its essence; what Florence Lipsky calls the "fundamental figure" that dictates a city's urban morphology.[1]

Nearly any city could provoke such a study. I have come to see how Pittsburgh *deserves* such a study. Travel to Italy, where architecture and landscape have been intertwined for centuries, and in the Pacific Northwest, where volcanic mountains hover constantly in your field of vision, helped me to see Pittsburgh in a new way.

Human occupation in general, and cities in particular, are commonly seen to impose upon the land. In Pittsburgh, under the extreme conditions of rapid industrialization, the land was written off as ruined as early as the mid-nineteenth century. Yet, despite the despoilments of industry, the density and reach of urban development, and the dominating stance of contemporary skyscrapers, the land remains, and arguably has the upper hand.[2]

While Pittsburgh was, for a time, the quintessential industrial city, it was always and is today the quintessential topographical city. It is among those cities that, in the words of Spiro Kostof, "respond so fatefully to the sculpture of the land that it is impossible to isolate the urban experience from earth-induced affects."[3] The land generates its own history, and the built environment—whether by design, intuition, or coincidence—is an act of topographical response.

Pittsburgh stands at the intersection of land and city, landscape and architecture, the natural and the man-made; yet this dichotomy has been little acknowledged. Written works about Pittsburgh frequently start with a few paragraphs in praise of the terrain—and then move on to other topics at hand.

That Pittsburgh has been slow to remark its fundamental figure is a by-product of the city's 150-year romance with industry. Yet Pittsburgh is not alone in this, for modern writers and designers have commonly failed to explore the intersection of the land and the city. A synthesis that had prevailed for centuries was broken when landscape and architecture emerged as separate disciplines in the eighteenth century, and the intersection of these disciplines has been insufficiently explored ever since.[4]

It is the land that is usually overlooked. As William Rees Morrish observes, "earth and mountain have lost their power to evoke civic action to join with the geomorphic landforms to construct a collaborative terrain. . . . We have lost contact with the earth."[5] Yet Pittsburgh is a collaborative terrain. Despite its famous ills, and often unknowingly, it has never lost contact with the earth. Today Pittsburgh displays a growing awareness of its fundamental topographical figure as a generator of urban history and a framework for contemporary life.[6]

Our experience of the land and the city is closely associated with images. Pittsburgh's topographical space is pictorial space. Gina Crandell defines the pictorial as elements of unity, balance, distance, and elevation that capture the glance of the spectator. Pictorial space "favors, freezes, and frames particular views, or pictures, of the landscape."[7]

The role of landscape in our culture, as it has emerged since the eighteenth century through landscape design, landscape painting, and the romanticism of nature, has left us unable to talk about or look at landscape without conjuring up pictures. Equally, the axial-view corridors of the urban street grid and urban open spaces such as public squares make the city an inherently pictorial place.[8] Images of the city and its buildings have been widely recorded and popularized since the nineteenth century through bird's-eye views and picture postcards, photographs and films. Consequently, suggests M. Christine Boyer, "merely looking at architecture and urban space for their visual excitement . . . became a spectator habit."[9]

Pittsburgh amplifies these tendencies. The countless vantage points of the topographical city encourage an active perception of its visual qualities. In Pittsburgh, everyone is a spectator.

Like Pittsburgh itself, the current study is an act of topographical response. It is a chronicle of the engagement of the land and the city, and it records the spectator's perceptual experience in this place.

A number of key books have contributed significantly to the conceptual shape of this study including: William R. Morrish's *Civilizing Terrains: Mountains, Mounds and Mesas* (Los Angeles: Design Center for American Urban Landscape, 1989; rev. ed., San Francisco: William Stout Publishers, 1996); Paul Shepheard's *The Cultivated Wilderness, or, What is Landscape?* (Cambridge, Mass.: MIT Press, 1997); David E. Nye's *American Technological Sublime* (Cambridge, Mass.: MIT Press, 1994); Vincent Scully's *Architecture: The Natural and the Manmade* (New York: St. Martin's Press, 1991); and Clemens Steenbergen and Wouter Reh's *Architecture and Landscape: The Design Experiment of the Great European Gardens and Landscapes* (New York: Prestel, 1996; rev. ed., Basel and Boston: Birkhäuser, 2003).

Instructive models for this sort of idiosyncratic urban study have included Reyner Banham's *Los Angeles: The Architecture of Four Ecologies* (New York: Harper and Row, 1971; reprint, Berkeley: University of California Press, 2001); Rem Koolhaas's *Delirious New York: A Retroactive Manifesto for Manhattan* (New York: Oxford University Press, 1978; reprint, New York: Monacelli Press, 1994); and Florence Lipsky's *San Francisco: la grille sur les collines = The Grid Meets the Hills* (Marseille: Parenthèses, 1999).

Like all who explore Pittsburgh's built environment, I am greatly indebted to the chroniclers of Pittsburgh architecture. Historians and writers James D. Van Trump, Walter C. Kidney, and Franklin Toker have studied Pittsburgh from the scale of the building to the scale of the metropolis, and have turned many a memorable literary phrase.

Their work is cited repeatedly throughout this study. Kidney's article, "Pittsburgh: A Study in Urban Identity," *Progressive Architecture* 49, no. 3 (March 1968), 116–27, was especially revelatory for my purposes.

My special appreciation goes to Barry Hannegan, Edward K. Muller, and Charles Rosenblum, who reviewed the manuscript at my request and urged it onward. Hannegan, a landscape historian, supplied an important seed for this study with his insights about Carnegie Tech that were published in the late 1950s. Years later he was the first key supporter of my work. Muller, an urban historian, who has written more than anyone else about the regional landscape, supplied academic grounding and a knowledgeable urban eye. Rosenblum, an architectural historian, sharpened my architectural thinking and enthusiastically engaged issues related to architect Henry Hornbostel.

Kenneth Kolson and Lu Donnelly reviewed the manuscript for the publisher. Their comments led to many improvements in the work. I thank Cynthia Miller, director of the University of Pittsburgh Press, for seeing the potential of this project, and senior editor Deborah Meade, production director Ann Walston, and everyone at the press who worked to make this book a reality. A grant from The Graham Foundation for Advanced Studies in the Fine Arts has enhanced the quality of the publication and its illustrations.

Thanks for their various contributions and support go to Behula Shah, Paul Tellers, Kevin Lamb, Douglas Cooper, Patricia Lowry, Gerard Damiani, Chuck Biddle, Albert Tannler, and Jack Consoli; past and present colleagues at Carnegie Mellon University Libraries, especially Henry Pisciotta, Bella Karr Gerlich, Mo Dawley, Jillian Chisnell, Jennifer Aronson, Jennie Benford, and interlibrary loan staff; Photography and Graphic Services at Mellon Institute, Carnegie Mellon University, specifically Gary Thomas, Stephen Baden, and David Little; Louise Sturgess and the Pittsburgh History and Landmarks Foundation; Gil Pietrzak and the Pennsylvania Department of the Carnegie Library of Pittsburgh; David Grinnell and the Library and Archives of the Historical Society of Western Pennsylvania; and Miriam Meislik,

Michael Dabrishus, and the Archives Service Center of the University of Pittsburgh.

Visual images are vital to this study. The illustrations reproduced here record the visions of many cartographers, photographers, artists, architects, and engineers who have lingered for a day or a lifetime in the topographical city. I am grateful to the creators, individuals, and organizations that have made these images available. Most importantly, I thank artist Clayton Merrell for creating artwork specifically for this project. His three featured illustrations contribute immensely to the character and meaning of this work.

Finally, I am grateful to Joann, my wife, and Yoshi, our dog, my companions and fellow spectators in the topographical city.

The Spectator and the Topographical City

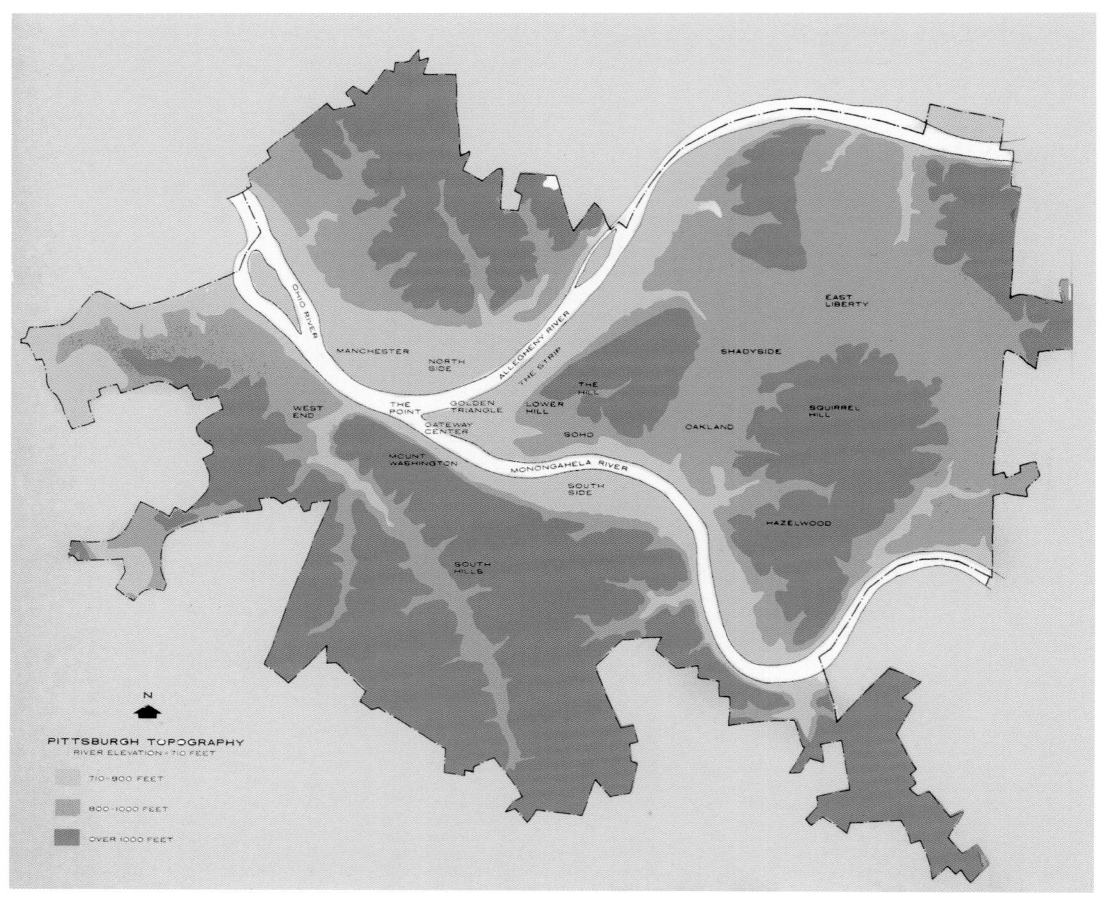

Fig. 1. *Pittsburgh Topography.* Reprinted from Walter C. Kidney, "Pittsburgh: A Study in Urban Identity," *Progressive Architecture* 49, no. 3 (March 1968), 118.

Perceiving the Topographical City

American school children are commonly taught (or used to be) about Pittsburgh's three rivers, the Allegheny, the Monongahela, and the Ohio. The confluence of the three rivers is Pittsburgh's reason for being more than a frontier outpost. The Allegheny and the Monongahela were not readily navigable, and approach their juncture from the north and south rather than from the more populous east; but the so-called Forks of the Ohio marked the head of navigation on that great river, and thus functioned as a gateway to the American west.

Less well known is the topographical setting through which the

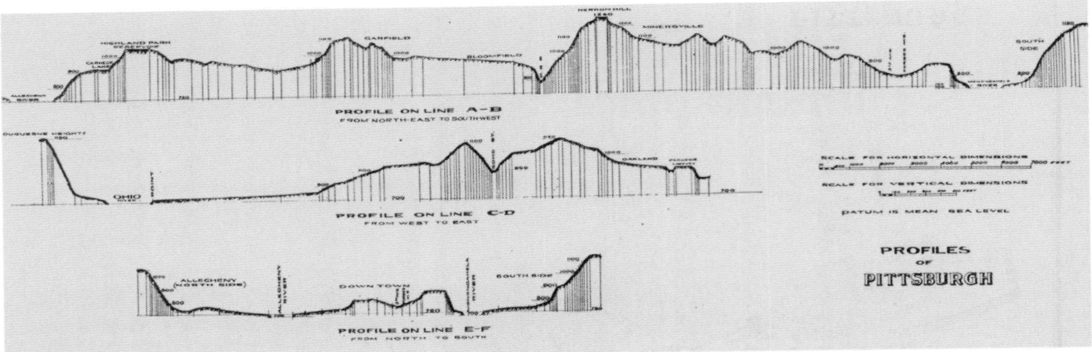

Fig. 2. *Profiles of Pittsburgh.* Reprinted from *The Pittsburgh District Civic Frontage,* vol. 5 of *The Pittsburgh Survey* (New York: Survey Associates, 1914), 6.

rivers course (figs. 1 and 2). Pittsburgh is built on a portion of the Appalachian Plateau that extends westward from the Allegheny Front, a high escarpment that slices diagonally across Pennsylvania and assures that the western part of the state is substantially higher than the east. Elevations in the Pittsburgh region range from 710 feet above sea level where the rivers meet, to 1,200 to 1,300 feet at the highest points. There are three primary topographical conditions from datum line to datum line: floodplains and bottomlands in the river valleys, uplands midway between rivers and hilltops, and high land at the prevailing level of the plateau.[1] Slopes tie it all together.

Consequently, the city of Pittsburgh lies unevenly upon unruly land. Communities and neighborhoods are variously defined by hills and demarcated by hollows. Buildings may be two stories on one side and four or five on another. There are a great number and variety of contrivances for scaling, connecting, and otherwise negotiating the terrain, ranging from bridges to tunnels to inclined planes and public steps.[2] Landforms shape topographical space and the city occupies that space with tenacity and verve.

Pittsburgh's topographical space provides the context for everyday experience. Bruce Lindsey relates how the rivers and the hills "are always present in your mind as behind you, or on your right, or below."[3] What is in the mind is also in the eye (figs. 3 and 4). In Pittsburgh, says Patrick Horsbrugh, "the topographic form and the consequences

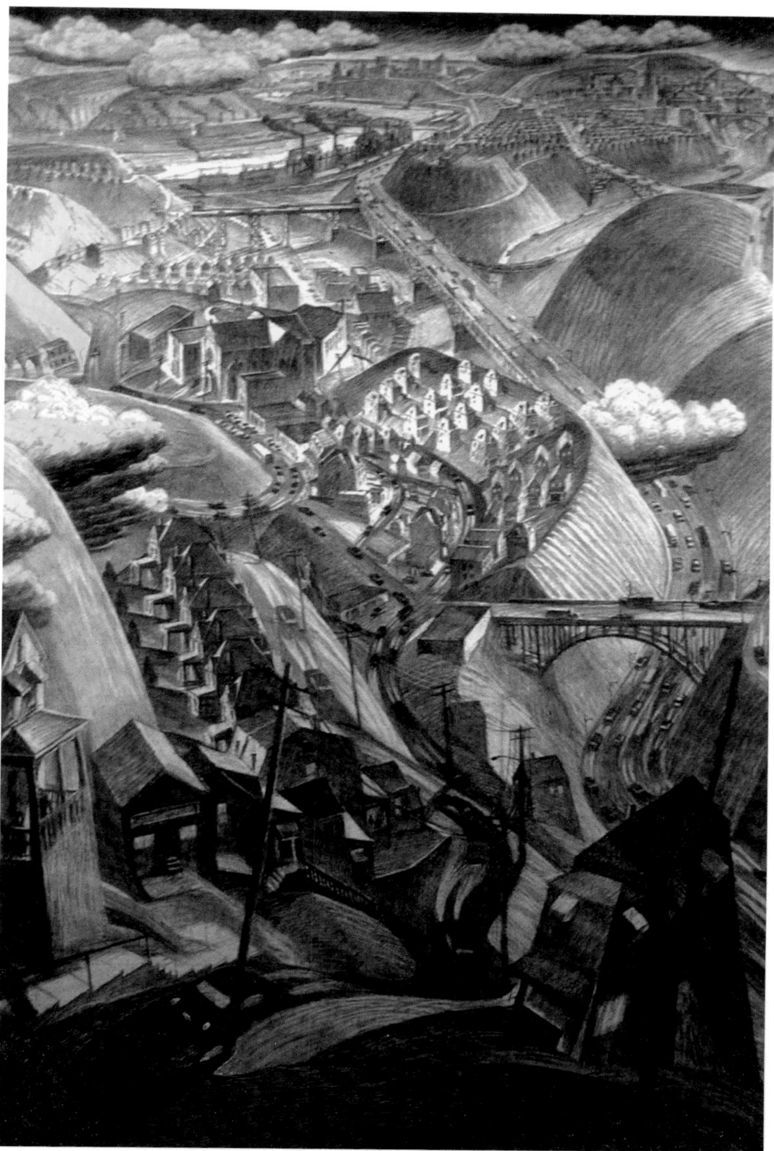

Fig. 3. Douglas Cooper, *Five Saltbox Hill,* 1997. Private Collection. Courtesy of Douglas Cooper.

Fig. 4. Diane Burko, *Three Rivers #2*, 1982. Courtesy of Diane Burko.

thereof, are inescapable. They condition every action, they confine every vista, they expose every prospect." Walter Kidney observes that in Pittsburgh, "more than in almost any other city, the third dimension is important in the look of things. You cannot go far before you find yourself looking up the side of a hill, or forward into empty space." Pittsburgh, says photographer Clyde Hare, "stands up and looks you in the face."[4] And we look back.

Perceiving the topographical city entails simultaneous perception of the land and the city. A classic bird's-eye view of Pittsburgh depicts urban development and the underlying terrain with equal weight (fig. 5). Foliage acts as both pictorial frame and pastoral setting. Figures in the foreground are a familiar presence from the tradition of landscape painting; they are denizens of a romantic scene. Yet they are also inhabitants of a bustling city and spectators actively taking in the view. They see an expansive panorama that appears to encompass the curvature of the earth. In fact, the view focuses on one discrete space in the topographical city.

Pittsburgh's topographical and pictorial space is organized into what William Rees Morrish calls "terrestrial rooms." Morrish contends that our concept of the room, and of human occupation generally, is

Fig. 5. William Gillespie Armor, *City of Pittsburgh,* 1888. Courtesy of The Hillman Company and Concept Art Gallery. Photograph by Chuck Biddle.

Fig. 6. Oakland, from the so-called lost neighborhood to the skyline. Reprinted from Pittsburgh Regional Planning Association, *A Plan for Pittsburgh's Cultural District, Oakland* (Pittsburgh: The Association, 1961), 1.

derived from spaces that are enclosed by surrounding landforms. For "within the . . . uncultivated landscape, the landforms contain resources, rooms to contain the heterogeneity of urban growth."[5]

Within the local Appalachian Plateau, "all the hills and stream divides rise to about the same elevation, the sky line as viewed from a hilltop appearing like that of a flat plain."[6] Thus the hills are not really hills; it's the valleys and the hollows that are real, voids in the solid of the overarching plateau. Pittsburgh, notes Horsbrugh, is "a city of spatial volumes, mostly enclosed."[7] When James Parton, writing in the *Atlantic Monthly* in 1868, famously called industrialized Pittsburgh "Hell with the lid taken off," his prose was shaped not only by the prevailing fire and smoke of the city's ironworks, but also by his specific viewpoint, looking "over into" a valley that he perceived as an abyss. Elsewhere in his essay, Parton writes of the "deep chasm in which Pittsburgh lies," as "at the bottom of an excavation."[8] In *The Mysteries of Pittsburgh*, contemporary novelist Michael Chabon describes the so-called lost neighborhood at the bottom of Junction Hollow, "the mysterious couple of streets and row or two of houses—a diorama, which one sees only from above . . . at the bottom of Pittsburgh" (fig. 6).[9]

The topographical city encompasses many terrestrial rooms that contain the heterogeneity of urban growth (see fig. 7).[10] They are *omnium-gatherums* full of buildings, industrial infrastructures, and engineered landscapes. Yet they are more than collections of random objects; for Pittsburgh's urban growth responds to the conditions of its topographical space. Frederick Law Olmsted Jr. praised "the bold picturesqueness of the [Pittsburgh] landscape—the deep ravines, the lofty hills, the precipitous declivities, the plunging prospects from hilltops into river valleys." At the same time, he perceived "a similar quality of forcefulness, activity, and bold irregular adaptation of means to ends" in the "dominant and impressive works of man in the city—the steel works, the bridges and viaducts, the jagged sky-line of office buildings."[11] This study singles out three terrestrial rooms that are at once essential to any understanding of Pittsburgh, singular in their scope and qualities, and representative of the spaces and visual experiences of the topographical city.

Pittsburgh's greatest room is the so-called Golden Triangle, the city's point of origin and downtown core. The Golden Triangle lies within the basin at the confluence of the three rivers, one of America's great natural settings. Hemmed in by land and water, the Golden Triangle is densely concentrated and has been rebuilt a number of times over. It is a place of multiple eras and multiple visions and varieties of topographical response. Because of the terrain, downtown Pittsburgh is the "most 'down' of downtowns in the country," its ground plane deeply recessed below the surrounding hills.[12] At the same time, its urban form reaches for the sky. The Golden Triangle is replete with vantage points and focal points composing views for the spectator, and its visual appearance is a key part of the city's identity.

Some ten miles east of the Golden Triangle, Turtle Creek empties into the Monongahela River at the mouth of the Turtle Creek Valley. The lower end of the valley is a room that is more like a passage, yet it holds a quintessential industrial landscape of waterways and railroads, factories and machines, and a great bridge. This landscape was largely realized in a discrete period of time (1877–1932), the product of powerful forces and a topographical response that was equal parts ac-

Fig. 7. Henry Koerner, *Oh Fearful Wonder of Man*, 1962. Carnegie Museum of Art, Pittsburgh; Purchase: The Henry L. Hillman Fund. Courtesy of Mrs. Henry Koerner.

commodation and exploitation. Here topography and technology forge a fantastic scene that evokes the technological sublime, brings a new scale and drama to the landscape, and plays as cinema for the spectator.

Between the Golden Triangle and the Turtle Creek Valley, Junction Hollow and Panther Hollow penetrate inland from the Monongahela

River and issue in an upland ringed by higher ground. Here, within the rich urban fabric of Pittsburgh's Oakland district, is one of the great, albeit little known and not fully realized, sites of American architecture, landscape, and urbanism. The historical campus of Carnegie Mellon University (once known as Carnegie Tech) is the progeny of Thomas Jefferson's University of Virginia and the City Beautiful Movement. Yet it is also a distinctive vision and topographical response, sprung from the mind and hand of architect Henry Hornbostel. Though seemingly complete in itself, it broadly engages, and is contingent upon, the larger landscape, including two successive campuses of the University of Pittsburgh. Together, these elements compose a complex vista for the spectator.

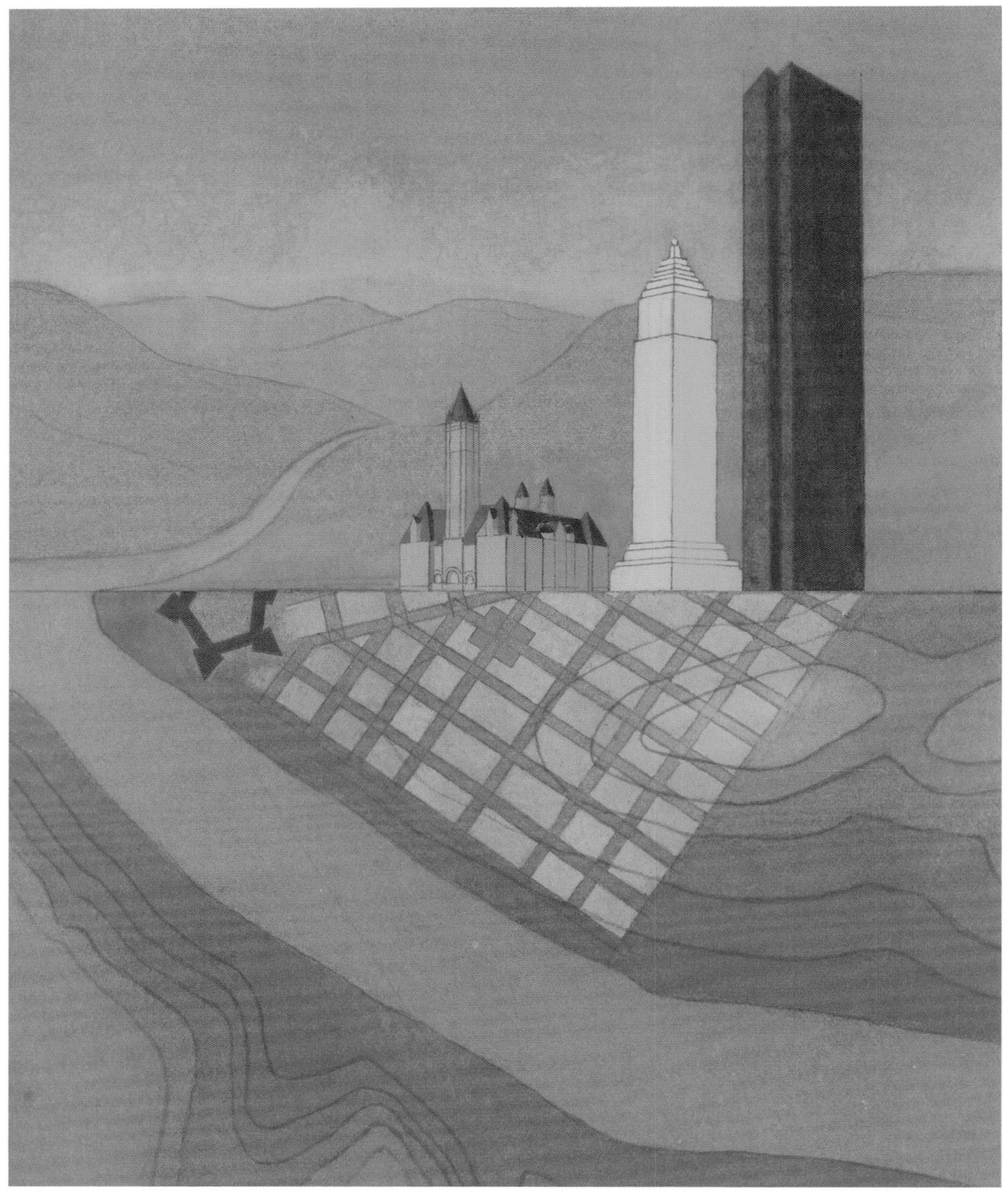

Fig. 8. Clayton Merrell, *The Golden Triangle*, 2005. Courtesy of Clayton Merrell.

In View of a Golden Triangle

The Point is the Alpha and Omega of the city, the place of arrival and departure, the beginning and the end of the land.

James D. Van Trump, *Landscape Architecture* (January 1975)

Cosmological Terrain

Pittsburgh's Golden Triangle is defined by the topographical elements of the basin at the Forks of the Ohio: the three rivers themselves, the floodplains and river flats, and the slopes and heights of the surrounding hills (fig. 8). William Rees Morrish writes of such a place:

In many cities, the mountain and a body of water are used to establish the basic organizational elements of each city's form. Traditionally, this civic mount is either an artificial construction or the city is formed around an existing landform. This geomorphic element is the *axis*

> *mundi,* signifying this urban place as a world city. To balance this aggressive declaration, water is used to describe the outer boundary of the mountain's power. It sets the city in a proper geomorphic position between the mountain and the sea, or lake, within the protective eye of the mountain and within reach of the life-giving resources of water.[1]

Pittsburgh's civic mount, which Morrish elsewhere calls the "sacred mountain," stands east of the original city. The rivers are the city's life-giving water. Pittsburgh lies within the protective eye of the former and within close reach of the latter. A Chinese word for landscape is written with two characters: *shan* (mountains) and *shui* (water). It follows that mountains are *yang* to the *yin* of water. These are opposites, yet complements: each shapes the other.[2] In Pittsburgh the region's complex geological history reveals that the rivers have shaped the land as the land has shaped the rivers.[3] George Beck's painting *View of Pittsburgh, 1804* makes these archetypal relationships clear (fig. 9).

This topographical setting casts Pittsburgh as what Morrish calls a "world city," or a city at the center of the world. Mircea Eliade argues that any act of settlement invariably involves the establishment of a center: "If the world is to be lived in, it must be founded. . . . The discovery or projection of a fixed point—the center—is equivalent to the creation of the world."[4] The center is a cosmological point of orientation that establishes order within the preexisting chaos of undifferentiated space.

Many cultures represent the center as the sacred mountain and *axis mundi,* the place of connection between the cosmic realms of heaven, earth, and the underworld, or as the *omphalos,* the navel or point of creation.[5] Pittsburgh is, by its topographical nature, a place of differentiated space, prone to centering. As a real city may deviate from the archetype, Pittsburgh developed a cosmological terrain with two primary centers—the sacred mountain and the point of creation—in counterpoint to one another, formed from the mountains and the rivers.

Far from the looming mountain depicted by Beck, or even the highest point of land, Pittsburgh's sacred mountain was a hill about eighty

Fig. 9. George Beck, *View of Pittsburgh 1804,* 1804. University Library System, University of Pittsburgh.

feet high. This hill was a key topographical figure in the landscape, however, projecting into the land between the rivers like a thrust stage in a theater. Like the hills of Rome, it served as a central stage for drama, ceremony, and power. It ultimately became known as Grant's Hill.

The rivers marked a periphery for the power of the sacred mountain, but they also formed a second center point or *omphalos*. The rivers' point of confluence was and is the primary point of reference in the region. It projects a centrifugal form of control over its hinterlands as the datum point from which distances are commonly measured.[6] It is the point of creation for the city as we know it. It is a center point owing to topography and history, and it came to be called the Point.

At these two centers, and in their interplay, humans began to "undertake the creation of the world that [they chose] to inhabit" and to imprint the land with their presence.[7] They started by marking and imitating the natural forms of the landscape in their own constructions as a type of mimetic architecture.

Prehistoric Native Americans frequented this place as early as 500 BCE. The so-called mound builders are now understood as a variety of cultures that built sites and settlements throughout the Ohio and Mississippi Valleys over the course of a thousand years or more. They were North America's first architects.[8] Their architecture consisted of mounds or tumuli, often shaped as cones, which Morrish calls "the simplest geomorphic construction"; complex earthworks of rings, squares, octagons, and other geometrical enclosures; flat-topped pyramids; effigy mounds; and engineered roads. These earthworks served funerary, religious, celebratory, and boundary demarcation functions and were commonly sited and oriented in relation to natural topographical features.[9]

The Hopewell and Adena cultures occupied the Ohio Valley and extended as far eastward as the Monongahela River Valley. Roger G. Kennedy suggests that Hopewell and Adena population centers constituted ancient cities, and asserts: "The new cities of the central valley—Cincinnati, St. Louis, Marietta, Portsmouth, Lexington, Pittsburgh, and Nashville—had to be built by clearing away evidence of older ones."[10] In the case of Pittsburgh, at least, this is almost certainly a vast overstatement, but there were at least two major Adena burial mounds in the immediate Pittsburgh area. Both were sited in conjunction with key topographical features: one on a prominent outcropping at McKees Rocks, three miles below the Point on the Ohio River at Chartiers Creek (fig. 10); and the other on the aforementioned hill that stood within the land at the Forks of the Ohio.[11]

This ancient American landscape endured for centuries. Later generations of Native Americans also knew the Forks of the Ohio well, though they apparently never established more than transient settlements here. When the Europeans arrived, they found remnants of a

Fig. 10. *Vicinity of Pittsburgh, McKees Rocks and Ancient Mound.* Reprinted from *History of Allegheny Co., Pennsylvania* (Philadelphia: L. H. Everts and Co., 1876), plate 16.

civilized and cosmological terrain in the seeming wilderness. Judge Hugh Henry Brackenridge wrote from Pittsburgh in 1786: "To the eastward is . . . a beautiful rising ground discovering marks of ancient cultivation, the forest having long ago withdrawn and shown the head and brow beset with green and flowers. . . . On the summit of the hill is a mound of earth supposed to be the catacombs or ancient burying ground of the savages. There can be no doubt of this, as on opening some of the tumuli or hills of earth, bones are found."[12]

Brackenridge may have thought of the Native Americans as savages, but he and others were curious about these structures in their midst. His son, Henry Marie Brackenridge, investigated this mound, and went on to write extensive archeological reports about prehistoric Native American sites and settlements throughout the Ohio and Mississippi Valleys.[13] As late as 1817, John Palmer reported a tumulus "in the form of a truncated cone, thirty feet in diameter by ten feet high" overlooking the settlement of Pittsburgh from the hill within the Forks of the Ohio.[14]

With this mound, prehistoric Americans reshaped the chosen hill in acknowledgment of its inherent form, accentuating its presence as a focal point, and investing it with cosmological significance. As a raised burial ground on a hill, the mound was a literal *axis mundi,* providing connection and passage between cosmic realms. As the first known work of man in the region, it designated the sacred mountain. The hill had the benefit of being above the floodplain, but it also had an apparent role within its larger topographical setting. It was a natural promontory that commanded a more or less symmetrical swath of flat land to the west, and it directly faced the region's primary topographical feature, the Forks of the Ohio. The sacred mountain was doubtless chosen with reference to the Point.

Events in the middle of the eighteenth century put this prehistoric landscape at risk. French and British interests increasingly focused at the Forks of the Ohio in the early stages of the War for Empire on the American frontier. Native Americans had supporting roles, and soon no role at all. George Washington was among the first people of European ancestry to reach the Forks of the Ohio, and was also one of the first recorded spectators in this place. When Washington viewed the Point in 1753, his first impressions were both topographical and practical: "I spent some time in viewing the rivers, and the land in the fork, which I think extremely well situated for a fort, as it has the absolute command of both rivers. The land at the point is 20 or 25 feet above the common surface of the water, and a considerable bottom of flat, well-timbered land all around it, very convenient for building: the rivers are each a quarter of a mile, or more, across, and run here very near at right angles."[15]

Washington did not dwell on the beauty of the natural landscape or on any preexisting cultural presence, but instead saw a place of military advantage and topographical control deep in contested territory.

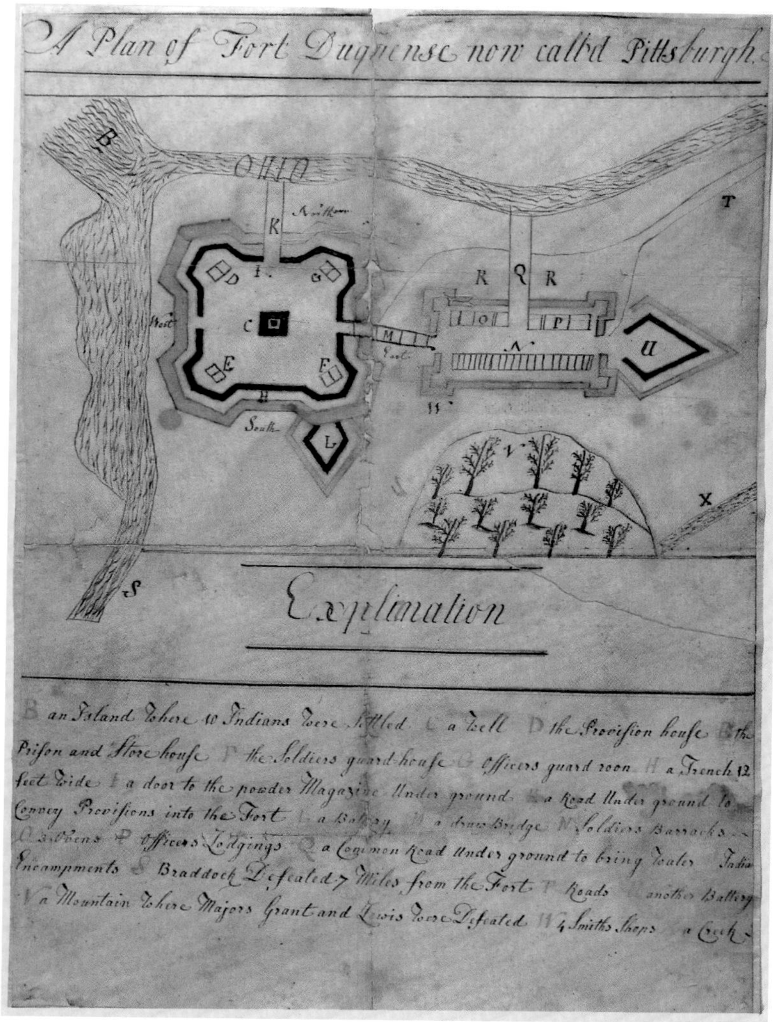

Fig. 11. *Map of Fort Duquesne Now Called Pittsburgh,* ca. 1759. Note the hill shown at the bottom right, and the notation: "a Mountain where the Majors Grant and Lewis were Defeated." The Historical Society of Pennsylvania (HSP), Norris Family Papers, Collection 454.

He further forecast a new intersection of land and city at this place. Soon the Europeans staked their claim and settled at the Point, establishing it as the *omphalos,* the point of creation of the community.

Despite Washington's best intentions on behalf of the British, the

Fig. 12. Charles Morse Stotz, *Fort Pitt,* 1976. Library and Archives Division, Historical Society of Western Pennsylvania, Pittsburgh, Pa.

French built the first substantial fort at the Forks—Fort Duquesne (1754–1758) (fig. 11). When the French ultimately abandoned the site, the British erected Fort Pitt (1759–1761) (fig. 12). Both forts were made, like the ancient burial mounds before them, principally and simply from the land itself. Both had mostly dry moats dug out from the land, and a variety of defenses built up and formed from the earth. At the same time, these forts introduced the dual disciplines of European landscape design—fortification and gardening—to this place.[16] Fort Duquesne was a rectangular fort with four arrow-like bastions and a high wooden stockade. Fort Pitt was a pentagonal fort with five arrow-like bastions faced in brick and additional fortifications arrayed beyond the walls. The French cleared the land around Fort Duquesne and planted cornfields and vegetable gardens. Fort Pitt, in turn, featured the adjacent King's Gardens. Both formal and agrarian, it encompassed as much as ten acres of vegetable plots and an orchard, with an ornamental layout of promenades and radial walks.[17]

War conclusively interconnected the Point and the sacred mountain. Major James Grant led an advance force of the expedition of the British Brigadier General John Forbes to the hill overlooking Fort Duquesne in September of 1758, and foolishly provoked the French and their Native American allies to battle. As had been the case three years earlier at nearby Braddock's Field, the French outmaneuvered and routed the British to an inglorious defeat. Nonetheless, the subsequent approach of the Forbes expedition prompted the outmanned French to burn and abandon Fort Duquesne, never to return. The occupying British force recovered their dead from the sacred mountain.

Although the British did not win the battle, they won the war, and with it the right to name the sacred mountain. Because of its role in the fierce struggle for the American West, Grant's Hill has been called "one of earth's immortal hills."[18]

A cosmological terrain of intrinsic order, community origins, and life and death would subsequently yield to a new landscape of imposed order and urban development. Yet Grant's Hill and the Point would persist as powerful organizing devices within the terrain, retain their position and memory as cosmological centers, and reemerge as key sites in the new civic topography.

Civic Topography

George Washington had noted "flat, well-timbered land . . . convenient for building," and with the modicum of security that emerged from the British conquest, attention turned to the approximately 255 acres of flat land that lay within the Forks of the Ohio. Here a fort became a settlement, and a settlement became a city. In this context, the Point and Grant's Hill suggested a physical axis that would link them in the new civic topography as they were already linked in the cosmological terrain and in history. Landscape architect Ralph E. Griswold

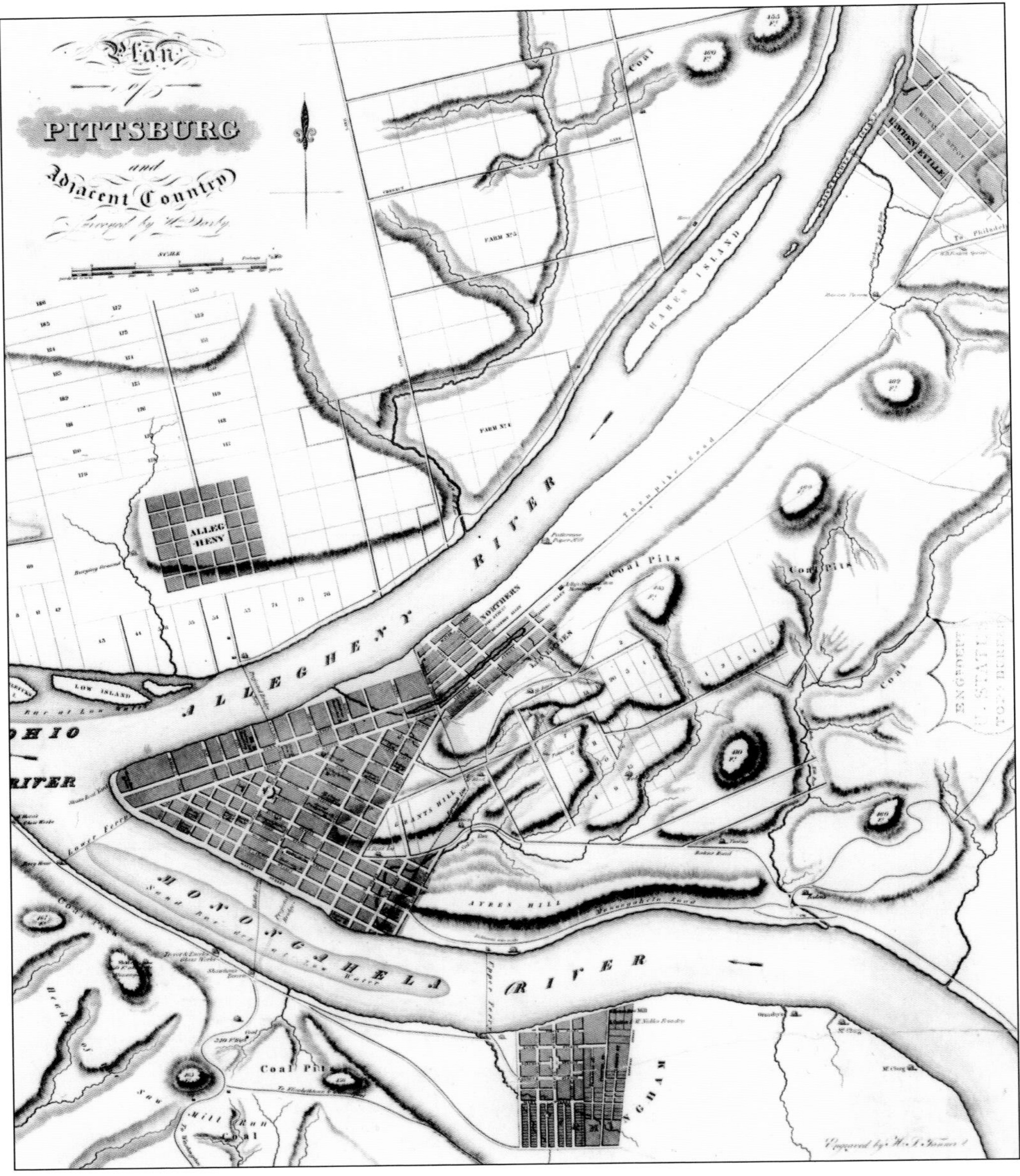

Fig. 13. William Darby, *Plan of Pittsburgh and Adjacent Country,* 1819. Map published by R. Patterson and William Darby. Library of Congress, Geography and Map Division.

would later wonder, "what might this embryonic city have been if the French had defeated the British?" He speculated: "With their characteristic flair for 'le grande plan' they most certainly would have created a monumental park at the Point with avenues radiating along the river fronts and a central mall bisecting the triangle terminated by some spectacular building on the hill overlooking the city."[19]

But it was the British and then the newly independent Americans who went to work instead, and slowly at that. In 1764 Colonel John Campbell planned a tiny town comprised of a four-block grid. Then in 1784 the Penn family commissioned a survey of all land between the Point and the hills to the east. Surveyors George Woods and Thomas Vickroy employed conventional gridiron planning to lay out the future city. A primary grid established street sizes (typically less than 60 feet wide) and block sizes (typically 100 by 250 feet). A secondary grid subdivided the blocks into saleable parcels. This plan provided the framework for urban development.[20]

The grid was a regularized and preconceived system of land division that spread the order of a new civilization across the terrain with scant regard for local topographic conditions (fig 13). Even so, Pittsburgh's grid—and the city's subsequent urban form—responded to the prevailing topography in a number of significant ways.

It was common procedure to orient a street grid to a waterfront. In Pittsburgh, however, two equally extensive river frontages met an acute angle. Consequently, the Woods-Vickroy plan incorporated two distinct street grids: most of the new blocks were platted parallel to the Monongahela River, while a two-block-wide strip was laid parallel to the Allegheny River. Liberty Street (now Avenue) was the seam "joining two pieces of tartan."[21] This clash of grids yielded unconventional triangular lots and increased the visual density along Liberty Street, while it foreclosed any potential views through the compact city. At the same time, it allowed the city to open squarely out to the rivers at the end of every street, and assured that both of the city's river frontages were orthogonally composed, enhancing their visual legibility when viewed from on or across the water.[22]

The Woods-Vickroy plan included a single open square—subsequently known as the Diamond and later as Market Square—to interrupt the grid. The Penn family donated this space for public use, and Allegheny County built its first courthouse there in 1799. The otherwise modest building featured a tower in an initial attempt to establish a visual presence for the civic authority and a focal point for the city. As remarked in 1826: "As for lofty glittering spires and cupolas no such necessary objects to direct the way-faring man and embellish the city withal are to be seen among us. The only ambitious structure that aspires to any height . . . is the steeple of the county court."[23]

By the mid-nineteenth century, however, as James D. Van Trump describes it, the Diamond, the courthouse, and its tower had all "come to look rather meager" for the government seat of a growing region. "Why not look to the hills—and especially to one of no great altitude which would 'command' the city slightly and sufficiently but not too much? Grant's Hill, if it *was* a little steep on the western side, was just the right height for a subtle and yet majestic architectural dominance by the law."[24] Spectators could gaze from below Grant's Hill at a fine monument silhouetted against the sky and the hills beyond; or gaze from its height at the city and the rivers laid out at one's feet. This site recalled the Capitoline Hill in Rome, and Capitol (*née* Jenkin's) Hill in Washington, D.C. Pierre L'Enfant, planner of the District of Columbia, had identified Jenkin's Hill as "a pedestal waiting for a monument."[25] Within sight of both the Potomac and Anacostia Rivers, it became the nation's civic mount after 1800, when it was crowned with the U.S. Capitol (fig. 14).

Grant's Hill, in the meantime, had become a popular pleasure ground at the edge of an increasingly crowded and untidy city. As Henry Marie Brackenridge wrote: "The hill was the favorite promenade in the fine weather, and on Sunday afternoon. It was pleasing to see the line of well-dressed ladies and gentlemen, and children, nearly the whole population repairing to this beautiful green eminence. It was considered so essential to the comfort and recreation of the inhabitants, that they could scarcely imagine how a town could exist without

Fig. 14. George Cook, *City of Washington from Beyond the Navy Yard,* 1834. View across the Anacostia River showing the U.S. Capitol on Capitol Hill. Library of Congress, Prints and Photographs Division, LC-USZC2–1826. Engraving by William Bennett.

its Grant's Hill."[26] Van Trump called Grant's Hill "paradise."[27] At the same time, the hill had begun to assume a civic identity as a site for civic celebrations and Fourth of July festivities, often marked with bonfires visible over great distances.

Grant's Hill received its monument in 1841 when architect John Chislett designed Pittsburgh's second Allegheny County courthouse (fig. 15). This was a rather sophisticated building in the then-fashionable Greek Revival style, constructed of "polished yellowish gray sandstone obtained from the neighboring hills." It featured a Doric portico, lateral wings, and a central dome that rose to a height of 148 feet (fig.

Fig. 15. *Pittsburgh (Pennsylvania),* ca. 1850. View across the Monongahela River showing the Allegheny County Courthouse on Grant's Hill at the far right. Carnegie Library of Pittsburgh. Engraving by Edouard Willmann.

16). Like the Native American tumulus that came before it, and the dome of the U.S. Capitol that it emulated, Chislett's hillock of a dome was a mimetic reflection of the hill that it crowned.[28]

These developments enhanced the significance of the sacred mountain but transformed its shape and its meaning. The plinth for the courthouse flattened the hilltop, obliterating what may have remained of the Adena burial mound. Chislett cast the new courthouse as a Greek temple, surrounded by a fenced *temenos,* or sacred precinct. Such a temple, says Eliade, is in itself a replica of the sacred mountain.[29] Moreover, the building's location, design, and assignation to the civic authority made it the *caput mundi,* the center of civilization and the capital of the world.[30] Published views show how the second courthouse dominated the city and the land (although they tend to exagger-

Fig. 16. John Chislett (architect), Allegheny County Courthouse, 1841. Pittsburgh History and Landmarks Foundation.

ate its scale). This dominance conveyed legitimacy and power to the civic authority in a time and place not far removed from (perceived) wilderness.

Van Trump imagines the spectator's perception of the courthouse: "The building was most majestic from a distance. Seen through mists of smoke as in a luminous twilight it was not too difficult to think of ancient Greece and the Athenian Acropolis."[31] Grant's Hill and its courthouse may not have been the climax of a formal French city plan or a nation's capital, but it is where mid-nineteenth-century Pittsburgh turned from the deterministic order of the grid and the parcel to embrace a civic topography reminiscent of Athens, Rome, and Washington, D.C. Grant's Hill had been transformed into what Morrish calls a "site": "Parcels are uncultivated fragments of land. They have been designated by speculators who lack vision or speculation about their place in the terrain. Parcels have not had their resources properly gathered and governed. A site is a parcel whose role, function and obligations to the terrain have been defined in terms of vision and spirit. It is full of latent formal and functional resources. To inaugurate a parcel into a site requires the merging and balancing of geomorphic landform and functioning city into a governed urban terrain."[32] As *caput mundi,* Grant's Hill and its courthouse literally governed the urban terrain.

Nevertheless, Grant's Hill would experience ever-increasing pressure from an advancing Monongahela River street grid. The grid extended eastward from the Point without regard for the ponds and gently rising land in its path, and Pittsburgh could grow further only by way of strenuous engagement with the eastern hills.

When an ideal grid confronts highly irregular land, it must deform in some way in deference to the relief of the land. As Pittsburgh's bottomland filled and the grid encountered the eastern hills, some streets climbed the hills at precipitous angles. Other streets turned to mount the hills from better angles, causing a major break and redirection in the street grid. And in time, means were mobilized to reshape the hills themselves.

Ultimately, the economic logic of the grid and the parcel eroded the natural and civic virtues of the sacred mountain and the site. Soon Pittsburghers would unceremoniously refer to Grant's Hill as "the hump." The 1830s and 1840s saw the first efforts to level the hill, and additional cuts proceeded throughout the remainder of the nineteenth century. As late as 1910, Frederick Law Olmsted Jr. recommended a further "hump cut" to facilitate the movement of street traffic and to "reduce the obstacle which appears to be offered by the steep gradients to the expansion of the district available for high-class retail trade and offices" (fig. 17). Altogether, as much as sixty feet was cut from the hill, leaving behind only a slight rise in the street grid.[33]

Thus Pittsburgh's topography was changed, and the sacred mountain virtually disappeared. Morrish laments the loss: "[When a] land-

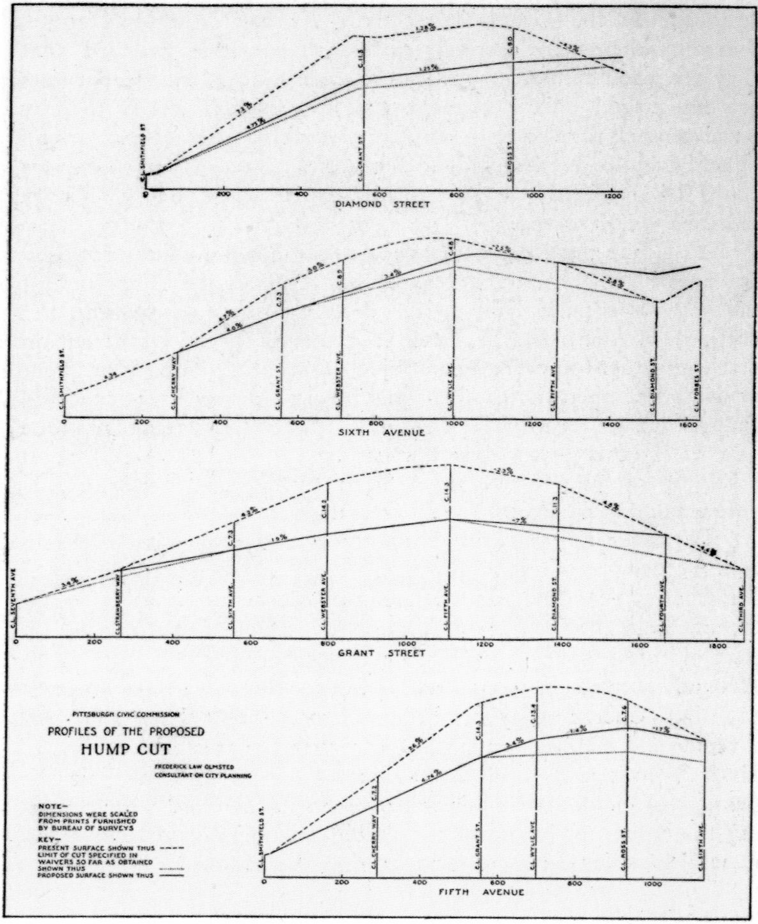

Fig. 17. Frederick Law Olmsted Jr., *Profiles of the Proposed Hump Cut.* Reprinted from Frederick Law Olmsted Jr., *Pittsburgh, Main Thoroughfares and the Down Town District: Improvements Necessary to Meet the City's Present and Future Needs* (Pittsburgh: Pittsburgh Civic Commission, 1911), 131.

form is graded level, the undulations of the geomorphology are rendered neutral. The earth has lost resident status as a fundamental citizen to the creation of urbanity. The urban terrain of our modern cities are groundless worlds in our minds as we attempt to ignore the foundations upon which we are intimately linked to the earth. They have lost a key element in the definition of urbanity, the sacred urban mountain."[34]

The gradual cutting of the hump and the associated lowering of street levels "tended to 'sky' the courthouse, making it difficult to see it properly from the street," and diminished its strength as a governing site within the civic topography.[35] In 1882, the courthouse burned.

An Architecture of the Land

The courthouse marked a new incarnation for Grant's Hill, and was soon joined on the hill by St. Peter's Episcopal Church (1851–1852) and St. Paul's (Roman Catholic) Cathedral (1855 and after). The churches sought to associate with the sacred mountain and the seat of civil authority, and in their own way, acknowledge and extend its dominance. St. Paul's two tall, spiky towers and octagonal dome now competed with the courthouse for visual attention on Pittsburgh's newly variegated skyline (fig. 18).

A skyline is an inherently topographical condition, as architecture intersects the horizon and the city engages the sky. At the same time, says Wayne Attoe, "the way mankind intervenes at the junction of land and sky . . . is one of the meaningful measures of human civilization."[36] Skylines proclaim a hierarchy of cultural institutions and values. For centuries, that intervention and those institutions and values were fairly consistent across cultures. Spiro Kostof explains, "the dominant accent of the skyline was the architecture of sacred buildings. These were often situated on eminences, natural or artificial, their architectural mass was piled up high, and their visual prominence was enhanced by sky-aspiring props."[37] With the coming of the secular state in the Western world, cathedral and town hall shared the skyline. In medieval Florence, for example, the dome of the Duomo, representing the religious authority, and the tower of the Palazzo Vecchio, representing the civic authority, rose together above the city. In early America, too, notes Paul Spreiregen, "the skyline consisted of church steeples at a high point with a domed building, usually a seat of government, as the focus."[38] Pittsburgh followed suit. William Schuchman's view of the city from

Fig. 18. William Schuchman, *View of Pittsburgh, Pa.,* 1859. Pittsburgh History and Landmarks Foundation.

1859 showed courthouse and churches jostling for position on Grant's Hill and the skyline.

Pittsburgh's third courthouse was built within this context, on the Grant's Hill site of its predecessor, once that site was further lowered to match the surrounding streets. America's premier architect of the time, Henry Hobson Richardson, designed the new courthouse and jail, often referred to as the County Buildings. Richardson was a mountain of a man, and his buildings reflected his appearance even as they took their cue from American topography and geology.[39] As Thomas C. Hubka remarks, "even a casual observer of Richardson's work is repeatedly struck by the force of his rugged, naturalistic expression, . . . Richardson's attempt to distill nature's powerful forces into his trademark expression of a bold, lithic monumentality."[40]

Fig. 19. H. H. Richardson (architect), The County Buildings, 1883–1888, perspective view, with inset site elevation view. Pittsburgh History and Landmarks Foundation.

Pittsburgh's County Buildings, realized between 1884 and 1888, were built firm and immutable, as appropriate for a civic institution (fig. 19). Richardson explained, "the intention has been to produce that sense of solidity requisite in dignified monumental work . . . by a quiet and massive treatment of the wall surface."[41] Critics have often praised these stone walls for their rugged simplicity, particularly those at the jail (fig. 20). Henry Russell Hitchcock cites precedents in seventeenth-century fortifications that Richardson had visited in France.[42] Yet the walls were deeply rooted in the local terrain.

Margaret Henderson Floyd asserts: "the rough-hewn geology of Pittsburgh, with its craggy granite outcroppings, provided an ideal setting for Richardson's use of masonry at the Allegheny County Build-

entire city and a visible expression of the *axis mundi.* At the same time, as *caput mundi,* the County Buildings reasserted the role of the civic authority. With the land—Grant's Hill—no longer much apparent in the landscape, the County Buildings assumed the role of the sacred mountain. In these buildings, Grant's Hill—like a true immortal—remains present to this day.

The County Buildings' rugged materiality, picturesque massing, and towering monumentality achieve a unique affinity with their setting. As Franklin Toker asserts, "the Courthouse exemplifies . . . the expression of the place (what the Romans called *genius loci*). The Courthouse does not merely stand in Pittsburgh—it is *about* Pittsburgh."[49] Richardson famously said, "If they honor me for the pigmy things I have already done, what will they say when they see Pittsburgh finished?"[50] The County Buildings were Richardson's personal achievement, but his words also suggest the extent to which these buildings represented an entire city. Richardson, it seems, built not mere buildings but Pittsburgh itself, reaffirming and granting new dimensions to the civic topography.

Privatizing the Skyline

In nineteenth-century Pittsburgh, as elsewhere, parcels of land were commonly small, and numerous small buildings stood side by side. But the borders of Schuchman's 1859 view suggested that some individual buildings—from churches to government buildings to commercial blocks—were beginning to take on their own architectural identities and distinguish themselves one from another (see fig. 18). The County Buildings exemplified and punctuated this trend.

Richardson's buildings were about as big as they could be. There was no *temenos* this time—the buildings' footprints matched the limits established by the grid, abutting streets and sidewalks on all sides, even while bridging a street to encompass a second block (the irregular shape of which was determined by the rise and shift of the grid). Load-bearing stonework could not be piled much higher. A building complex of this scale—like a cathedral or a castle—was envisioned to be the exception, a site among mere parcels.

Yet by the late nineteenth century, new building technology, commercial and institutional imperatives, and corporate aggrandizement led to unprecedented changes in scale in downtown Pittsburgh. Lots were commonly combined and redeveloped, and buildings grew in footprint, bulk, and height. As the new buildings proliferated they challenged the preeminence of the County Buildings. The material and psychological influence of the County Buildings waned, and, ultimately, even the courthouse tower could not keep its head above the architectural fray.

Growing commercial interests, like the churches before them, were attracted to the sacred mountain and the seat of civil authority, and the County Buildings became a locus for new and increasingly ambitious commercial development. By 1895 the fourteen-story Carnegie Building stood a short block from the courthouse door. This was the first steel-framed skyscraper in Pittsburgh, and its frame, made of Carnegie Steel's own commodity, was left exposed for an extended time during construction (fig. 23). This gesture may have been rooted in a nationwide recession, but it also served to advertise the Carnegie product and its new application to the spectator.[51] Steel-framed skyscrapers captured the grid's repetitive multiplicity and potential for growth and carried it into three dimensions. This newfangled materiality did not so much emerge from the earth as it climbed to the sky.

The Carnegie Building housed the offices of the Carnegie Steel Company and its subsidiaries, and later the offices of its successor, U.S. Steel Corporation. As a base of industrial power, it staked a claim to downtown Pittsburgh for commercial interests in general and Big Steel in particular, and foreshadowed Pittsburgh's role as a corporate center. The Carnegie Building was named for and constructed as a memorial to Thomas M. Carnegie, Andrew Carnegie's brother. But the Carnegie name also reflected Andrew Carnegie's personal claim to the city. Before long, Andrew Carnegie would be so identified with Pittsburgh that he was depicted as an embodiment of its topographic form (fig. 24).

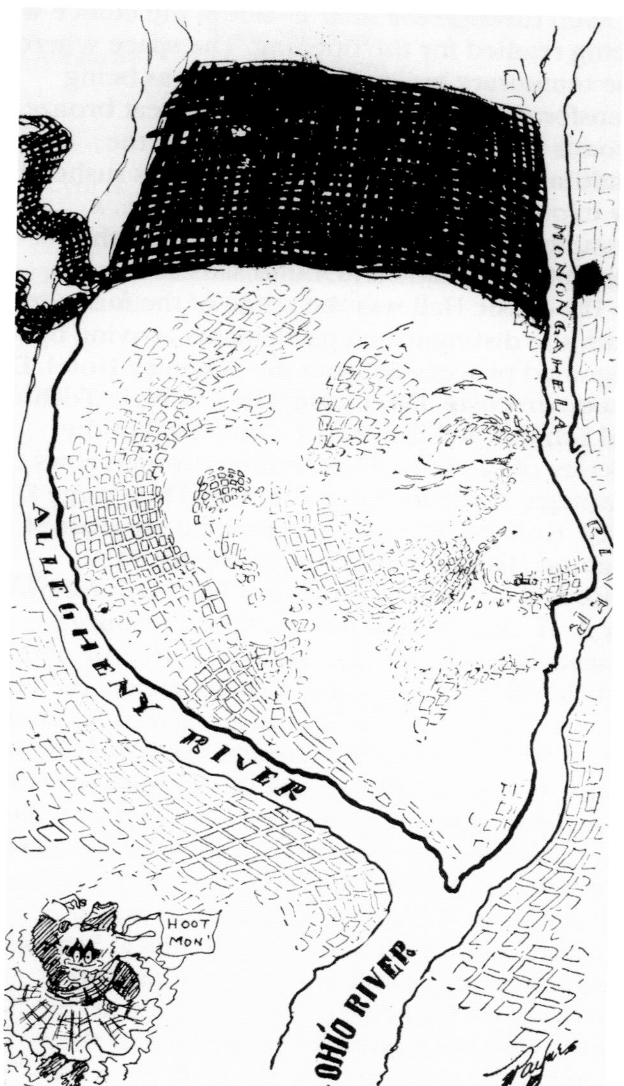

Fig. 23. Carnegie Building under construction, ca. 1894. Carnegie Library of Pittsburgh.

Fig. 24. Andrew Carnegie cartoon, *Pittsburgh Gazette Times* (April 10, 1907). Carnegie Library of Pittsburgh.

These developments introduced a new element of personal giantism into Pittsburgh's urban landscape.[52]

Carnegie's palpable presence would have appalled his rival, Henry C. Frick. In 1900 Carnegie ousted Frick as chairman of the Carnegie Steel Company, bought out Frick's interest in the company, and took over the H. C. Frick Coke Company (forming the Carnegie Company) after a virulent legal battle. Margaret Frick Symington Sanger has documented a complex Carnegie/Frick rivalry that ranged from business to art collecting.[53] Real estate and architecture were flash points.

In 1901, Frick built the 330-foot, twenty-one-story Frick Building, designed by D. H. Burnham and Company of Chicago, on a lot adjacent to the Carnegie Building. Daniel H. Burnham, who became famous for his maxim, "Make no little plans," was no shrinking violet. But Frick was apparently the aggressor here, driven by an obsessive competitive impulse to erect a building that literally overshadowed that of his former partner, now his foe. Sanger calls the Frick Building "perhaps [Frick's] most cynical gesture." Frick's later annex (1905), also by Burnham, further boxed in the Carnegie Building, blocking all southern light. Van Trump called the two Frick buildings "an architectural *riposte* in the great Frick-Carnegie battle."[54]

More important for the shape of the city, however, was the fact that the Frick Building was now the tallest structure in Pittsburgh, taller than Richardson's courthouse, which stood right across the street (see fig. 25). "From 1901 on," Kidney writes, "the Frick Building confronted the Courthouse, its slab-like form and its smooth, simply detailed granite walls almost like a cool aristocratic snub to the romantic towers, roofs, and dormers . . . of the older building." Van Trump laments, "No longer did the soaring tower, the symbol of the majesty of the law, front grandly toward the west."[55] No longer did the courthouse visually dominate the city.

Frick went on to be a major landowner, developer, and shaper of Pittsburgh's urban form. Not only did he subordinate the Carnegie Building and blunt the power of the courthouse, but in subsequent building campaigns he demolished St. Paul's Cathedral and exiled St.

Fig. 25. Frank E. Bingaman (photographer), vicinity of Grant Street, ca. 1905. Shows Allegheny County Courthouse, Frick Building, and Carnegie Building, from left to right, with the cleared site of St. Paul's Cathedral in the foreground awaiting Frick's Union Arcade. Carnegie Library of Pittsburgh.

Fig. 26. *Henry Phipps Properties,* ca. 1911, postcard. Private collection.

Peter's Episcopal Church to be rebuilt elsewhere. In their places Frick built the Union Arcade and the William Penn Hotel.[56] With these aggressive moves on the chessboard of the urban grid, Frick singlehandedly replaced Pittsburgh's nineteenth-century skyline by 1917.

The sale of the Carnegie Company in 1901 and the subsequent formation of U.S. Steel Corporation prompted Andrew Carnegie to exit

Fig. 27. Lycergus S. Glover [?], Detroit Publishing Company (photographer), "Pittsburgh, Pa.," 1908. Carnegie Museum of Art, Pittsburgh; Purchase: Second Century Acquisitions Fund.

the downtown scene, leaving the exploitation of area real estate to three of his former colleagues—Frick, Henry Oliver, and Henry Phipps. These men all realized large sums of money from the breakup of the Carnegie interests and subsequently engaged in what Toker calls the "real-estate War of the Three Henrys." As Toker notes, "no Renaissance pope could have carved up Rome more effectively." Van Trump adds, "like the princes of the Renaissance, the masters of these great fortunes loved to build."[57]

Frick raised his four buildings on adjacent lots in the Grant Street district, in close proximity to the County Buildings. Oliver (and his estate) developed a number of buildings further west, principally along what became Oliver Avenue. These included the Henry W. Oliver Building (1910), also by D. H. Burnham and Company, which became the city's tallest at twenty-five stories and 347 feet. And Phipps built seven buildings even further west (fig. 26). The Bessemer Building (1903) and Fulton Building (1906) flanked Sixth Street at the Allegheny River, where they formed "a kind of Phipps triumphal arch," says Van Trump, a gateway to downtown Pittsburgh.[58]

Like the medieval Italian city-state of San Gimignano, where families added masonry towers to the skyline to proclaim identity, wealth, and power, in downtown Pittsburgh, industrialists asserted their significance by the height, extent, and number of their buildings, which frequently bore their patrons' names.[59] This competition-by-architecture yielded a landscape of pervasive personal giantism.

Most of the new buildings were blunt, businesslike office blocks extruded from the grids on which they stood. Together, their boxy, flat-roofed forms thickened the skyline with architecture and gave the city new shape for the spectator (see fig. 27). In some cases, individual buildings displayed more purposeful visual qualities. Frick's Union Arcade, for instance, with its ornate architectural design and its location "where the city's two main streams of motor and traction traffic meet," boasted "a conspicuous figure in an uncommonly conspicuous neighborhood" (fig. 28).[60] And some of the new tall buildings sought an even more dramatic presence on the street and on the skyline. Gail Fenske and Derek Holdsworth attribute these changes to the emergence of large-scale commercial enterprise in the American economy and a sub-

Fig. 28. Union Arcade Building, shown in splendid isolation. Reprinted from *Union Arcade Building* (Pittsburgh: Union Arcade Building, 1916), n.p. Carnegie Mellon University Architecture Archives.

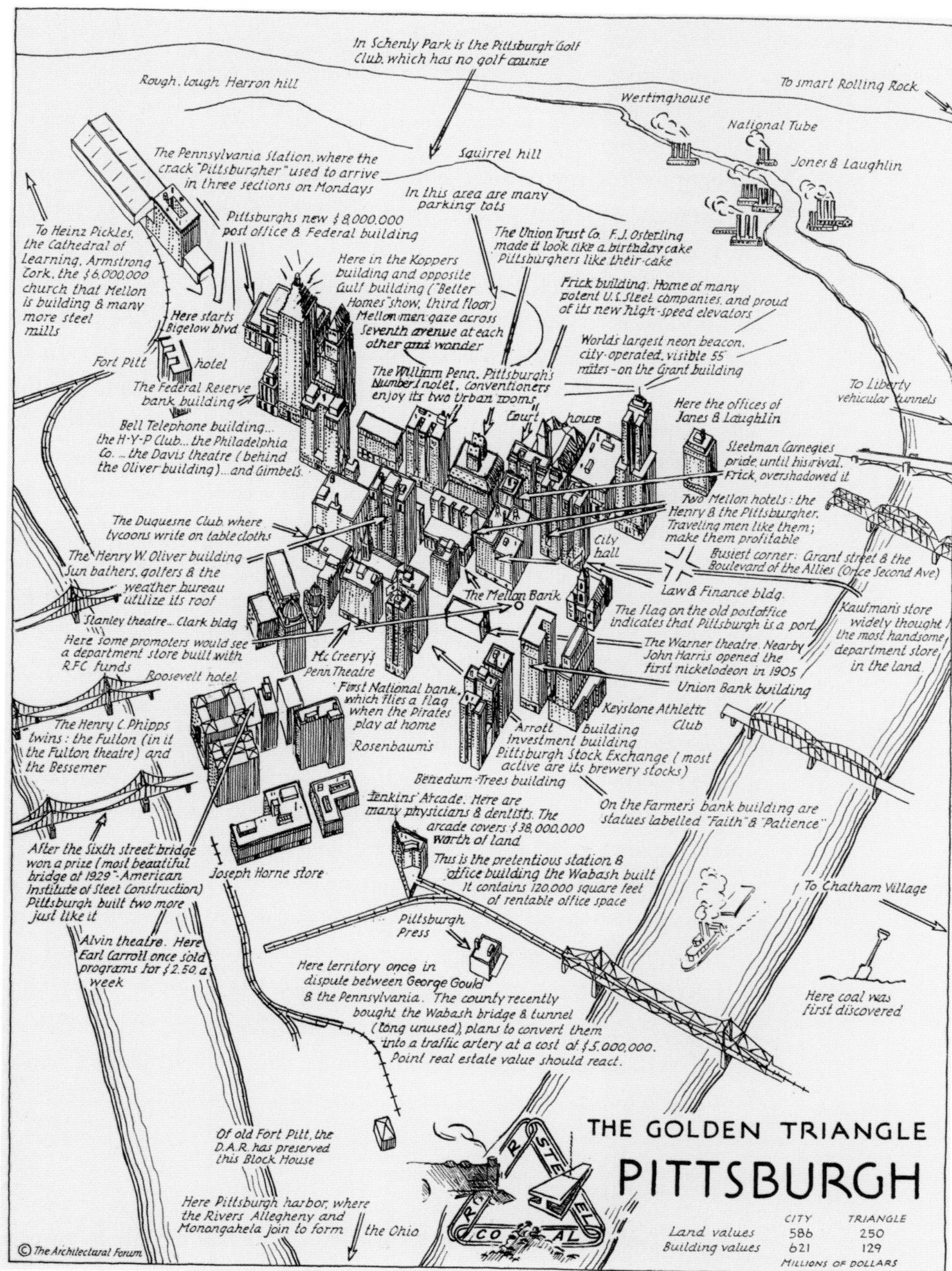

Fig. 29. *The Golden Triangle, Pittsburgh*. Reprinted from *Architectural Forum* 58, no. 6 (June 1933), 524.

sequent desire for commercial identity and "increased visibility on the urban scene. Visibility was achieved through the sheer scale and lavishness of construction—ornate and stylistically up-to-date office blocks and conspicuous crested towers stood out from the 'standard,' typically speculative, steel-framed office building construction—but also through siting the new construction such that it had high exposure to urban crowds. Becoming a highly visible architectural presence in the city marked a critical turning point, for now the enterprise began to exercise some control over its urban surroundings. It exerted this control visually—as a dominant structure in its setting, it radiated its influence outward."[61]

The key to this trend, and to the further transformation of the urban skyline, was the skyscraper. Height afforded an inherent visibility, and this visibility "legitimized a newly powerful commercial order. The unabashed appropriation of a form [i.e., the tower] reserved in earlier civilizations for ecclesiastical or civic purposes vividly conveyed the dominance of commercial affairs in American life."[62] The commercial skyscraper came to dominate the civic topography, and Americans increasingly found communal identity in private enterprise and commercial giantism.

When *Architectural Forum* magazine featured Pittsburgh in its June 1933 issue, it focused almost exclusively on the commercial city—its values, buildings, and visual image (fig. 29). Commerce had gilded the Forks of the Ohio, which was now commonly known as the Golden Triangle.[63] Commerce had replaced the church and the civic authority in the skyline, and visibility had become a commercial value in a contest that required more and more initiative to stand out.

Manhattanization

The Golden Triangle was fertile ground for tall buildings. By one assessment, downtown Pittsburgh had a dozen structures of skyscraper height by 1905. "Let them multiply," cheered the *Bulletin*. "There is no sky in the world which needs scraping more than that which arches over the Iron City."[64]

The skyscraper emerged due to the availability of new building materials and technologies such as the steel frame and the elevator, which were in some cases the products of Pittsburgh industry. It also benefited from a booming commercial climate, which in Pittsburgh was a reflection of industrial expansion. A lack of land may have been a factor in Pittsburgh as well, as commercial development in the Golden Triangle was hemmed in by topographical conditions: two flood-prone rivers and high land to the east. Noted architectural writer Montgomery Schuyler wrote in 1911 that "the skyscraper was in Pittsburgh an urgent necessity" because of the limited area for downtown expansion. "It follows of necessity," he added, "that the collection of skyscrapers in Pittsburgh should be more crowded and more impressive than the like collection in any other American city, New York and Chicago alone excepted."[65]

Most shadows were not as deep and purposeful as Frick's, but as the skyscraper gained a foothold in the American city, many noticed that the tall buildings were draining daylight from urban streets. New York City's zoning act of 1916, followed by Pittsburgh's similar law of 1923 (amended in 1927), combated tall, blocky buildings by enforcing stepwise setbacks in the building envelope and encouraging towers that emerged at a setback, centered on a point, and were carried to the skyline.[66] The Pittsburgh code, for instance, set a maximum height limit of 265 feet to the first setback, but allowed towers of unrestricted height. The result was the classic Art Deco–age skyscraper.

The essence of the skyscraper lay in what Diane Agrest calls its "upward transition to a point of culmination." That point was often articulated as a crest, and increasingly assumed emblematic distinction. Tall buildings with unique crests—such as New York's Woolworth and Singer Buildings—caught the spectator's eye and could be readily identified with their occupant or owner. Architects, faced with a new typological problem, initially turned to precedents from the past. The skyscraper crest was "often designed as an exemplar of an individual building in itself," like a temple or a chapel, set upon a high podium, and might reflect any architectural style or period from the Roman to the Gothic.[67]

Long before zoning, the Keenan Building (1907) was Pittsburgh's first tall building to thrust a notable crest onto the skyline (fig. 30). Built for newspaperman T. J. Keenan, founder of the *Pittsburgh Press,* it was sited at the intersection of the two downtown street grids and followed an early skyscraper tradition of newspaper buildings with elaborate crowns.[68] All of eighteen stories tall, the Keenan Building culminates in a concrete dome, covered in copper tiles. This dome was originally surmounted by a globe topped with an eagle, and was surrounded by four smaller domes at the corners, all topped with flagstaffs. Schuyler disparagingly called the copper dome a "gilt umbrella," and Kidney described the overall effect as that of "a Prussian general with four aides."[69] An account in Keenan's own *Pittsburgh Press* suggested that visibility was the key: "Located at the conjunction of three wide streets and facing up Sixth Avenue, the building will be one of the most conspicuous in the city. For this reason, Mr. Keenan has adopted a more impressive and naturally more expensive style of architecture than would be called for were the structure to face on one of the narrow streets of the lower city."[70] The building remains readily visible to the spectator today.

The Keenan Building anticipated three important skyscrapers, built just before or in spite of the Depression. Each was broadly Deco in massing, was taller than any previous Pittsburgh building, had an emphatic crest, and was highly visible.[71]

The Grant Building (1927–1930) was a speculative project of W. J. Strassburger, designed by architects Henry Hornbostel and Eric Fisher Wood (fig. 31).[72] Toker likens its "dramatically proportioned setbacks" to a "giant's throne."[73] At forty stories, it tops out at about 485 feet. Spiky Art Deco finials originally topped the body of the building, yet the crest is atypically nonhistorical: a boxy penthouse crowned by a thirty-eight-foot tall steel tower.

The Koppers Building (1927–1929) was built for the Koppers Corporation, a chemical company controlled by Mellon family interests (fig. 32). Designed by Graham, Anderson, Probst, and White, a Chicago architectural firm, its frontal setback design was related to Eliel

▲◀ Fig. 30. Thomas Hannah (architect), Keenan Building, 1907, postcard. Pittsburgh History and Landmarks Foundation.

▲▶ Fig. 31. Henry Hornbostel and Eric Fisher Wood (architects), Grant Building, 1927–1930, postcard. Carnegie Mellon University Architecture Archives.

◀ Fig. 32. Graham, Anderson, Probst, and White (architects), Koppers Building, 1927–1929. Shows illumination for Light's Golden Jubilee (1929). Carnegie Mellon University Architecture Archives.

Fig. 33. Trowbridge and Livingston (architects), Gulf Building, 1929–1931, postcard. Pittsburgh History and Landmarks Foundation.

Saarinen's celebrated but unsuccessful entry in the Chicago Tribune Tower Competition (1922), an event that more than any other displayed the eclectic possibilities for skyscraper design. Thirty-four stories tall, it reaches approximately 475 feet in height, with setbacks at the twenty-first and twenty-ninth floors. The crest is a medieval château in form, capped with a copper roof that is both corporate advertisement and pun.

Across the street, the Gulf Oil Company—also a Mellon concern—built the Gulf Building (1929–1931), now known as the Gulf Tower (fig. 33).[74] Designed by Trowbridge and Livingston of New York, it was, for many years, the tallest building in Pittsburgh at forty-four stories and 582 feet. After an initial setback at 108 feet, the building climbs as a tower—a campanile to echo and succeed the courthouse tower. The crest is a pyramidal adaptation of the Greek Mausoleum at Halicarnassus (353 BCE), one of the seven wonders of the ancient world.[75]

Architects and clients who favored the high visibility of tall buildings and emphatic crests also focused on nighttime visibility through illumination. New lighting technologies provided new possibilities for an "architecture of the night."[76] Setbacks accommodated floodlights, and skyscraper crests could be outfitted with beacons, searchlights, and time and weather signals. The beginnings of aviation called for navigational lighting in high places, but there were promotional motivations as well. When lighted, Rem Koolhaas says, "Building becomes Tower, landlocked lighthouse, ostensibly flashing its beams out to sea, but in fact luring the metropolitan audience to itself."[77]

The steel tower on top of the Grant Building carried what was then the world's largest neon beacon light (fig. 38). With 300 million candela visible for up to 150 miles, it flashed P-I-T-T-S-B-U-R-G-H in Morse code.[78] The Koppers Building's crest was lighted by 197 lights between 250 and 1,000 watts each.[79] The Gulf Building culminated in a beacon light, and after 1956 in a "Weathergide," which gave weather forecasts by means of light signals in the corporate blue and orange.[80]

As the skyscrapers grew, glowed, and multiplied, they began to interact with each other. Agrest suggests: "the relationships between buildings are complex insofar as they are established not only in terms of entire buildings or of the building's body to the crest, but also in terms of relations between crest and crest, and between the body of one building and the crest of another, etc." At times, the dialogue may border on the erotic. Horsbrugh notes that the Koppers Building acts as an "admirable foil" for the adjacent Gulf building.[81] In fact, Gulf and Koppers stand virtually body to body, cheek to cheek, tête-à-tête, joined together as a couple under the auspices of the Mellon family (see figs. 33 and 34). If the Gulf Building is Pittsburgh's Empire State Building, as has often been suggested, then the Koppers Building is Pittsburgh's Chrysler Building. And, in the bedroom scenario imagined by Madelon Vriesendorp and Rem Koolhaas (see fig. 35), the Grant Building stands in for Rockefeller Center (as the jilted lover?).

Skyscrapers came to interact most explicitly in the competition for sheer height. In Pittsburgh, as elsewhere, height mattered; and each new skyscraper upped the ante. Yet despite their competitive nature, the skyscrapers contributed to the greater whole of the skyline (see figs. 36 and 37). "Like the beauty contest," Koolhaas says, the skyline "is the rare format in which collective success is directly proportionate to the ferocity of individual competition." As Schuyler wrote of Manhattan, "it is in the aggregation that the immense impressiveness lies."[82]

"The Trend is to Grant Street," announced a Grant Building promotional flyer, and the three Deco-age skyscrapers ratified that claim.

Fig. 34. John Kane, *From My Studio Window,* 1932. The Metropolitan Museum of Art, Bequest of Miss Adelaide Milton de Groot (1876–1967), 1967, 67.187.164. Photograph ©1984 The Metropolitan Museum of Art.

On Grant Street, at the eastern end of the Golden Triangle, they broke free from the extruded grid and transformed the boxy skyline with their sheer height and eye-catching crests. As the Pittsburgh skyline grew and changed, it assumed a cumulative and characteristic profile—or rather two profiles, for the nighttime skyline became an alternative skyline of glowing disembodied crests and scanning/flashing beacons.

The Gulf Building has been called "an important element in the visual impact of downtown as seen by the visiting eye, whether from distant points in the hills, from some of the entry points of the city, [or] from the air."[83] The height, lively crests, and lighting schemes of all three skyscrapers gave them ready identity and wide visibility, and enabled them to communicate with the spectator over an expansive terrain. Consequently, these attributes were assumed by the skyline as

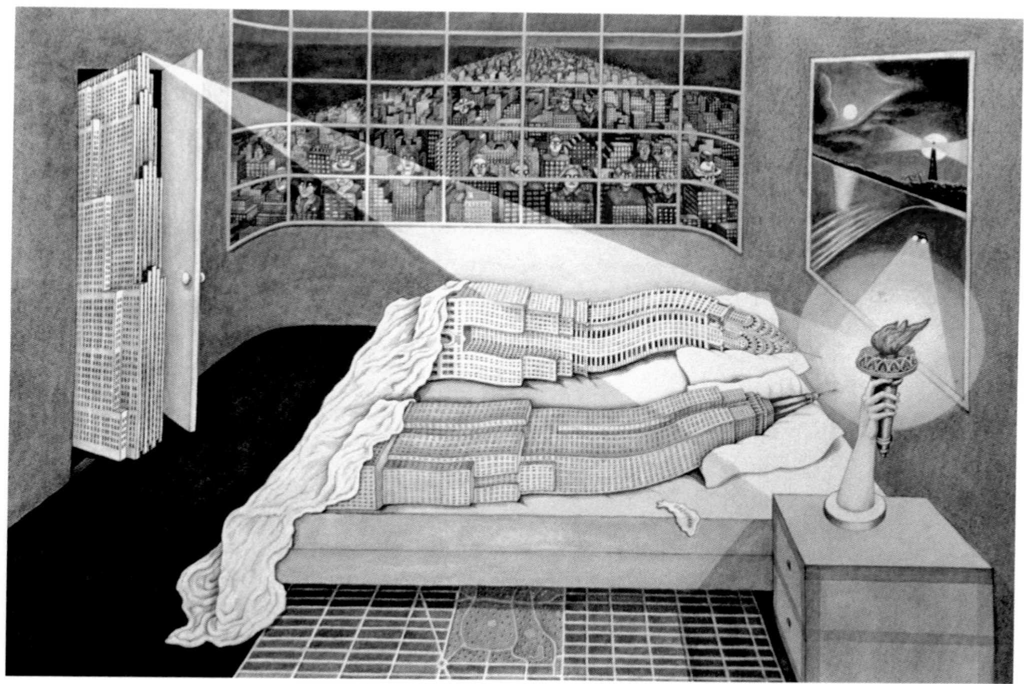

Fig. 35. Madelon Vriesendorp, *Flagrant délit*, from *Delirious New York: A Retroactive Manifesto for Manhattan* (New York: Oxford University Press, 1978). Courtesy of the Office of Metropolitan Architecture (OMA).

a whole. Thus Pittsburgh experienced a process of Manhattanization whereby the skyline became a distinctive and recognizable visual entity in and of itself, and a device of communication within the larger landscape.[84]

The Aerial Point of View

The neon beacon high atop the Grant Building was a skyline device and a practical government-sanctioned response to the advent of regular airmail flights and the desire for nighttime flying (fig. 38).[85] This height and flight synergy between the skyscraper and the airplane was emblematic of the age. During the 1920s and 1930s, as Adnan Morshed recounts, the skyscraper and the airplane were the "soaring icons of the modern world." Each was a symbol of technological progress that

Fig. 36. Skyline from Mount Washington, ca. 1937, postcard. Pittsburgh History and Landmarks Foundation.

struck a chord with the popular imagination. Together, they marked the advance of civilization; and not so incidentally, changed the ways that "people experienced and viewed the physical world."[86]

Skyscrapers are for seeing as well as being seen. Agrest observes that structures like the Eiffel Tower and the Empire State Building are defined in part "in terms of [their] own gaze."[87] The skyscraper is a surrogate spectator, calmly observing the surrounding landscape. It also, of course, can provide a platform for human sight. In Pittsburgh, the Grant and Gulf Buildings had observation decks on the thirty-seventh and forty-second stories, respectively, that were open to spectators and afforded outward and downward views (fig. 39).[88]

The airplane provided a related, if more extreme, aerial viewpoint, and its popularity resulted in what Charles Waldheim calls a "new form of mass spectatorship."[89] Pittsburgh embraced the airplane as it had the

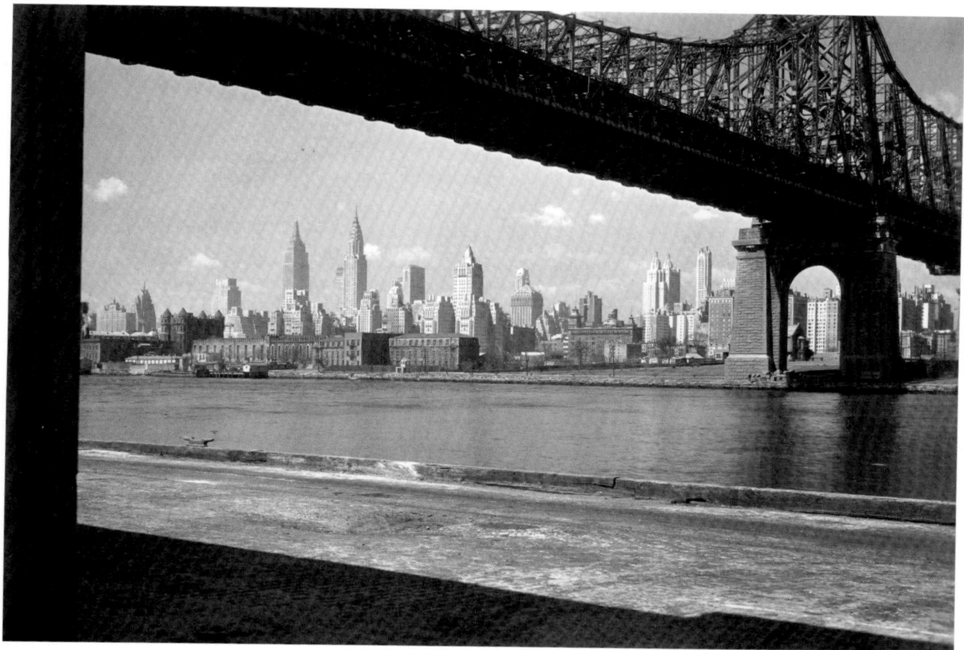

Fig. 37. Samuel H. Gottscho (photographer), New York City midtown skyline framed by Queensboro Bridge, 1932. Library of Congress, Prints and Photographs Division, Gottscho-Schleisner Collection, LC-G612-T01-17838.

skyscraper, and all things aviation were prominently covered in the Pittsburgh Chamber of Commerce magazine *Greater Pittsburgh* during the late 1920s and early 1930s. The new Allegheny County Airport opened in 1931, and by 1936 an average of 250,000 people visited the airport each month, many simply to experience the "modern landing field spectacle" of "the coming and going of huge passenger planes." Three commercial airlines carried an average of 6,093 passengers per month, and four companies provided sightseeing rides for more than 25,000 people per year.[90]

All of these eyes in the sky held potential implications for the built environment below. Thus, contemporary concerns for skyline and nighttime visibility were joined by a concern for aerial appearances. In a 1927 article entitled "Architecture and Aeronautics," Raymond M. Marlier addressed his fellow Pittsburgh architects, saying: "The project

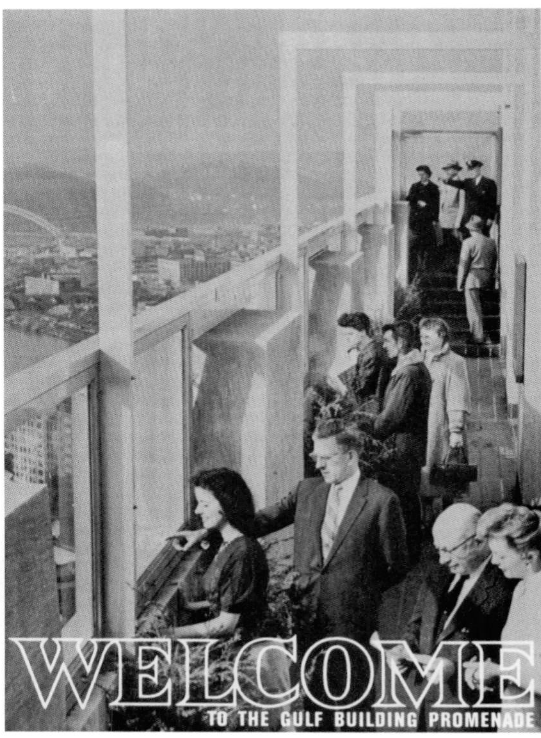

Fig. 38. Grant Building beacon. Reprinted from *Greater Pittsburgh* (March 23, 1929), cover. Carnegie Library of Pittsburgh.

Fig. 39. *Welcome to the Gulf Building Promenade,* ca. 1960, brochure. Pittsburgh History and Landmarks Foundation.

you are now designing will, while it stands, be viewed by thousands of aerial travelers. . . . The time is near when no architect can continue a successful general practice while ignoring the aerial age we are now entering." Marlier, who was a pilot, urged the architects to take a "fly on him" and see Pittsburgh from the air, with an eye toward designing from this new point of view.[91]

The significance of the new aerial point of view was perceived far beyond Pittsburgh, and had profound implications for urban planning as well as architecture. For some observers, including trend-setting French architect Le Corbusier, the high vantage points provided by tall buildings and the airplane came as a revelation indeed. And the new view, it seemed, wasn't pretty, revealing the "hitherto hidden and monstrous corruption of our cities," which were "terrifying in [their] confusion." In *Aircraft: L'Avion accuse . . .* he wrote, "The airplane is an indictment. It indicts the city. It indicts those who control the city. By means of the airplane, we now have proof, recorded on the photographic plate, of the rightness of our desire to alter methods of architecture and town-planning."[92]

Le Corbusier concluded that "cities, with their misery must be torn down. They must be largely destroyed and fresh cities built." Rebuilding would begin with a clear site, and proceed according to the new insights afforded by high vantage points; the viewpoints that indicted also suggested new possibilities.[93] For Le Corbusier, says M. Christine Boyer: "When the eye took in the urban panorama, optimism reigned and there the imagination conceived of vast new arrangements of space. This aerial perspective implied a new way of seeing and knowing—by analysis, comparison, and deduction. From this vertical perspective, Le Corbusier noted, the eyes see clearly, the mind makes wise decisions, and the city planner knows what to do."[94] The wise city planner would replace the dense and ineffectual urban layout of the past with a purposeful new order at a new scale. "The old limited dimensions, doors thirty or forty feet apart, narrow streets . . . will have ceased to exist. A new scale, a new and nobler dimension will animate the architecture of cities"(fig. 40).[95]

The new city would be characterized by boundless space, functional order, serial repetition, and scenic unity. Le Corbusier prescribed a continuous open landscape studded with widely spaced skyscrapers. The preferred skyscraper was flat-topped (Le Corbusier detested crests), and cruciform in plan. This urban model was codified as the so-called *ville radieuse,* or Radiant City.[96] As Waldheim explains, "the idea of landscape . . . shifted from scenic and pictorial imagery to a highly managed surface best viewed, arranged, and coordinated from above."[97]

When Pittsburghers looked out from their skyscrapers and down from their airplanes, they saw that what had appeared picturesque from oblique viewpoints on the surrounding hills now appeared chaot-

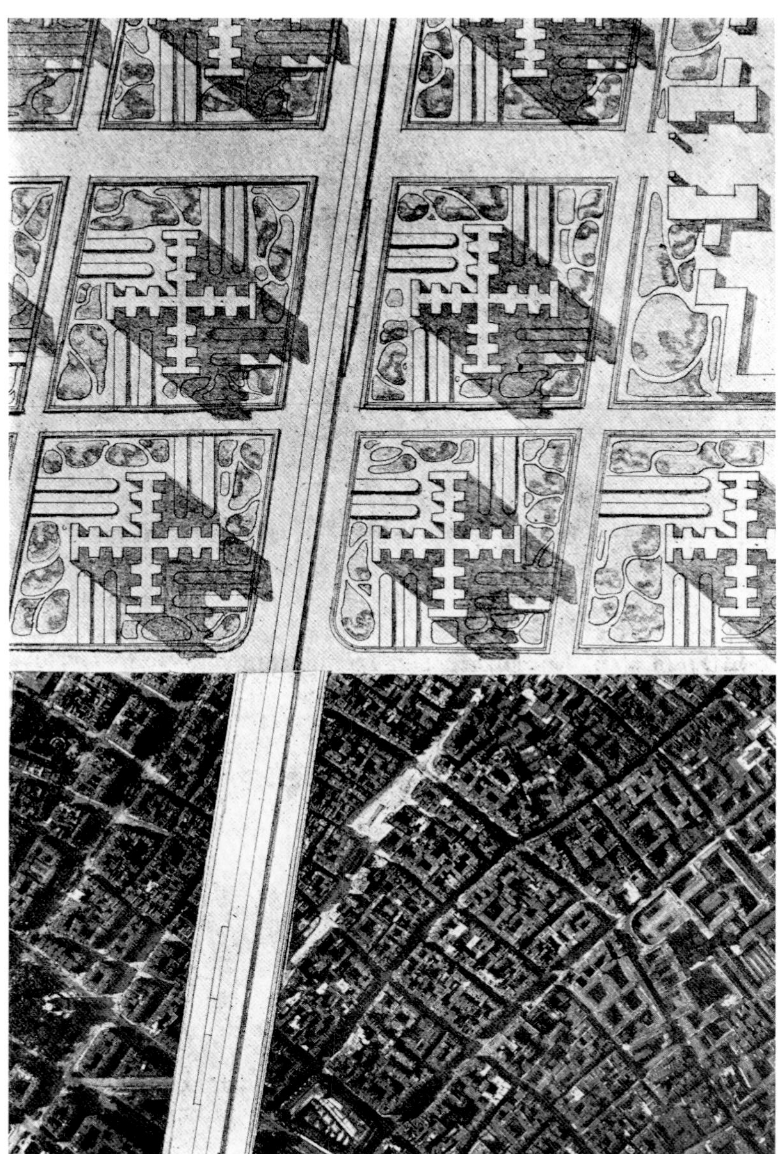

Fig. 40. Le Corbusier, *Paris: Plan Voisin,* 1925. The caption in *Urbanisme* (1924) reads: "Here are the districts which it is proposed to demolish and those which it is suggested should be built in their place. Both plans are to the same scale." © Artists Rights Society (ARS), New York/ADAGP, Paris/FLC.

Fig. 41. Mitchell and Ritchey, *Pittsburgh in Progress*, 1947. Note the inset photograph taken from the observation deck at the Grant Building. Reprinted from Mitchell and Ritchey, *Pittsburgh in Progress* (Pittsburgh: Kaufmann's, 1947), cover. Carnegie Mellon University Architecture Archives.

ic and congested. *Life* magazine photographer Margaret Bourke-White took indicting aerial photographs of Pittsburgh in 1936 and 1944.[98] As Pittsburgh attacked its smoke problem, the view looked clearer and clearer, and the city looked worse and worse to the spectator.

In 1947, Edgar J. Kaufmann commissioned architects James Mitchell and Dahlen K. Ritchey to envision Pittsburgh seventy-five years in the future, in honor of the seventy-fifth anniversary of Kaufmann's Department Store. Their study took the form of an exhibit and publication called *Pittsburgh in Progress* (fig. 41).[99] This was, it turned out, a far more important vision for Pittsburgh than Frank Lloyd Wright's celebrated Point projects, which Kaufmann commissioned at virtually the same time. Wright's plans would have spectacularly transformed Pittsburgh's Point, but did not find civic support. The Mitchell and Ritchey plan significantly reshaped the city.[100]

As if seen through the eyes of Le Corbusier, *Pittsburgh in Progress* presented views of the congested present and an ideal future, almost exclusively as seen from above. Pittsburgh's present was smoke and

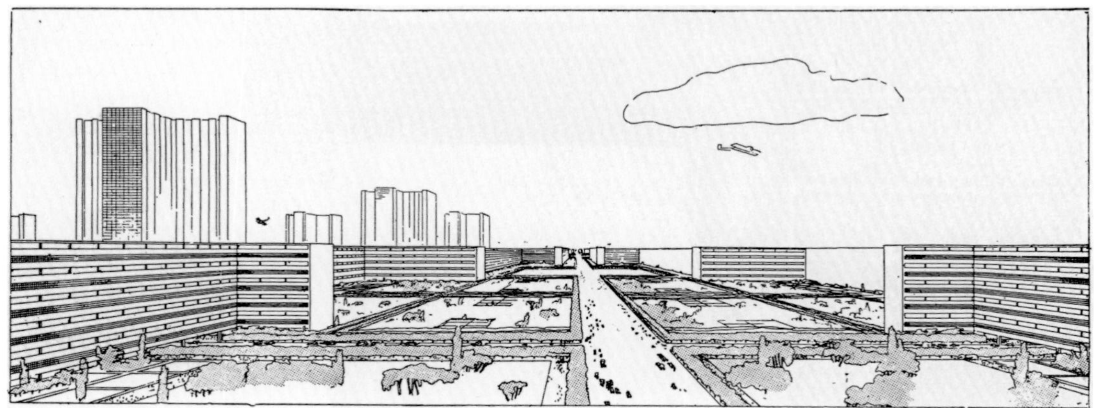

Fig. 42. Le Corbusier, *Cité contemporaine de 3 millions d'habitants,* 1922. The caption in *The Radiant City* (1935) reads: "There are no more pariahs deprived of sun and of space. Equipment worthy of a machine-age civilization." Note the airplanes. © Artists Rights Society (ARS), New York/ADAGP, Paris/FLC.

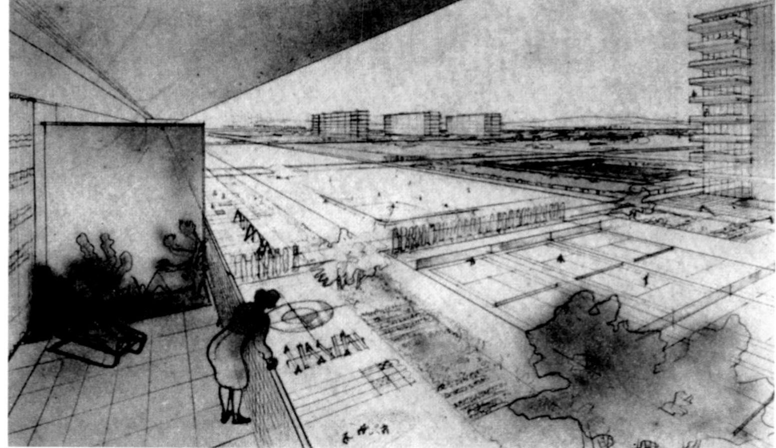

Fig. 43. Mitchell and Ritchey, illustration from *Pittsburgh in Progress*. The original caption reads: "Spaciousness, light and air—hallmarks of the new Pittsburgh." Reprinted from "*Pittsburgh in Progress*: Towards a Master Plan," *Progressive Architecture [Pencil Points]* 28, no. 6 (June 1947), 72.

problems with housing and recreation and parking. It was "tangled traffic with bottlenecks of narrow intersections . . . close-walled streets . . . ever-increasing multitude of autos, street cars, busses . . . lack of parking facilities for them in the heart of the city . . . growing numbers of children seeking places for their games on streets . . . families living cramped and crowded in inadequate, unsanitary dwellings" (see inset fig. 41). Here, it seemed, were findings to rival the urban problems that had been detailed in the Pittsburgh Survey of 1908–1909, all newly diagnosed nearly forty years later from the observation deck at the Grant Building, and from Marlier's airplane.[101]

Pittsburgh's future was a City for Tomorrow (or Radiant City), represented as a series of large-scale group plans. This approach, the architects said, "strives to broaden our imaginations so that we may not hesitate to plan the rebuilding of the city in bold terms." It would require Le Corbusier's clear site; Pittsburgh would need to be destroyed to be renewed. "The old city wilderness will be cleared away. New pioneers will have cleansed and opened the land for living areas of noble proportions." The new Pittsburgh would "have tall buildings so more space will be available for playgrounds, parks, schools, sports, and homes" (see figs. 42 and 43).[102] The conceptual irony of introducing boundless space into an inherently bounded place like Pittsburgh was seemingly not apparent.

Fig. 44. Margaret Bourke-White (photographer), "Richard King Mellon," 1955. Gateway Center appears in the background below. Time and Life Pictures, Getty Images.

So Pittsburgh got to work building the City for Tomorrow. If *Pittsburgh in Progress* provided the vision, it was the unlikely political and economic alliance of Democratic mayor David L. Lawrence and the powerful Mellon family that choreographed the partial realization of that vision. In 1955 Margaret Bourke-White and *Life* magazine returned to America's so-called Renaissance City to record Pittsburgh's new role as a celebrated exemplar of post–World War II urban renewal. Bourke-White took new aerial photographs of the city. And she photographed mover and shaker Richard King Mellon in his aerie on the thirty-ninth floor of a new skyscraper, looking down on a city that was radically changing its urban form as a Radiant-City wannabe (figs. 44 and 45).[103]

Panorama Field

The Radiant City and its widely spaced buildings called for ample expanses of open land targeted for transportation, recreation, and plantings. Le Corbusier purposefully placed his skyscrapers in parkland, and sought, says Caroline Constant, to "dissolve the polarity of

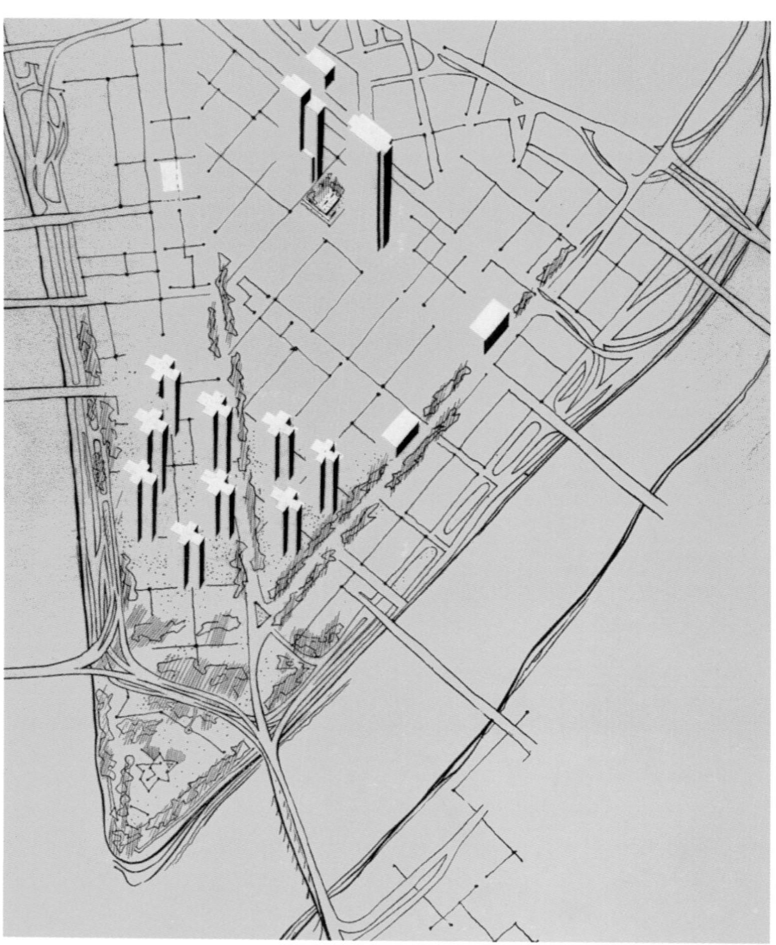

Fig. 45. Helen Benz Schiavo, *Map, Golden Triangle, Pittsburgh, Pa.* Reprinted from *Architectural Forum* 91, no. 5 (November 1949), cover.

city and country, merging the density of the former with the '*soleil, espace, verdure*' of the latter."[104] In turn, Mitchell and Ritchey referred to their future Pittsburgh as Park City, and proposed "a spacious triangle of green" for the Point where "towering office buildings are set in the midst of the expanding green of nature." Here, "The clear sky, clean air, pure water, green leaf and open vista of life in nature will replace the dusty, dry, and crowded city. Nature will be as much a part of the city as it is of the country. And Pittsburgh, with its naturally dramatic setting, will then offer panoramas of unmatched beauty."[105]

The legacy of American postwar urban renewal obscures the fact that one of its aims was to green the city. When urban renewal ultimately laid bare Pittsburgh's Point, it was in fact transformed into parkland—complete with Radiant City office towers and panoramas (figs. 46 and 47).

The eighteenth-century forts at the Point had wasted away when no longer needed. A park was proposed in their stead as early as 1836, recalling the common conversion of outdated fortifications to green space in European cities. And similar recommendations periodically followed. Yet the Point was ultimately subdivided into streets and parcels and was largely developed as part of the commercial city. Its role as a cosmological center point was disregarded and virtually lost. In 1956, landscape architect Ralph E. Griswold commented, in a diagnosis and prescription worthy of Le Corbusier and in sympathy with Mitchell and Ritchey, "Not a vestige of the natural beauty that [George] Washington had seen withstood the onslaught of industrial and commercial invasion. The Point became an indiscriminate hodgepodge of urban chaos. . . . When the air was cleared and the black, ugly confusion of the Point was revealed in full sunlight, a civic shudder shook the citizens. . . . A complete new life, urban reincarnation, was the only hope. This was the challenge—a drastic challenge requiring equally drastic measures."[106]

So Pittsburgh set about renewing the Point, starting with a clear site.[107] A Point Park Commission was appointed in 1940, and the Commonwealth of Pennsylvania sanctioned a state park in 1945. Subsequently, Griswold and the firm of Clarke and Rapuano planned Point State Park, which was slowly realized between 1948 and 1972.

Despite Griswold's indictment, the Point's topographical setting remained largely intact and inspired park designers to restore "the rivers, forest and view of surrounding hills as nearly as possible to the scene George Washington had in looking out over the Point in Pioneer

Fig. 46. Julian Michele, Point State Park and Gateway Center, ca. 1953. Reprinted from *Charette* 35, no. 1 (January 1955), back cover.

days."[108] To this end, they sought to restore the Point's natural conditions as much as was feasible. Native trees were grouped naturalistically as "token forests." An open meadow separated the groves of trees "like the clearing for a pioneer enterprise."[109] The early forts were evoked, and in the case of Fort Pitt, partially rebuilt of reconstructed earthworks.

Point State Park was staked to an eighteenth-century ideal, but it was also a very modern place.[110] Streets were replaced by contemporary highways that were as prominent and integral to the design of the park as were the historic fortifications. The Portal Bridge, an elegant underpass beneath the highways, was designed in part by Gordon Bunshaft, one of America's premier modernist architects. A 150-foot high fountain inserted at the very tip of the Point was a modern technological marvel. It was also a conscious and conspicuous topographical response, evoking the proximate confluence of the three rivers and "rising majestically against the horizon of the western hills" (see fig. 50).[111]

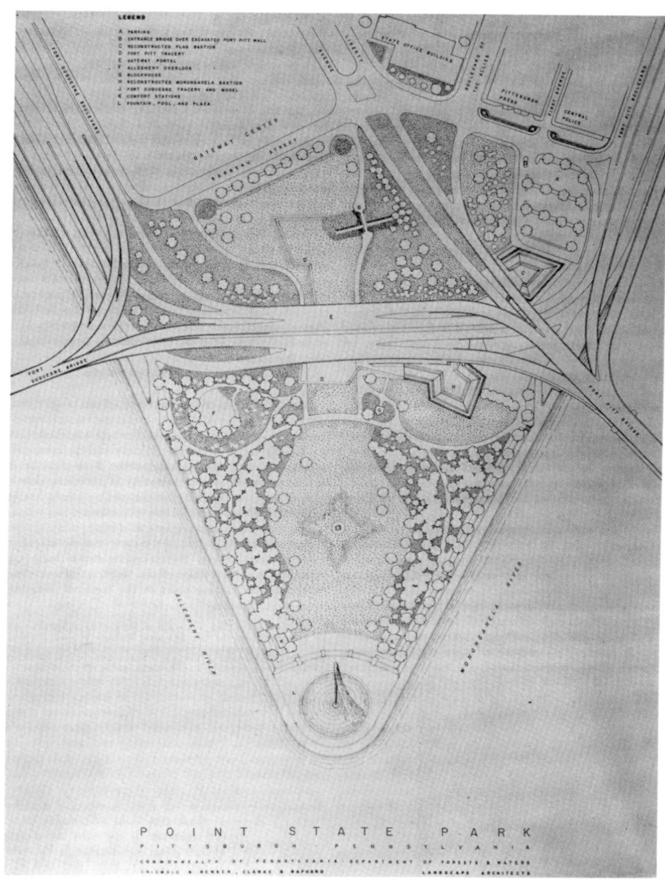

Fig. 47. Griswold and Renner with Clarke and Rapuano (landscape architects), *Point State Park*. Reprinted from Ralph E. Griswold, "From Fort Pitt to Point Park: A Turning Point in the Physical Planning of Pittsburgh," *Landscape Architecture* 46, no. 4 (July 1956), 201.

The Point State Park Committee further proposed an adjacent commercial development "to supply a setting for Point Park itself, since the park would be spoiled if it was separated from the city by a blighted and decayed area." Subsequently, as many as nine widely spaced office towers were planned for the new Gateway Center development, featuring cruciform building footprints with clear Radiant City precedents (fig. 48).[112] The three buildings that were built in this manner (1950–1953) were clad in a first-time-ever skin of chromium stainless steel.[113] With this, Pittsburgh metals provided architectural finish as well as structural brawn on the skyline. The Gateway Center buildings were much criticized, however, at least by architects. *Architectural*

Fig. 48. Gateway Center. Reprinted from *Charette* 31, no. 4 (April 1951), cover.

Forum conceded that they "proclaim[ed] the Steel City through its own metallic glitter," while opining that they were not much differentiated from "up-ended diners."[114]

But these were up-ended diners in a park! Not only was Gateway Center adjacent to Point State Park, but it incorporated its own landscape plan as well: a formal plan in the European manner with fountains and strong axes, an echo of Fort Pitt's King's Gardens on virtually the same site (fig. 49).[115] This landscape provided a lush green ground plane for the office buildings, which covered only 20 percent of the site. "Now, at last," proclaimed *Architectural Forum*, Le Corbusier's Radiant City had been realized, some thirty years after its conception: "Here, for the first time in US city planning, the concept of office towers in a park

Fig. 49. Clarke and Rapuano (landscape architects), Gateway Center landscape, ca. 1954. Carnegie Library of Pittsburgh.

has made good sense in economic terms. It has made sense to men who may have never heard of Le Corbusier's 'Ville Radieuse.' And having once made sense to these eminently practical men the concept can no longer be shrugged off as the dream of some unrealistic visionary."[116]

Point State Park and Gateway Center are the principal Pittsburgh legacies of the Radiant City's aerial imperatives and point of view. As such, they are best perceived and understood from the air; and they were, it seems, at least partly conceived from the air. Griswold recorded at least one instance in 1952 when the park designers and other officials visited the aforementioned thirty-ninth floor offices of Mellon Bank to visually survey the area of the park from above (see fig. 44). Fort perimeters, highway ramps, and building footprints appeared as if

Fig. 50. Newman-Schmidt Studios (photographer), view of Point State Park with fountain. Reprinted from *The Allegheny Conference on Community Development . . . Presents . . . Pittsburgh and Allegheny County: Planning to Reality* (Pittsburgh: 1956), 6. Carnegie Mellon University Architecture Archives.

drawn on the land from above (see fig. 47).[117] Aerial views of Point State Park and Gateway Center were widely published during the projects' long gestation period so that this new part of the city became known from the air long before it could be experienced on the ground (fig. 46).

In addition, the Gateway Center towers themselves provided purposeful aerial views. The wide spacing between buildings, cruciform floor plates, and in-the-round plans fostered views from the interiors in all directions. The single-pane windows, considered large for the time, promoted expansive and unobstructed views. They were picture windows, and for most of the occupants/spectators, the picture was the park below.[118]

But there were also key new viewpoints on the ground. At Point State Park, the reconstitution of a westward view was key. Here, said Griswold, the spectator "will behold a beautiful landscape of rivers, forests, and hills" (fig. 50).[119] As Robert C. Alberts explains further: "The basic concept had been set forth in the early years to build and maintain a simple, unified park of monumental sweep, uncluttered by

Fig. 51. View of Gateway Center from Point State Park. The photograph was taken before the completion of the park and its highways. Reprinted from *The Allegheny Conference on Community Development . . . Presents . . . Pittsburgh and Allegheny County: Planning to Reality* (Pittsburgh: 1956), 7. Carnegie Mellon University Architecture Archives.

buildings, memorials, and statues, with the open space that is so rare in modern cities. The hills and rivers, little changed by man since the eighteenth century, would provide a majestic memorial far more impressive than any man-made monument. The dramatic view to the west, down the Ohio River, the nation's first highway to the heartland of America, should be open and unimpeded."[120]

This westward view of a neo-eighteenth-century landscape was balanced by a view back toward the east—a new view to a new city edge that had been opened by urban renewal. When the preexisting panorama was deemed lacking, a new one was built in the form of Gateway Center (fig. 51). So the new Point provided the spectator with a 360-degree panoramic view that scanned from the natural wilderness to the modern city and back again.

Paul Shepheard says of London what could be said of Pittsburgh: it is a very congested place, so it is difficult to see the city without climbing hills or venturing out on a river where there are wide panoramic views. Shepheard speaks almost wistfully of the wide swaths of open land left in London after the Great Fire of London, and again after the

Fig 52. Harrison and Abramovitz with Mitchell and Ritchey (architects), Alcoa Building, 1952. Carnegie Mellon University Architecture Archives.

aerial bombing of World War II. Each time the dense city was laid open, creating new spaces and sweeping new views; and each time the city was thoroughly rebuilt. What if, he asks, these spaces had been left undeveloped, as permanent "panorama fields"?[121]

Urban renewal brought to Pittsburgh a panorama field that remained when all the rebuilding was done, a place of reconnection with the terrain. The panorama field opened up both air and ground space for the spectator. It is thus a place of new and improved views from above and from the ground. With this, Pittsburgh reestablished the Point as the city's *omphalos*, specifically embodied in the renewed forts, and celebrated the birth of the modern city, as symbolized by the great fountain and reflected in the metallic sheen of Gateway Center. Land that had been converted to parcels had reemerged as a key site in the civic topography, showcased for the spectator.

The Eye of the Landscape

Meanwhile, uptown, Richard King Mellon had been building that office from which to look down on the city and the Point. The office was housed in one of two new corporate skyscrapers that were designed by New York architects Harrison and Abramovitz and built almost simultaneously—one for the Alcoa Corporation (1952) and one for Mellon Bank and U.S. Steel (1953) (figs. 52 and 53).[122]

These buildings displayed their materials first and foremost—an aluminum curtain wall for Alcoa and stainless steel spandrels for U.S. Steel. When it was built, the Alcoa Building was explicitly promoted with the slogan, "Aluminum on the Skyline." Here was a type of corpo-

Fig. 53. Harrison and Abramovitz with William York Cocken (architects), U.S. Steel Building, 1953. Reprinted from "From Trains to Trim," *Charette* 31, no. 3 (March 1951), 13.

rate giantism whereby tall buildings could be identified with their corporate owners by their materials alone, and corporate products served an emblematic function in lieu of crests. The zoning rules that had so shaped the Deco-age skyscrapers were circumvented with street-level setbacks, so the resulting buildings were blocky flat-topped towers (again). Yet both buildings contributed to a distinctive Pittsburgh skyline whose corporate constituency *and* materials reflected Pittsburgh's industrial strength.[123]

The new skyscrapers were conceived in conjunction with a new square that would occupy the entire city block that lay between them. This block contained a motley collection of buildings and parking lots suitable for clearing, as shown by the requisite indicting photograph taken from above (fig. 54). Richard King Mellon, inspired by Union Square in San Francisco, first envisioned the square at his feet; and Mellon Square (1949–1955) subsequently became a gift to the city from

Fig. 54. Before Mellon Square. Reprinted from John Mauro, "Magnificent Square in the Triangle," *Charette* 35, no. 12 (December 1955), 14.

three Mellon family foundations (fig. 55). Here architects Mitchell and Ritchey made their first major contribution to the actual rebuilding of Pittsburgh, in association with Simonds and Simonds, landscape architects.

These were not exactly office towers in a park, but the new skyscrapers and the square were designed—and designed to be seen by the spectator—with reference to one another. The square serves as both foreground and focal point for the surrounding buildings.[124] Architects' renderings depicted both skyscrapers as seen from across the proposed square (see figs. 52 and 53). As a condensed panorama field, the square

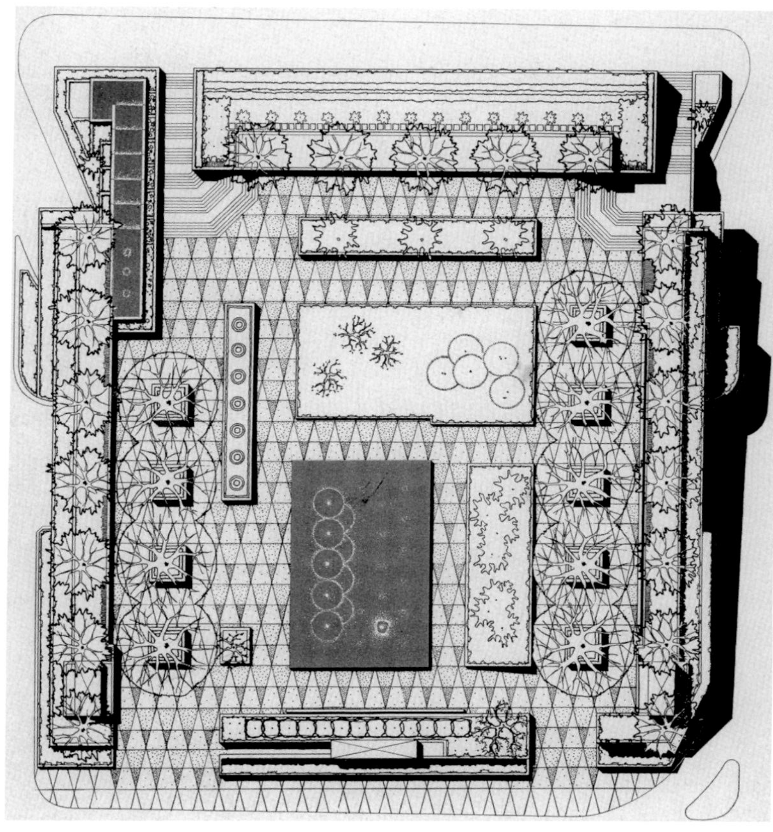

Fig. 55. Mitchell and Ritchey (architects) and Simonds and Simonds (landscape architects), Mellon Square, 1949–1955, site plan. Reprinted from "An Open Place at the Heart of a City," *Architectural Record* 121, no. 2 (February 1957), 196.

provides a 360-degree showcase of downtown buildings, and full-height views of the new towers. Both buildings face the square with their narrow sides, displaying an elegance of line that is lost when they are seen broadside. In turn, the square enhances views from the towers themselves. Frederick Gutheim remarks that Mellon Square "furnishes plenty of eye-food for the fortunate ones whose offices overlook it."[125]

Mellon Square was a precursor to the skyscraper plaza required by many urban zoning codes in the late 1950s and early 1960s. Such plazas sought to add open space to the city while providing economic and aesthetic benefits for their corporate parents. The Mellons created Mellon Square with an eye toward the benefits that it would afford the new Mellon offices. The square's striking pattern of terrazzo paving acknowledges this dual role as public space and private amenity: the triangle motifs in alternating hues purposefully suggest both the Golden Triangle and a series of Ms for the Mellons.[126]

Mellon Square has a diagrammatic quality, as if it, too, had been designed from an aerial point of view, perhaps from the adjacent skyscrapers. The geometric forms of planters and fountains are broadly dispersed in an ordered but asymmetrical way that suggests a Radiant City site plan at a reduced scale.[127] But the square is, at the same time, closely related to traditional urban spaces like the English (and American) square and the French *place*. Like the English square, Mellon Square has the nature of a cavity, scooped (literally in this case) out of existing urban space, with a variable architectural surround. Equally, like the *place*, Mellon Square was conceived as one component of a larger urban fabric, with a complementary architectural backdrop (in this case limited to the two new skyscrapers at an un-*place*-like scale).[128] Unlike many such precedents, however, Mellon Square features no market or civic center, no monument or memorial, no proscribed ritual activity or definitive communal purpose.

Built over a multistory parking garage, Mellon Square functions most explicitly as an automobile destination.[129] As with many such urban spaces, busy streets surround the square on all sides. But Mellon Square's surface was "lifted up above the streets to lose by elevation and sight lines the street and traffic confusion. . . . [By] the fact of the lifting up, the apparent limits of this volume were extended beyond the screened-off streets to the facades of the flanking buildings on all sides."[130] Thus, by hiding the surrounding traffic, and extending the visual space of the square to a walled perimeter, Mellon Square became less like an urban square or *place* and more like an enclosed park or garden (fig. 56).

John Ormsbee Simonds called the square "an oasis in an asphalt desert." Our new American cities, he claimed, "are oriented to the noise and fumes and frictions of our traffic-glutted streets" and are as deserts. In contrast, "A park must be . . . a cool and refreshing oasis. . . .

Fig. 56. Cy Hungerford, *How the Old Place Has Changed!* from *Pittsburgh Post-Gazette,* October 19, 1955. Library and Archives Division, Historical Society of Western Pennsylvania, Pittsburgh, Pa.

it must give the welcome relief of foliage, shade, splashing water, flowers, and bright color. Like the oasis it is, the urban park must be a place of pure delight—an inviting refreshing environment."[131]

This metaphor places Mellon Square within a long tradition of garden design. As Rob Aben and Saskia de Wit recount, the Eastern archetype of the desert oasis long ago led to the enclosed paradise gardens of Persia and other Islamic lands. This genre was gradually assimilated by medieval European culture, combined with the Western archetype of the clearing in the forest, and transformed into the enclosed pleasure gardens of castles and contemplative gardens of monasteries. The enclosed garden is a condensed and bounded place, walled off from the

Fig. 57. *Fountain of Youth,* from *De Sphaera* (ca. 1470). Biblioteca Estense Universitaria Modena, Modena, Italy. Courtesy of the Ministry for Cultural Assets and Activities.

surrounding context. It is a place of visual and multisensory appeal, with fountains, canals, and pools, and fruit trees, flowers, and herbs. It is a private place to contemplate, or a romantic place to flirt (fig. 57).[132]

Mellon Square is a modern-day urban manifestation of the enclosed garden. It is a bounded place set apart from everything outside it. It is, despite its extensive hardscape, a green and watered place; a sensuous place of plantings and the gentle sounds and cooling effects of pools and fountains. The donors intended the square to be "a quiet and unspoiled haven of beauty, rest and relaxation." To this end, they expressly encouraged horticultural displays and forbade organized gatherings, commercial programs, advertising, charitable solicitation, and rallies.[133]

In these respects, and in spite of its contextual design, Mellon Square is in but not of the city. As Aben and de Wit explain, when the garden is brought into the city "[it takes] the landscape with it. . . . The changeover from dark, winding alleys to the openness, light and tranquility of the garden is utterly unexpected; the garden makes spatial reference more to the landscape than to the city of which it is a part." When the enclosed garden "takes the landscape with it," it captures that landscape at a different scale. "Against the scale of the landscape it sets the scale of the room."[134] At Mellon Square, in the Golden Triangle, this means a room within a terrestrial room, and an enclosed garden that is both a microcosm and a simulacrum of the landscape that lies beyond.

When Mellon Square was built, one article commented, "perhaps no other American city has ever so much needed . . . a garden at its heart. This bright mosaic of water and terrazzo and green growth is giving back to the people of Pittsburgh something of their long-lost hill and river heritage."[135] It is this evocation of the land that the spectator senses in coming upon Mellon Square among the dense city streets, or when peering down upon it from a neighboring skyscraper. Quoting artist Winslow Homer from a different context, Gutheim calls Mellon Square "the eye of the landscape."[136] As such, it is the quiet eye of the swirling landscape that is the topographical city.

Taking on the Terrain

In 1907, architect Henry Hornbostel proposed a 700-foot addition to Richardson's Allegheny County Courthouse in downtown Pittsburgh. The stated rationale for this towering structure was to provide much-needed office space. Yet it also indulged in the romance of the bold gesture and the ideology of sheer height. It would have spectacularly reasserted the primacy of the courthouse, which had been the tallest structure in Pittsburgh until it was trumped by Burnham's Frick Building. Hornbostel would trump Mr. Make-no-little-plans Burnham, so that the courthouse could again regain the "prominence that it should have." The tower, Hornbostel contended, would: "make the old city of Pittsburg loom up into the most prominent and conspicuous place among modern cities. A 700 foot tower over the courthouse with a belfry and tower clock would dominate all of Allegheny county and be an expression of Pittsburg's enterprise, typically American and artistically striking."[137] The proposal was much criticized, however, for its disregard for Richardson's masterwork and for the presumed folly of its height, which was thought likely to induce pneumonia in its occupants.[138] It was never built.

Hornbostel's tower would have been the tallest building in the world—taller than the Singer Building in New York, then under construction. Such competitive comparisons among man-made structures are fairly common, and became nearly ubiquitous in the skyscraper era (fig. 58). Comparisons of man-made objects with the natural terrain are less common; perhaps because man generally loses in any such contest of superlatives (fig. 59). But tall buildings may establish significant relationships with the surrounding terrain by virtue of their relative height.

Paul Shepheard reports, for instance, that the dome of London's St. Paul's Cathedral is one thousand meters in elevation—the same height as the hills around the city. The spectator who climbs to the top of St. Paul's assumes the same topographical position as the spectator standing on a hill. The cathedral's cupola extends above the dome, and is—at least theoretically—visible from great distances above the crests of the surrounding hills. The cathedral is a pervasive visual object in the terrain. Its cupola tops the terrain.[139]

Grant Street lies at approximately 760 feet in elevation (and would have been even higher in 1907, before the final cutting of the hump). Add 700 feet, and the top of Hornbostel's courthouse tower would

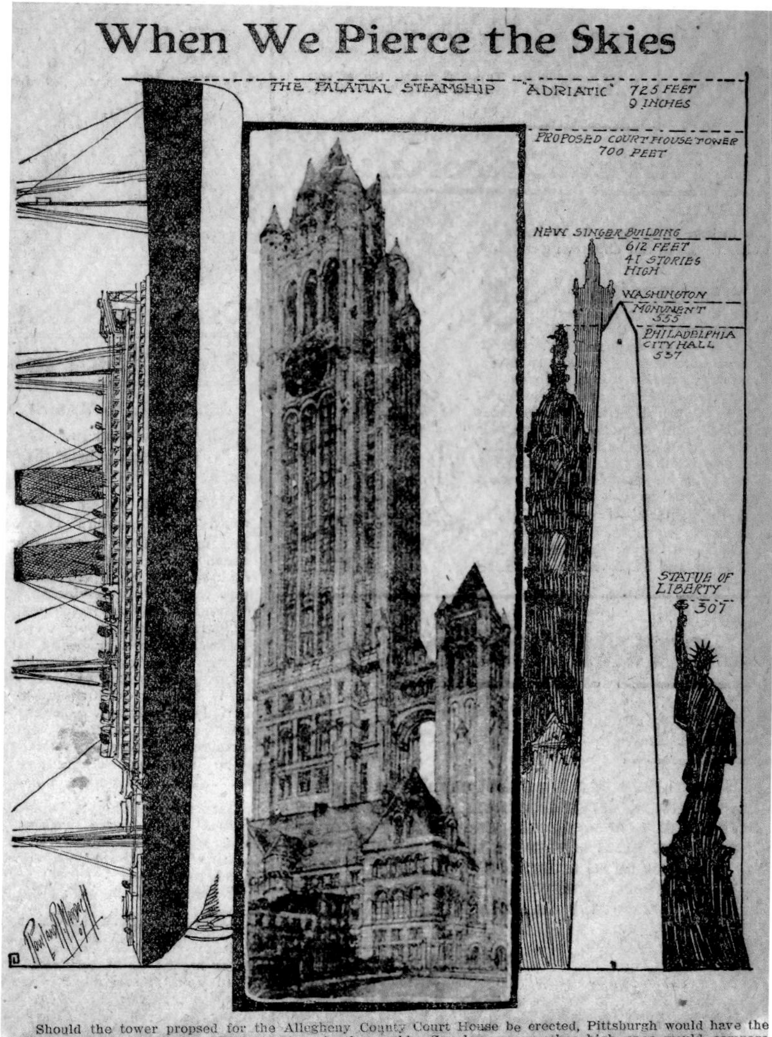

When We Pierce the Skies

Should the tower propsed for the Allegheny County Court House be erected, Pittsburgh would have the distinction of possessing the tallest structure in the world. See how some other high ones would compare with it. Only one ocean vessel, if stood on end, would reach further into the clouds.

Fig. 58. *When We Pierce the Skies.* This drawing ignores the existence of the Eiffel Tower. Reprinted from *Pittsburgh Chronicle Telegraph* (April 19, 1907), 13. Carnegie Mellon University Architecture Archives.

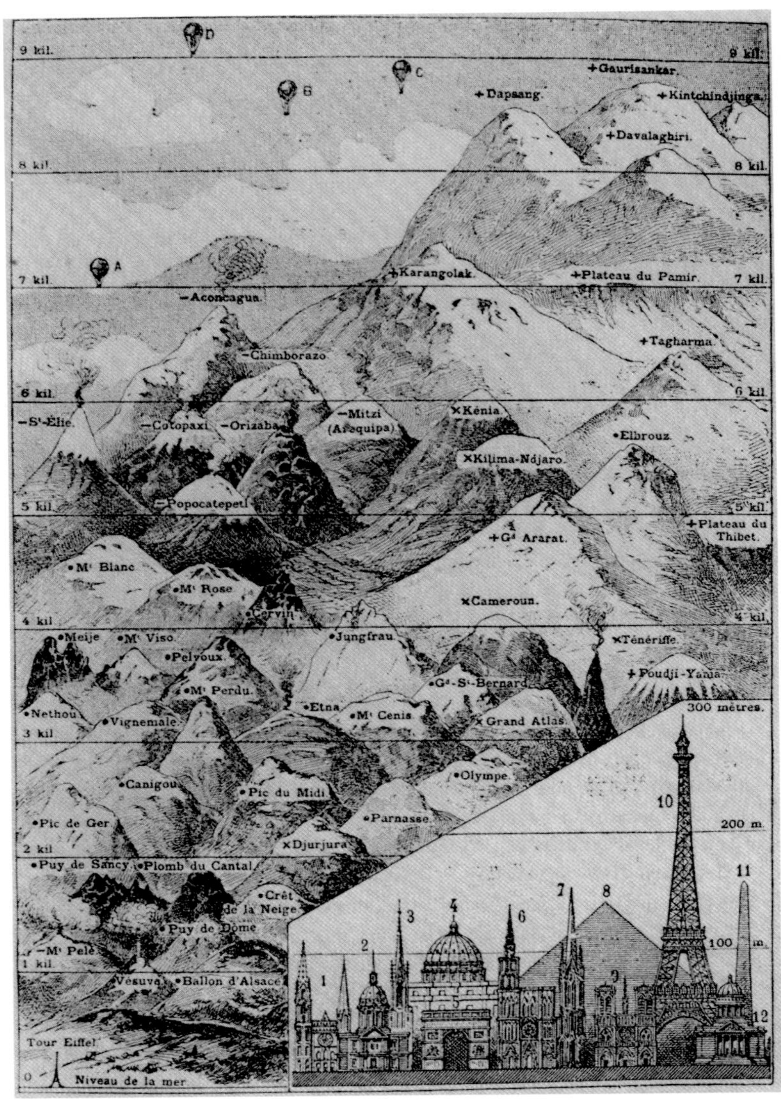

Fig. 59. *Montagnes.* Note the Washington Monument as shown in this and the previous illustration, and the Eiffel Tower, as transposed from the bottom right corner to bottom left corner. Reprinted from *Petit Larousse Illustré* (Paris: Larousse, 1925), 485. Courtesy of Librairie Larousse. Rights reserved, Petit Larousse, 1925.

have surpassed the 1,200- to 1,300-foot height of the surrounding plateau. The tower would have dominated views of the Golden Triangle and been visible from high points throughout the region—more or less "all of Allegheny county" as Hornbostel had promised. Subsequently, a number of buildings in the Grant Street corridor took on the challenge of the terrain and achieved superior heights. The Grant Building topped off at about 1,200 feet in elevation, with its beacon at 1,240 feet. The Gulf Building reached 1,380 feet, with its crest extending above the prevailing terrain, appearing from certain vantage points like a pyramid resting on the plateau. The flat-topped U.S. Steel Building, at Mellon Square, measured approximately 1,350 feet in elevation.

The critical skyward thrust came in 1971, however, when U.S. Steel built a new headquarters building on Grant Street (figs. 60 and 61). Designed, like its predecessor, by Harrison and Abramovitz, it was conceived as an even greater showcase of the corporate product line. The building is a matrix of Cor-Ten steel, exposed as an external skeleton. Exposed steel normally corrodes, but Cor-Ten steel rusts instead and forms a protective coating at the same time. Thus the spectator reads the building as a raw industrial artifact like an upended mill building or bridge. When seen from a distance, it is a monolith—a single steel column supporting the sky; a steel spike driven into the land. Van Trump called it "a Cyclops which forcibly captures the eye," referring simultaneously to its size, singularity, visual magnetism, return gaze, and service to steel.[140]

Like the Eiffel Tower in Paris and the Duomo in Florence, the U.S. Steel Building asserts control over its environs. Leon Battista Alberti said of Filippo Brunelleschi's great red dome in Florence that it was "ample to cover with its shadow all of the people of Tuscany."[141] In Pittsburgh, the steel industry and the tower substitute for the church and the dome, and the U.S. Steel Building casts its own ruddy shadow of sorts. Cor-Ten rust flakes off and rains over the city—as if, by the dispersal of molecules and the application of pigment on the terrain, to mark steel's Rust Belt domain. Triangular in plan, the U.S. Steel

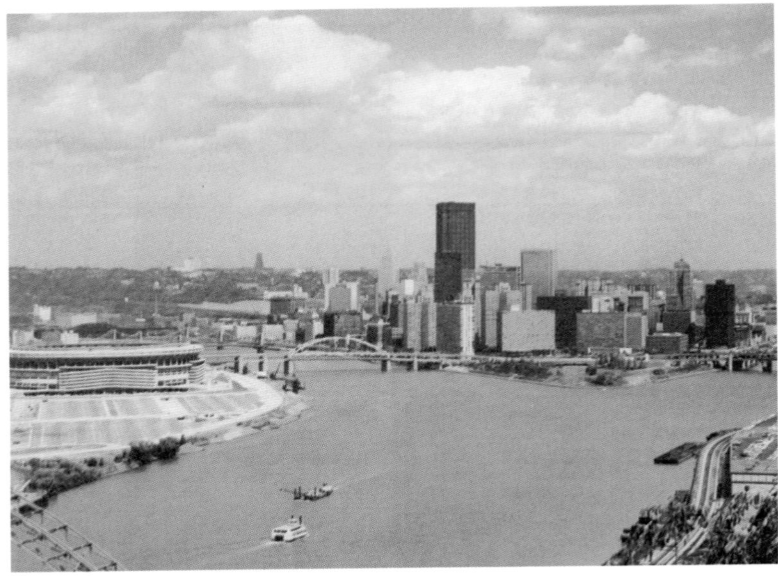

Fig. 60. The Golden Triangle. Reprinted from *The Steel Triangle in the Golden Triangle* (Pittsburgh: ca. 1971). Carnegie Mellon University Architecture Archives.

Fig. 61. U.S. Steel Building and environs. Reprinted from *The Steel Triangle in the Golden Triangle* (Pittsburgh: ca. 1971). Carnegie Mellon University Architecture Archives.

Building was publicized as the "Steel Triangle in the Golden Triangle," and was intended to symbolize both the corporation and the city.[142] It is a triangular extrusion of the terrain on which it stands: two of the building's walls parallel the rivers and their meeting point reprises the Point. U.S. Steel, like Richardson years before, constructed not just a building but Pittsburgh itself, again granting new dimensions to the civic topography.

At sixty-four stories, the U.S. Steel Building is Pittsburgh's ultimate act of corporate giantism and the tallest building in the city. The city's man-made skyline builds gradually to a climax, but does not prepare the spectator for this. At 841 feet, on a 760-foot site, the U.S. Steel Building's 1,600-foot elevation lifts it high above the prevailing plateau. It is almost twice as tall as the apparent height of the surrounding landforms; it outclasses the architectural and natural competition and dominates the larger landscape as the central reference point in its topographical setting. It links heaven and earth. It is the new *axis mundi.*

Four downtown skyscrapers built in the 1980s—One Mellon Bank Center (1983), One Oxford Center (1983), PPG Place (1984), and Fifth Avenue Place (1985)—are also tall enough to peer over the horizon. Even as they partially dilute the singular power of the U.S. Steel Building, they create a critical mass of buildings that breaks above the plateau and dominates views around Pittsburgh beyond the immediate topographical setting as a cluster of pervasive visual objects in the terrain. Paul Ostergaard has dramatized this effect in a fantastic drawing that reconstitutes the region's prehistoric inland sea, flooding the city to the rim of the plateau, and leaving only skyscraper crests to project above sea level (fig. 62).

Dense urban centers assume topographical form as they rise above the land and create artificial horizons. This man-made topography of tall buildings and interstitial spaces has often been likened to mountains and canyons. The setback skyscrapers that emerged from New York City zoning were high and tapered like mountains. Skyscraper architects and image-makers like Raymond Hood and Hugh Ferriss exploited the skyscraper-as-mountain metaphor (fig. 63).[143] The sky-

Fig. 62. Paul Ostergaard, *Pittsburgh: City of Water*, 1991. Courtesy of Paul Ostergaard and Urban Design Associates.

scrapers of a dense skyline may collectively emulate a mountain range, or a singular mountainous mass. Thus urban centers may become what Kenneth Frampton calls "megaforms": man-made constructions that "have the potential of gathering the contingent landscape around them by virtue of their anthrogeographic character, so much so that they may, at some juncture, appear to merge with the ground or alternately to become, through their topographic presence, the status of being a landmark."[144]

Over time, Pittsburgh's Golden Triangle became a triangle in mass as well as in plan. The tendency for intensive development to focus inland from the riverfronts shaped a triangle in elevation.[145] The trend toward skyscraper development at downtown's eastern edge transformed the triangle into a wedge-shaped form, with its tip at the Point, and its base aligned with Grant Street and the eastern hills. High at its

Fig. 63. Hugh Ferriss, *The Business Center.* Reprinted from Hugh Ferriss, *The Metropolis of Tomorrow* (New York: I. Washburn, 1929), 113.

center, sloped at the edges, descending to the rivers at its feet, the Golden Triangle is at one with the prevailing topographical conditions. It is a reef emerging from the inland sea, an outcropping eroded from the plateau.

Thus the Golden Triangle becomes a surrogate landform and claims the role of the sacred mountain. Though it breaks above the region's upper datum line as an exceptional topographical condition, it literally takes its place within the terrain. It is a megaform that merges with the ground *and* attains the status of a landmark. What seemed for a time like a competition between land and city ends (for now) as it began—in mimetic geomorphic construction whereby the city takes on the mantel of the terrain and centers the terrain for the spectator.

In the guise of the mountain, the Golden Triangle may inspire its own topographical response. Pittsburgh's David L. Lawrence Convention Center (1999–2003) is such a response (fig. 64). For architect Rafael Viñoly, "Pittsburgh is . . . defined by its rivers, and sculpted as

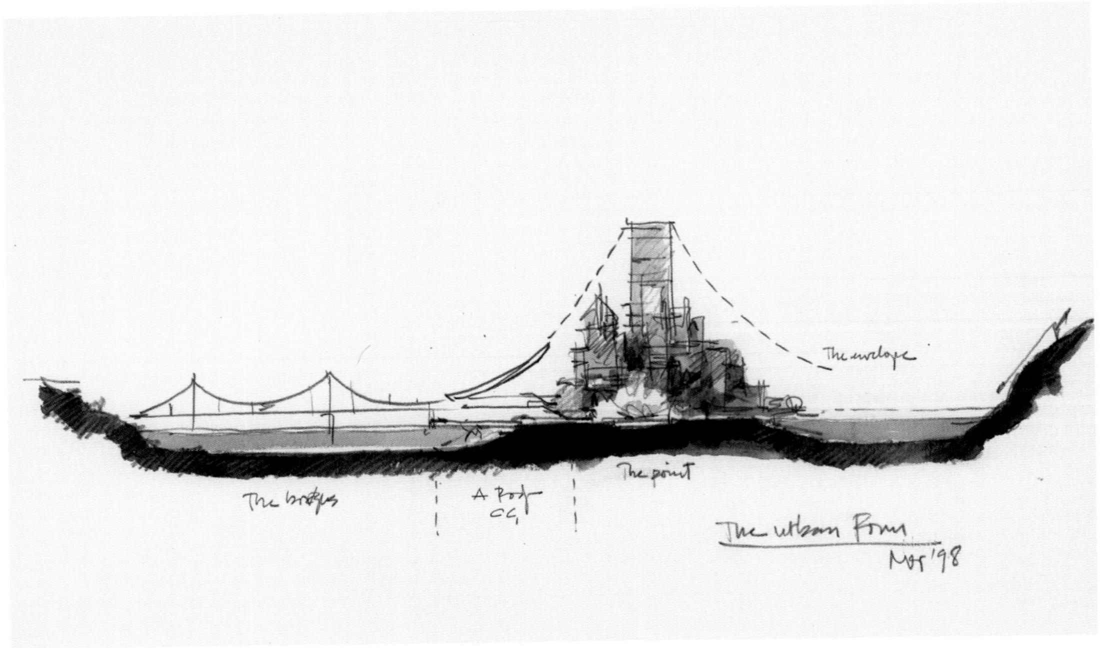

Fig. 64. Rafael Viñoly Architects, David L. Lawrence Convention Center, ca. 1998. Courtesy of Rafael Viñoly Architects, PC.

Fig. 65. Dollar Bank, "Currency of Growth and Opportunity," ca. 2000, advertisement. Courtesy of Dollar Bank and Dymun + Company.

an urban wedge." The new building pays homage to Pittsburgh's rivers and its "powerful urban form." Its roof responds to the slope of the bridges that cross the Allegheny River, and connects to the slope of the urban wedge or megaform.[146] In this way it mediates between the water and the sacred mountain, and reinvigorates Pittsburgh's status as a world city.

The View from Mount Washington

The image of the Golden Triangle has become the image of Pittsburgh; it prompts the spectator to identify, and identify with, the city.[147] For the resident, says Kostof, the image of the city "is the familiar fond icon of the city-form, a vision to cherish and come home to." It is also an "urban advertisement to the world."[148] Consequently, this image plays an important role in both cultural representation and civic boosterism, and serves as a common vehicle of communication with a consumer audience. For close to two centuries, images of the Golden Triangle have been consistently pictured in such mediums and venues as paintings, lithographs, photographs, logos, souvenirs, advertisements, and television studio backdrops. An advertisement for Dollar Bank, for example, depicts Pittsburgh within its topographical setting, as a land of growth and opportunity. The hills are planted with greenbacks, and the Golden Triangle beckons like Oz (fig. 65).

Of many potential city views, one commonly takes precedence as the image of a city. Traditionally, this view is a panoramic profile of the face of the city that is best suited for pictorial representation, often as viewed by the spectator from across a body of water or from a high vantage point. The most common and emblematic image of Pittsburgh is the view from Mount Washington, high land that rises about four hundred feet above the river datum line across the Monongahela River from the Golden Triangle.[149]

George Washington may or may not have viewed the Forks of the Ohio from the vantage point that would be named in his honor, but views from Mount Washington have been the stuff of Pittsburgh since its earliest times. A map of the city from 1826 shows this height labeled: "Spot from whence one has a view of the Town, Forts and Rivers."[150] Because the mountain follows the course of the Monongahela and Ohio Rivers, it boasts multiple vantage points that yield panoramic views of the city, ranging from orthogonal views of the southern flank of the Golden Triangle to views that face the Point more or less head-on.

Fig. 66. R. W. Johnston Studios (photographer), "Official Sesqui-Centennial Photograph of Pittsburgh," 1909. Incorporates an 1849 view inset at bottom center. Library of Congress, Prints and Photographs Division, Panoramic Photographs Collection.

Views from almost any angle feature serendipitous attributes of unity, balance, distance, elevation, and sunlight. The view from Mount Washington is the quintessential pictorial view for the urban spectator.[151]

The "Official Sesqui-Centennial Photograph of Pittsburgh," published and marketed in 1909, makes this view, and at least some of its meaning, explicit (fig. 66). The photograph's very existence indicates the significance of this viewpoint for Pittsburgh. As a commemorative document, it says that this view is the appropriate record of the city at an important celebratory moment in its history. As a montage of three separate elements it has a more complex message.

The primary image, an angled view of the contemporary city, celebrates Pittsburgh in its 150th year. An 1849 bird's-eye view of the city, drawn from a similar vantage point and incorporated into the photo-

graph as a tiny foreground inset, represents all that Pittsburgh has been. And the villa and spectator that are introduced on the right side, formal and dignified in their architectural and sartorial dress, suggest that the view and the city itself are the province of the city's elite, who are paternalistically entitled to take in the view. With this, the photograph supports what Peter B. Hales calls an "urban mythos built on [the] Gilded Age concept of merchant princes and their agents remaking a city to their own image."[152] This is the Pittsburgh of Carnegie, Frick, and the Mellons.

The villa and its merchant prince, however, were literally mythical—the products of photographic manipulation. The elite have had little presence on Mount Washington. Van Trump describes the buildings that actually line the hilltop as "raffish and haphazard," as if one of the city's helter-skelter neighborhoods had "crept up the other side of the ridge, and with one eye closed, hair all anyway, and cap pulled down, was peering over the edge with a kind of friendly shyness down at the Golden Triangle."[153] The view from Mount Washington was accessible to all; and those who didn't go there in person could share the view and experience a sense of vicarious urban ownership by purchasing the sesquicentennial photograph and hanging it on the wall.

The view from Mount Washington was further democratized and formalized as a civic amenity about 1970 when terraces and overlooks were built along the edge of the mountain to make the view and the viewing experience explicit (fig. 67).[154] As public space, these platforms make the view available to large numbers of spectators—and now literally everyone comes to Mount Washington to take in the view. The overlooks showcase the view; and like the villa's imaginary terrace, they

Fig. 67. View from Mount Washington overlook, 1972. Carnegie Library of Pittsburgh.

Fig. 68. Aaronel de Roy Gruber, *Downtown Pittsburgh Skyscrapers from Mount Washington,* 1996. Carnegie Museum of Art, Pittsburgh; Purchase: Gift of Photo Forum Gallery. Courtesy of Aaronel de Roy Gruber.

showcase the spectator as a contributing part of the view. By extending into space beyond the side of the mountain, they suspend the spectator within topographical and pictorial space.

The view from Mount Washington reveals the Golden Triangle-as-landform within its topographical setting (fig. 68). By the act of viewing, the spectator, who identifies with the view and stands suspended within it, sees and assumes his or her place within the topographical city.

Fig. 69. Clayton Merrell, *The Turtle Creek Valley*, 2004. Courtesy of Clayton Merrell.

Scenes from the Turtle Creek Valley

The setting is a fantastic scene.

Carl Condit, *American Building Art: The Twentieth Century*

The Technological Sublime

For more than a century, industry was a fact—perhaps *the* fact—of life in Pittsburgh. The city and its environs hosted an extraordinary array of industrial activities and an inordinate amount of smoke. People all over the world knew Pittsburgh for its status as the world's primary steel producer and for its murky atmosphere. Today, much of the industry and nearly all of the smoke are gone, but Pittsburgh is still widely known as both the Steel City and the Smoky City.

Technology confronted topography in the regional landscape (fig. 69). Industry was present because of the land, or more specifically, the coal within the land, but the land itself was begrudging in its accom-

▶ Fig. 70. Skyline montage of industry and the civic authority. Reprinted from Pittsburgh Architectural Club, *Catalog of the Second Architectural Exhibition* (Pittsburgh: The Club, 1903), cover.

◀ Fig. 71. *Pittsburgh: Mills for Miles: Gigantic Manufacturing Establishments,* ca. 1911–1922. One of a series of stamps issued by the *Pittsburg Dispatch.* Carnegie Library of Pittsburgh.

modations. Valleys became industrial corridors as factories and mills sought locations adjacent to waterways and the railroads that frequently followed their banks. Yet while the valleys were commodious in spots, industrial development necessarily shifted from shore to shore as waterways meandered, bluffs loomed, and meager floodplains came and went.[1]

Industry incontestably despoiled the natural landscape. Industrial Pittsburgh was not a pretty sight. As Edward K. Muller writes, "The combination of Pittsburgh's dense smoke pollution, blackened surfaces, and the many bare and scarred hills presented a drab and depressing aspect about which travelers and journalists routinely and pejoratively commented." For many residents, it was not a very pleasant place to live either, as the Pittsburgh Survey, the sobering findings of which were publicized in 1908–1909, made abundantly clear.[2]

As industry became pervasive, representations of Pittsburgh that sought to be emblematic incorporated elements of the industrial landscape. A depiction of the Allegheny County Courthouse might place it within an industrial context, with smokestacks spliced into the scene (fig. 70). Other representations gloried in the sheer magnitude of the industrial presence as factories became vehicles of civic boosterism and of the rhetoric of technological progress (fig. 71).

Some spectators saw only a scarred landscape and a need for social reform, others saw civic identity and the fruits of progress, and still others saw power, mystery, and even beauty in the sensory experience of this place. Writers, artists, and other spectators often focused on industry to the exclusion of the rest of the city. Factories and mills were exposed along the waterfronts and prominently displayed for the spectator. They called attention to themselves with their scale, noise, and activity, and with their smoke. The industrial landscape was undeniably dramatic, especially at night. Representing the experience of many Pittsburgh visitors, Williard Glazier wrote in "The Great Furnace of America":

> By all means make your first approach to Pittsburg in the night time, and you will behold a spectacle which has not a parallel on this continent. Darkness gives the city and its surroundings a picturesqueness that they wholly lack by daylight. It lies low down in a hollow of encompassing hills, gleaming with a thousand points of light. . . . Around the city's edge, and on the sides of the hills which encircle it like a gloomy amphitheatre, their outlines rising dark against the sky, through numberless apertures, fiery lights stream forth, looking angrily and fiercely up to the heavens, while over all these settles a heavy pall of smoke.[3]

Aaron Harry Gorson (1872–1933) painted such scenes, initiating a Pittsburgh School of industrial artwork around the turn of the twentieth century (fig. 72). He particularly favored nighttime scenes, and painted the steel mill, observes Rina Youngner, as a "locus of light and atmospheric effects." Gorson frequently assumed a riverfront point of view, observing and painting (in his own words) "the most beautiful curving lines of opalescent water framed in huge, deep, dark, or turquoise haze, hills gracefully bowing against each other, studded with

Fig. 72. Aaron Harry Gorson, *Mills at Night*, n.d. From the Art Collection of Lucian Caste. Photograph courtesy of Spanierman Gallery, LLC, New York.

houses and broken up by tall slender smoke stacks from the massive mills softened by clouds of smoke."[4]

Such perceptions are perhaps best understood as experiences of the sublime. The sublime is about experiences of beauty, awe, and wonder, sometimes tinged with fear, in the presence of visual phenomena, when, as David E. Nye writes, "an object, natural or man-made, disrupts ordinary perception and astonishes the senses, forcing the observer to grapple mentally with its immensity and power." At first, in America, the spectator experienced the sublime in natural sites such as Niagara Falls and Yellowstone Park, and in the expansive and untouched natural landscape. But as the country developed, works of man emerged that were seen to embody what Nye, and Leo Marx before him, have called the "technological sublime."[5] The spectator experienced the technological sublime in the immensity and power and sensory stimulation of the industrial landscape, and in the human mastery and operation of these forces.[6] In Pittsburgh, major elements of a sublime industrial landscape included waterways and railroads, factories and machines, and bridges and tunnels.

Navigable waterways and railroad right-of-ways spread man-made technology across the terrain (fig. 73). Dams tamed Pittsburgh's flood-prone rivers, and high hardened bulkheads reshaped riverbanks to accommodate changes in water levels, docking, and various industrial activities.[7] At the same time, industrial valleys became engineered railroad landscapes replete with main lines, branch lines, sidings, industry spurs, ample yards, and an associated topography of cuttings, embankments, bridges, and tunnels. Towboats and barges and locomotives and rolling stock became ubiquitous and perpetually shifting components of the regional landscape. Spectators experienced the technological sublime in the reach, capacity, and motion of the waterways and railroads.

Factories, mills, and industrial plants engendered sprawling working sites (fig. 74). In Pittsburgh, iron and steel works were most in evidence, yet "the metropolitan industrial complex . . . included both a broad array of metal-working industries and substantial operations in aluminum, electrical equipment, glass, coke, machinery, and railroad

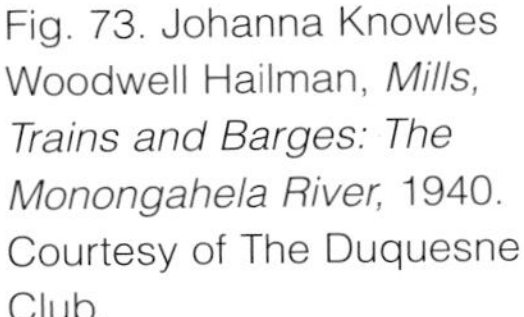

Fig. 73. Johanna Knowles Woodwell Hailman, *Mills, Trains and Barges: The Monongahela River,* 1940. Courtesy of The Duquesne Club.

equipment."[8] Large mass-production facilities were frequently conglomerated in the landscape. For the spectator, says Nye, the manufacturing district "evoked fear tinged with wonder. It threatened the individual with its sheer scale, its noise, its complexity, and the superhuman power of the forces at work." Newfangled industrial machines, such as engines, cranes, and blast furnaces suggested near-animate forces under human control. They awed spectators with their technological sophistication and recalled monsters or even visions of hell due to their speed, noise, and fire (fig. 75).[9]

Bridges confronted topographical voids (fig. 76); their lengths, heights, and structural types were largely determined by specific topographical conditions. The many bridges in the Pittsburgh region

Fig. 74. Jones and Laughlin Steel Mill, 1963. Library and Archives Division, Historical Society of Western Pennsylvania, Pittsburgh, Pa.

crossed waterways and valleys and linked topographical edges. Their steel trusses and concrete arches were always functional, frequently expressive, and sometimes innovative. Tunnels were the bridges' hidden counterparts, especially in Pittsburgh, where bridges may issue directly into tunnels, and tunnels may open directly onto bridges. Bridges and tunnels embodied the sublime as they conquered nature, spanned great distances, and assumed monumental forms.[10]

Since the early nineteenth century, according to Nye, "the technological sublime has been one of America's central 'ideas about itself.'"[11] In Pittsburgh, the technological sublime has been both idea and spectacle. Turn-of-the-twentieth-century Pittsburgh guidebooks included industrial and engineering sites and encouraged visitors to view and tour the manufactories that made Pittsburgh the workshop of the world and a tourist attraction.[12] When visitor James Parton described Hell-with-the-lid-taken-off Pittsburgh, it was, he said in a sublime analogy, "a spectacle as striking as Niagara."[13]

Fig. 75. Elsie Driggs, *Pittsburgh*, 1927. Whitney Museum of American Art, New York; Gift of Gertrude Vanderbilt Whitney, 31.177. Photograph by Geoffrey Clements, copyright © 1996; Whitney Museum of American Art, New York.

From Braddock's Field to Bessemer

Nowhere was the technological sublime more apparent than at the lower Turtle Creek Valley east of Pittsburgh, where Turtle Creek passes through a narrows before it empties onto a meander floodplain and into the Monongahela River. The narrows is an extreme topographical condition, but the floodplain was manifestly suitable for settlement. John Frazier, a trader reputed to be the first white settler west of the Al-

Fig. 76. Frederick T. Gretton (photographer), "Hot Metal Bridge," 1887. Library and Archives Division, Historical Society of Western Pennsylvania, Pittsburgh, Pa.

legheny Mountains, built a cabin here in 1742, and the towns of Port Perry (before 1840) and Braddock (1867) were founded nearby.[14] This was also the site of a major battle of the War for Empire. In 1755, British forces under General Edward Braddock and Virginian colonials under George Washington, having just crossed the shallow Monongahela River, came under preemptive attack here while marching to seize the Forks of the Ohio. The Battle of Braddock's Field resulted in the rout of Braddock's forces, a near-death experience for Washington, and a temporary stay in the fate of Fort Duquesne.

"In 1850," wrote Hugh P. Meese, "the Monongahela [River] at Braddock's Field rolled through a quiet scene of sylvan beauty. Thickly wooded hills shaded her peaceful waters on the south, while on the Braddock side long grassy swards dipped to the river's brim."[15] A published view of this locale from as late as the 1870s shows a lightly settled landscape well suited to the pastoral conventions of landscape painting (fig. 77). Yet a steamship, railroads, a factory, and their accompanying plumes of smoke promised new modes of human occupation. Sixty years later, John Kane's painting, *Turtle Creek Valley, No. 2* (1932), maintained a pastoral pretense even while it documented the expanded presence of technology in the landscape (fig. 78).

Fig. 77. *Braddock of Long Ago.* The mouth of Turtle Creek is visible at the far right. Reprinted from *The Unwritten History of Braddock's Field* (Pittsburgh: Nicholson Printing Co., 1917), 6.

Over time, what appeared to be immersed within the landscape utterly transformed that landscape for the spectator. Meese has described a land of the bullfrog and the meadowlark now filled with cinder, ash, and slag; flocks of pigeons in the clear sky replaced by clouds of smoke; orioles' nests swinging in hickory groves replaced by the operators' cages of industrial cranes; the call of the robin and woodthrush replaced by the plant siren, the woodpecker by the pneumatic riveter, the screech-owl by the rail-saw.[16] When artist Joseph Pennell visited in 1909 he portrayed the topographical setting while fully acknowledging its transformation (fig. 79). Pennell believed that the sites of human work were the wonders of the world. His gritty etchings recorded the reality of an industrial landscape under billowing clouds of smoke.[17]

Fig. 78. John Kane, *Turtle Creek Valley, No. 2,* 1932. The Roland P. Murdock Collection, Wichita Art Museum, Wichita, Kansas.

Industrial development began with the preexisting waterways. In 1850 Lock and Dam No. 2 was constructed on the river near the mouth of Turtle Creek, raising water levels and facilitating slack water navigation and direct access to the expansive Connellsville coalfield to the south. Riverbank bulkheads gradually reshaped both the water and the land, and Turtle Creek itself was ultimately channeled, and its mouth was moved 1,125 feet east of its original location to accommodate industrial development.[18] The waterways yielded floodplain building sites, provided the water resources and waste-disposal capacity that

Fig. 79. Joseph Pennell, *Edgar Thomson's Steel Works*, 1909. View from Dooker's Hollow. Library of Congress, Prints and Photographs Division, Fine Print Collection, LC-USZC4–5728.

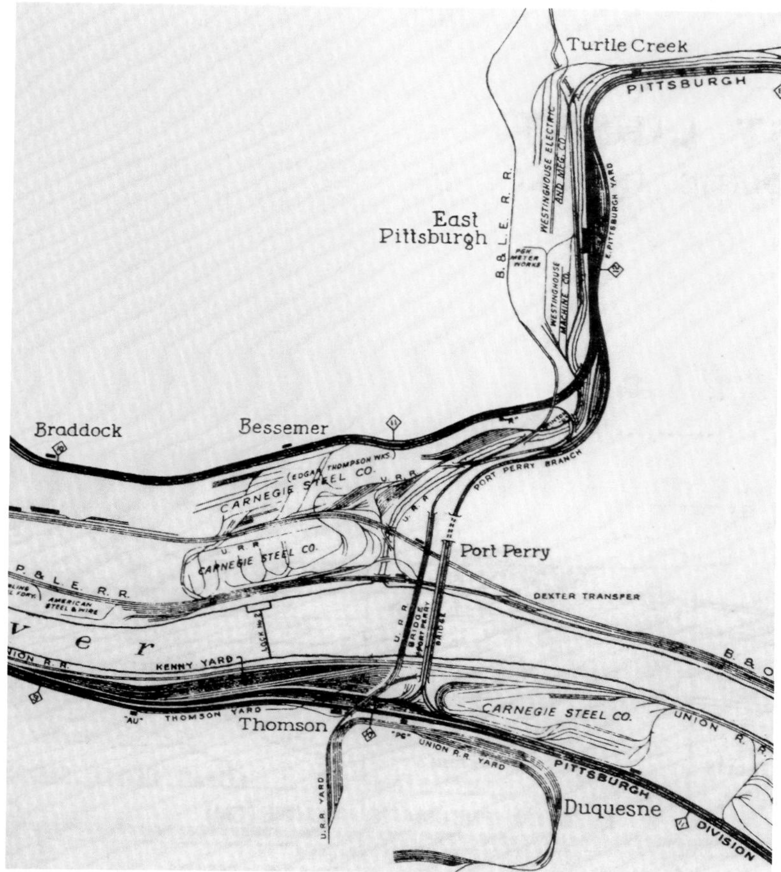

Fig. 80. *Pennsylvania R.R. System Central Region: Industrial Map of the Pittsburgh District* (detail), 1924. Pennsylvania Railroad Technical and Historical Society.

were necessary for industrial production, and facilitated the shipment of raw materials and finished products. But if waterways were the first fact of industrial development, railroads tracing the valley floors were the key to industrial growth.

Railroads, like the waterways, converged at the lower Turtle Creek Valley (fig. 80). In an environment of topographical constraints, the railroads were content to follow the waterways as paths of least resistance. After 1852 the Pennsylvania Railroad's main line ran the length of the Turtle Creek Valley, then turned west above the Monongahela

River to Pittsburgh. The Baltimore & Ohio Railroad ran along the north shore of the river after 1861. Other major players were the Pittsburgh & Lake Erie Railroad, which also followed the river's north shore, various Pennsy branch lines, and the regional Union Railroad. By the late nineteenth century, this extraordinary concentration of railroading assets was the point of highest railroad freight density in the world. By 1921, more than two hundred passenger trains a day were running through the Monongahela and Turtle Creek Valleys.[19] Over time, the railroads reshaped and consumed the land in many places, and obliterated the town of Port Perry at the mouth of Turtle Creek.

When Andrew Carnegie established a local steel mill in 1875, he purposefully chose a site that was adjacent to the Pennsylvania Railroad's main line.[20] Ease of shipping by rail was important, but Carnegie had another motive as well; he promptly named the mill after the railroad's then-president, Edgar Thomson, expecting to make the railroad the mill's best customer. As planned, the Edgar Thomson Works quickly became the nation's largest producer of steel rails. This relationship reflected a special synergy between the steel industry and the railroad in Pittsburgh and the Monongahela Valley. As Dan Cupper writes: "If Philadelphia was the brain of the Pennsylvania Railroad, then Pittsburgh was surely its heart. Pittsburgh was the railroad's western terminus, but in time it became an industrial vortex, with rich black bituminous coal and Great Lakes ore streaming through it and to its steel mills, and raw steel slabs and finished forged and structural steel products being turned out by the trainload."[21] As Pittsburgh evolved into the Steel City, both Andrew Carnegie and the Pennsylvania Railroad could claim the title of Steel King. Artist Grif Teller captured this shared identity in *The Steel King*, artwork commissioned for the Pennsylvania Railroad calendar of 1941, which shows PRR locomotive No. 6100 passing the north side of the Edgar Thomson Works in Braddock's Field near what was now known as Bessemer Station (fig. 81).

When the Westinghouse companies came to the Turtle Creek Valley beginning in 1889, they too sought proximity to the railroad. Westinghouse built a series of plants along the Pennsy main line, and then

Fig. 81. Grif Teller, *The Steel King*, from the Pennsylvania Railroad calendar (1941). Courtesy of Ken Murry.

built its own Interworks Railway joining those plants to one another. Throngs of Westinghouse employees commuted to work by rail (fig. 82). Westinghouse had strong business associations with the railroads, producing safety, signaling, and electrification advances that revolutionized railroad operations. But the Westinghouse name would be best known for its electrical products and advancements that impacted many fields.

When Aymar Embury II described the topographical circumstances and industrial development of the Turtle Creek Valley and environs in 1915, waterways, railroads, and industrial sites formed a continuous industrial landscape: "The [railroad] parallels the course of a small river, deep cut between the hills which rise for the most part steeply from the very banks of the stream, but occasionally opens out enough to give

Fig. 82. "Arrival of Employees on Morning Train." Reprinted from *The Pittsburg Electrical Hand-Book* (Pittsburgh: The American Institute of Electrical Engineers, 1904), 37.

space for little manufacturing towns. Where ever this happens, and in many places where it does not, manufacturing plants and factories have been crowded in between the railroad and the river, or between the railroad and the hills; so that for twenty or thirty miles east of Pittsburgh, the [railroad] seems to pass through one continuous manufacturing plant."[22] The burgeoning steel and electric industries dominated this terrain, and new identities emerged to mark the changed but closely joined relationship of technology and topography. The Steel Valley now met the Electric Valley at the confluence of the Monongahela River and Turtle Creek.

Steel Valley

"So the mills came to Braddock, stripping the hills bare of vegetation, poisoning the river, blackening heaven and earth," wrote Thomas

Bell in his novel *Out of This Furnace* (1941).[23] This was not fiction, but it was not the whole story, either.

The Monongahela Valley was the birthplace of the modern American steel industry.[24] The mills that lined the valley over a distance of nearly forty miles were sites of pivotal industry advancements in site planning, technology, and production. The Edgar Thomson Works (commonly called ET) was the flagship mill in the valley. Built on an ample floodplain site between Turtle Creek and the town of Braddock, the mill was a uniquely powerful presence in the landscape (figs. 79 and 83). "What a wonder Carnegie constructed at Braddock's Field," exclaims John N. Ingham, in an otherwise matter-of-fact account of Pittsburgh's iron and steel industry. ET, he asserts, was "a technological and organizational marvel of the modern world."[25]

As America's first major Bessemer plant for making steel rails, ET was an integrated mill that took in raw materials, made both iron and steel, and manufactured finished products. At the same time, ET represented a major breakthrough in the relationship between steel mill design and steel-making technology. Alexander Lyman Holley, who designed the works, had reportedly "taken a clean piece of paper, on which he drew the railroad tracks first and then placed the buildings and contents of each building with prime regard to the facile handling of material so that the whole became a body shaped by its bones and muscles, rather than a box into which bones and muscles had to be packed."[26] Thus "the buildings and equipment making up the new complex promoted a continuous flow of materials through the mill." Subsequently, "its layout design became the prototype for the construction of integrated steel mills in the industry."[27]

ET was wildly successful. Despite its initial rational skeleton, it underwent nearly constant growth and rebuilding. Holley had carefully oriented the mill with reference to preexisting railroads and a prominent bend in Turtle Creek.[28] Soon, however, the mill jumped the Baltimore & Ohio Railroad tracks and multiplied in size as new works were laid out parallel to the river. John R. Stilgoe observes that individual steel mills often "stretched for miles along rivers, their buildings and furnaces

Fig. 83. "Edgar Thomson Furnaces and Steel Works, Bessemer, Pa." Reprinted from *The Story of Pittsburgh and Vicinity: Illustrated* (Pittsburgh: *Pittsburgh Gazette Times,* 1908), 150.

Fig. 84. John McWilliams (photographer), "Edgar Thomson Works: Looking East at the Ore Yard and Blast Furnaces No. 3, No.5, and No. 6," 1989. Library of Congress, Prints and Photographs Division, Historic American Engineering Record, HAER,PA,2-BRAD,2A-2.

linked by conveyors, railroads, and catwalks." ET, says Ingham, became "a sprawling series of buildings, switchyards, engines, sheds, and smokestacks."[29]

The vital steel-making process took place in Bessemer or open-hearth furnaces inside more-or-less enclosed buildings. The manufacture of finished products took place in massive production sheds. Piles of raw materials (coke, iron ore, and limestone) and waste material (slag)

composed a constantly shifting mill site topography. Nevertheless, the buildings and other features of the site played a secondary role in the look of a mill. It was the blast furnace plants, where iron-smelting took place, which were the primary eye-catchers. For much of its history, ET has had the most active blast furnaces of any mill in the Pittsburgh district.

Two blast furnaces and a phalanx of hot blast stoves and smokestacks are commonly bundled together to comprise a blast furnace plant (figs. 84 and 86). The furnaces generally flank the hot blast stoves, with the smokestacks above or alongside. These individual elements, and the plant as a whole, are sculptural objects (fig. 87). Their massive cylindrical forms are sheathed in more-or-less monochromatic steel skins prone to rust; extended by various hoists, ore bridges, and cranes; and dressed in intermittent veils of mechanical parts. The blast furnace plants emerge from and visually dominate attached buildings called cast houses. Like railroad locomotives, the blast furnaces are outsized machines that are exposed and active in the landscape. This outward show attracts the spectator's eye, though their inner workings and the fire in their bellies remain shielded from the spectator's view.[30]

The blast furnace plants have striking commonalities with urban American grain elevators. Both consist of tall and more-or-less cylindrical forms that are repeated in series and displayed in full view, yet sealed from full sight. Like grain elevators, blast furnace plants assume monumental architectonic forms along waterways and railroads (figs. 84 and 85). At heights surpassing one hundred feet they operate at the scale of the landscape, creating their own skylines. Also like grain elevators, which in their most dramatic incarnation symbolize both a city (Buffalo, New York) and the commerce of the Great Lakes, blast furnaces assume iconic significance in the Pittsburgh region. The blast furnace plant acts as a technological totem. It is a visual surrogate and symbol for both the steel industry and Pittsburgh itself.[31]

America's urban grain elevators were much admired by Le Corbusier and other early modern architects for their straightforward concrete construction and simple geometric forms, but those architects took little notice of blast furnaces.[32] Grain elevators are more building than machine; while blast furnace plants are more machine than building. Le Corbusier and the others professed to favor the machine, but they focused on the aesthetics of functionalist structures and streamlined vehicles (ships and airplanes) and their potential for architectural form-giving, rather than on the gritty production-driven realities of industrial machines. The blast furnace was little acknowledged as a designed object and focal point in the landscape until the steel industry began to decline and photographers such as Bernd and Hilla Becher began to record surviving blast furnaces.[33] The Bechers photographed each aging furnace in a frank and consistent manner, like a series of portraits of old men (fig. 87).

The steel mill's visceral physicality and complex processes invite anthropomorphic analogies. Holley saw a body of bones and muscles in ET's layout; upright blast furnaces assume the anthropomorphic stance of statuary.[34] Joe Magarac, a steel-industry folk hero and figure of mythic giantism, was the personification of both the mill and the blast furnace (fig. 88). Magarac was reportedly conceived in legend at the Edgar Thomson Works; and Magarac—not Edgar Thomson or Andrew Carnegie—has been the dominant presence there.[35] He was born in an iron mountain, and literally made of steel. He worked day and night, producing two thousand tons of steel each day. He formed molten steel with his bare hands, cut sheets of metal with his teeth, and

Fig. 85. Jet Lowe (photographer), "Buffalo Grain Elevators: General View of Site from South," 1990. Library of Congress, Prints and Photographs Division, Historic American Engineering Record, HAER,NY,15-BUF,27–1.

squeezed out rails from between his fingers. Magarac was as powerful as a machine, was himself a machine.[36]

Machines are typically associated with maleness due to the normative conditions of industrial work. Machines extend the strength of the male worker. Pittsburgh industries were an almost exclusively male domain, and the coupling of man and machine was repeatedly trumpeted in the rhetoric of Pittsburgh industry. Machines also shared the hard contours of the ideal masculine physique that was on active display in the mills.[37] The frankly exposed blast furnaces embodied male erotic power.

Curiously, however, the Magarac-like steelworkers tended to view their mills and blast furnaces as female. Pittsburgh mills often had fe-

Fig. 86. *Pittsburgh, Workshop of the World. Night Mill Scene,* n.d., postcard. Eugene Levy Collection, Carnegie Mellon University Libraries.

▶ Fig. 87. Bernd and Hilla Becher (photographers), "Blast Furnace," 1979. Photograph taken at the Edgar Thomson Works in Braddock. Carnegie Museum of Art, Pittsburgh; Purchase: Gift of the Partners of Reed Smith Shaw and McClay. Courtesy of Sonnabend Gallery.

Fig. 88. William Gropper, *Joe Magarac,* 1946. Collection of the University Art Gallery, University of Pittsburgh.

male names (e.g., the Lucy, Isabella, Eliza, and Carrie Furnaces), as did individual blast furnaces (e.g., Dorothy, Ann). A Carnegie Steel Company handbook asserted that the steelworker "refers to his furnace in the feminine gender, because, he knows she is a fickle maid capable of acting in most unexpected and astonishing ways."[38] Writer Laurie Graham has a different reading of this practice. She notes that James Oppenheim, in his novel *The Olympian* (1912), portrays the steel mill as an

Industrial Mother that gives birth to steel. At the same time, "a blast furnace is female for obvious reasons," Graham explains. "She is charged with ore, then the ore is transformed in the fire of her voluminous belly. At the moment of birth molten iron bursts from her taphole amid a shower of sparks and light." The furnace is perceived as a womb-like chamber, and Graham discovers erotic overtones in the attentions of the steelworkers.[39]

Within the steel mill, it seems, a landscape of giantism and its superhuman machines may be viewed as embodiments of the male workers, and/or female beings with female bodies. Ultimately, Graham suggests, "Whether the conflagration of the furnace, the bubbling soup of molten steel, the tall, dark stacks spitting smoke or plumes of fire, the imagery of the steel mill is one of generative, erotic power. Male and female merge in its thunderous shapes and fires."[40]

Many vantage points opened onto the Edgar Thomson Works, and it was especially remarked for its fiery pyrotechnics and dramatic smokescape. When Otto Kuhler looked down at ET from the rim of the valley he saw "red clouds of smoke [rising] behind violent flames," as "long snakes of red-hot steel crept through the darkness."[41] ET captivated the spectator, and unleashed powerful forces in the Steel Valley. This sublime and sensual power extended to the mill's topographical setting, where technology and the land flow together as a single dynamic force (fig. 89). Rails, roads, and Turtle Creek spread loosely over the terrain, winding a course toward the river and the mill, like a pour of molten steel.

Electric Valley

Westinghouse ruled the Turtle Creek Valley as a realm of corporate giantism. The Westinghouse Electric and Manufacturing Company, the largest Westinghouse facility, was located in East Pittsburgh, a short distance up the valley from its mouth. Immediately adjacent was the Westinghouse Machine Company, and the two plants together became known as the Westinghouse East Pittsburgh Works (fig. 90). The West-

Fig. 89. Todd Webb (photographer), "Looking Towards Pittsburgh from Hill Near Westinghouse Bridge," ca. 1950. Courtesy of George Eastman House. Photograph © Todd Webb, Courtesy of Evans Gallery and Todd Webb Trust, Portland, Maine, USA.

inghouse Air Brake Company and Westinghouse Foundry were sited further upstream in Wilmerding and Trafford, respectively. Wilmerding was a Westinghouse company town. In time, Westinghouse territory spread to nearby upland communities where additional manufacturing and research facilities were built.

The Westinghouse companies were all about mechanical devices and electrical apparatus, from the turbine to the transformer, from the scale of the light bulb to that of the landscape. Westinghouse succeeded in two high-profile arenas of the sublime: the harnessing of Niagara Falls for electric power generation, and the lighting of the 1893 World's Columbian Exposition in Chicago. These achievements made long-distance power transmission a commercial possibility and gave impetus to the proliferation of incandescent electric lighting, populating the landscape with both transmission towers and streetlights.[42] Such Westinghouse innovations won acclaim and new business, and set the stage for the Westinghouse East Pittsburgh Works, which was established in 1894.

Innovative technology called for up-to-date architecture. Many nineteenth-century American factories were multistory buildings,

Fig. 90. Westinghouse East Pittsburgh Works. Note the railroad station to the right, the office building left of center, and the connecting viaduct. Reprinted from *The Pittsburg Electrical Hand-Book* (Pittsburgh: The American Institute of Electrical Engineers, 1904), 80.

boxy in plan and massing. They emphasized functionality over style, yet they blended substantially with the architecture of their town settings. By the turn of the twentieth century, however, factory buildings had evolved into variations on the theme of the production shed.[43] The common production shed featured a rectangular footprint and basilica-form massing, with a high central bay under a gabled roof, and lower bays to either side (fig. 91). Production sheds allowed for large unobstructed spaces (in both height and breadth), were expandable (along the primary axis), and were repeatable (in parallel rows). They could be combined and multiplied in large and ever-expanding complexes.

Over time, Westinghouse built numerous production sheds in adjacent parallel rows at the Westinghouse East Pittsburgh Works. The works grew to an awesome size, with many acres under roof and many

Fig. 91. Aisle inside Westinghouse Electric and Manufacturing Company. Reprinted from *Works of Westinghouse Electric & Manufacturing Company: Their Industrial and Sociological Aspect* (Pittsburgh: Westinghouse Electric and Manufacturing Company, 1904), n.p. Library and Archives Division, Historical Society of Western Pennsylvania, Pittsburgh, Pa.

miles of aisles, dwarfing its town setting.[44] In this, the Westinghouse Works embodied an aspect of the technological sublime: the suggestion of infinity due to sheer size and the repetition of elements. For the spectator on the valley floor, the works was a continuous brick facade, displaying window after window after window (see fig. 92). For the spectator on the surrounding hills, the works was a vast expanse of roofs, nearly filling the valley from side to side (fig. 90).

Factories could provide a measure of architectural familiarity even at this scale, but the turn-of-the-century factory was principally a container for the unfamiliar machines and processes inside. The Westinghouse plants were chock full of machines, and most of the action was internal. The high central bay of a production shed provided perfect accommodation for overhead cranes that spanned and traveled the length of the bay. In fact, the production shed and the overhead crane were so commonly matched that the existence of one suggested the presence of the other. There were more than sixty overhead cranes in the Westinghouse Electric and Manufacturing Company buildings by 1904.[45]

Such facilities marked a new era of industrial architecture and production through a merging of architecture and the machine.[46] It was no longer just a matter of machines inside of buildings (though there were many), or outside of buildings (as at the steel mill), but buildings *as* machines. As Lindy Biggs writes: "In the late nineteenth and early twentieth centuries, owners and engineers had begun to build a new kind of factory, and in so doing they recast the idea of what a factory should be. . . . No longer a passive shell simply to house machines, tools, and workers, the new factory embraced a more complex vision: it became 'the master machine,' organizing and controlling work. . . . [E]ngineers realized that, by rethinking the layout of buildings and the way things moved through them, they could approximate a factory that ran like a machine."[47]

This master machine concept, adds Betsy Hunter Bradley, "was based on the technological integration of machinery and the building that housed it." The fully realized master machine was first defined as a "steel-framed structure incorporating a powerful traveling crane and housing electric-powered machinery."[48] It later grew even more sophisticated with the growing influence of industrial engineers who advised on a wide range of topics including site selection, building design, heating and ventilation, natural and artificial lighting, shop floor layout, work flow, and materials handling.[49] The new factory embodied, as well as housed and manufactured, technology.

Electrical power was a key element of the master machine and a Westinghouse specialty. Not surprisingly, Westinghouse was an early advocate of electrically powered factories. Electrical power ran the machin-

Fig. 92. Westinghouse Electric and Manufacturing Company. Reprinted from *The Pittsburg Electrical Hand-Book* (Pittsburgh: The American Institute of Electrical Engineers, 1904), unnumbered plate.

ery, and electrical lighting allowed for round-the-clock operation (the ideal machine does not rest) and lit the buildings at night in a serene and steady glow. Though seemingly enhanced, a photograph of the Westinghouse Electric and Manufacturing Company forecast a prominent visual role for electricity in the industrial landscape (fig. 92).[50]

Thus the factory became sublime in functionality as well as scale, and the spectator saw the Westinghouse Works as a sublime master machine, with Westinghouse himself in control. Nye notes that the experience of the technological sublime involved "a celebration of the power of human reason, and . . . guaranteed special privilege to engineers and inventors."[51] George Westinghouse was the consummate engineer and inventor, with 361 United States patents to his name. He was commonly depicted against the backdrop of his various technological progeny, which together populated a landscape not unlike the Turtle

Fig. 93. George Westinghouse. Reprinted from *Scenes From a Great Life: George Westinghouse Centennial, 1846–1946* (Westinghouse Electric Corporation, 1945), n.p. Hagley Museum and Library.

Creek Valley (fig. 93). George Westinghouse was a larger-than-life figure, whose personal giantism matched the corporate giantism in the regional terrain.[52]

This constant presence was reflected in the physical layout of the Westinghouse Works. Many Westinghouse plants had a general office building for company executives and engineers. In East Pittsburgh, the original office building is seven stories tall (fig. 94). The building was sited to command the primary entrances to both the Westinghouse Electric and Manufacturing Company and Westinghouse Machine Company plants, as well as the main entrances to the combined works from the town to the west, and from the railroad station—by means of a viaduct—to the east. Here the general office building operated somewhat like a panopticon, an architectural device that facilitates visual surveillance in multiple directions.[53] Such oversight was both practi-

Fig. 94. General office building, Westinghouse East Pittsburgh Works, n.d., postcard. Eugene Levy Collection, Carnegie Mellon University Libraries.

Fig. 95. Westinghouse East Pittsburgh Works. Shows giant electric sign. Reprinted from *Ten Years with Westinghouse Electric & Manufacturing Company, 1921–1931* (New York: Carreau and Gnedeker, 1931), 5. Library and Archives Division, Historical Society of Western Pennsylvania, Pittsburgh, Pa.

cal—especially in times of labor unrest—and symbolic. Here Westinghouse and his surrogates were all-seeing eyes, at once spectators and masters of all that they surveyed.

If a multitude of corporate facilities, the prodigious productivity of the master machine, and the prevailing presence of the master himself were insufficient manifestations of Westinghouse territory, a new and taller general office building was built in 1930 and topped with a massive Westinghouse Electric (later just Westinghouse) sign (fig. 95). With this, the Westinghouse name and the corporate product (electrical apparatus) rose high above the Westinghouse Works and conclusively commanded the Electric Valley, or, as it was now clearly labeled for the spectator, the Westinghouse Valley.

The Great Bridge

After 1931, the Steel Valley met the Electric Valley under the George Westinghouse Memorial Bridge. The Philadelphia to Pittsburgh turnpike had crossed through the Turtle Creek Valley since the early nineteenth century. It descended a steep grade down the eastern slope and followed a circuitous path across the valley floor. In 1915, this road was incorporated into the Lincoln Highway, the first automobile route to cross the United States.[54] The popularity of the Lincoln Highway, the proliferation of the automobile, and continued industrial growth in the valley soon rendered the road slow and dangerous. So a new route was devised to cross over the valley at the height of the flanking hills (fig. 96). This new cutoff required the construction of 2.8 miles of new highway and a massive new bridge more than 1,500 feet in length and over 200 feet in height. The new road and bridge considerably upgraded the motoring experience on this part of the Lincoln Highway, accentuated the highway's prestige, and punctuated its unprecedented reach. It also transformed the spectator's experience of the Turtle Creek Valley.

If the waterways and railroads ran along the valley floor in a more or less parallel fashion as channeled by the topography, the Westinghouse Bridge was a great lateral and elevated stroke across the terrain.

Fig. 96. The Aerial Surveys of Pittsburgh, Inc. (photographer), "Air View of the Westinghouse Bridge." Reprinted from George S. Richardson, "The Design of Concrete Arches in Allegheny County, Pennsylvania," *Journal of the American Concrete Institute* 3, no. 10 (June 1932), 639.

An incisive 130-foot-deep cut through a high bluff provided access to the bridge from the east, and a viaduct and a bluff-side cut and embankment provided access from the west. The bridge spanned from bluff to bluff at a point where the valley narrowed but remained thick with infrastructure. More than two dozen railroad lines, a highway with a street railway, and Turtle Creek itself passed under the bridge (fig. 97). As stacked from top to bottom, the bridge became the fifth level of passage in the valley. Supervising engineer V. R. Covell described the scene: "One hundred and ninety feet below the new bridge, the trains on the main line of the Pennsylvania Railroad thunder past, crossed overhead by the Union Railroad, and underneath by a main highway carrying a street railway, and by Turtle Creek, the stream which drains the valley 220 feet below the floor of the structure."[55]

The Westinghouse Bridge responded to the facts of its setting and

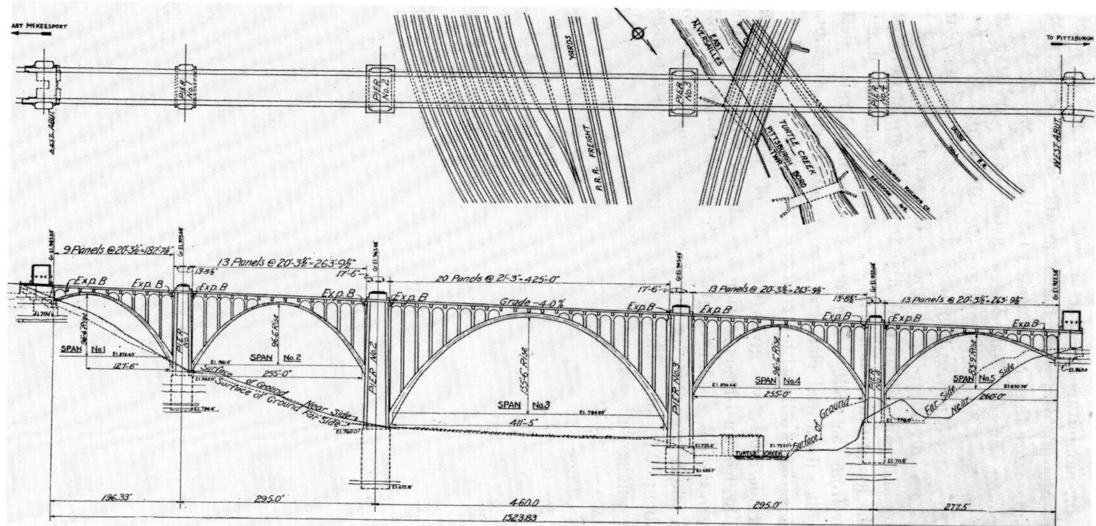

Fig. 97. *A General Plan and Elevation of the Westinghouse Bridge.* Reprinted from George S. Richardson, "The Design of Concrete Arches in Allegheny County, Pennsylvania," *Journal of the American Concrete Institute* 3, no. 10 (June 1932), 642.

rose to the challenge of its site. George S. Richardson, who designed the bridge, acknowledged that concrete-arch construction was not naturally suggested by the project and was more expensive than steel construction. Yet two studies for steel cantilever bridges were rejected. The deciding factor, Richardson reported, was "the belief that in the concrete design there had been created a structure of monumental character . . . which was warranted for this location."[56]

As a "structure of monumental character," the bridge plays a prominent visual and organizational role in the landscape (figs. 98 and 99). Though constructed at a topographical narrows it is massive in scale. It is a dominating focal point, inviting views from near and far, from below, and even from above. It gives form and scale to the void. It is a visual connector from point to point, a divider of topographical space, a hinge that interrelates the land and the sky, and a frame that controls what the spectator sees. It organizes and focuses the landscape for the spectator.[57]

As a work of engineering, the Westinghouse Bridge is both an amalgam of historic and archetypal precedents and a marvel of modern design. At its dedication, A. W. Robertson compared the bridge to the Appian Way; it readily recalls a Roman viaduct loping across the landscape.[58] For those passing through on the valley floor it is a triumphal arch, a point of entry to greater Pittsburgh. At the same time, when it was built, the bridge embodied the latest in contemporary bridge-building technology. It boasted at least one true superlative—the 460-foot center span was the longest concrete arch in America—and was deemed a peer of other monuments of contemporary engineering. According to the *Engineering News Record*:

> The George Westinghouse Bridge claims a place in the select company of other great engineering achievements in recent years such as the Holland Tunnel, the Hudson River [George Washington] suspension bridge and the Hoover Dam, all of which have captured the public imagination and offered a special appeal to the engineer. . . . There is a sound basis for this claim, for the new structure is spectacular in the service it renders, in the boldness of its design and erection, in the grace and symmetry of its architecture and in its location over a busy industrial valley in which three levels of highway and railway were already provided for.[59]

As a triumphal arch may honor an emperor, and a bridge or dam may honor a president, so the George Westinghouse Bridge honors a modern industrialist. It thereby suggests another form of personal giantism in the landscape: Westinghouse the man—a colossus—bestriding the valley. This evocation of George Westinghouse in a monumental structure within the context of the Westinghouse Valley suggests the existence of a prevailing mythology in this place, one seemingly spelled out on thirty-foot pylons at each end of the bridge. Here Art Deco sculptural reliefs, designed by sculptor Frank Vittor, feature styized industrial motifs, heroic figures, and high-minded inscriptions.[60]

Two of the reliefs—representing electricity and transportation—are directly associated with George Westinghouse (fig. 100). One depicts Westinghouse innovations in the distribution of electric power by

Fig. 98. Ernest Wilson Boyer, *Bridges,* 1933. Georgetown University Library, Special Collections Division. Gift of Helen King Boyer, 1985. Courtesy of Helen King Boyer.

way of alternating current. An inscription reads: "Wherever electricity has flowed, man's existence has been enriched and industry has grown." The other relief features trains foremost, acknowledging Westinghouse's role as a pioneer of railroad technology. The bridge's primary dedication statement is paired with this panel. It praises and honors Westinghouse the man, reading:

IN BOLDNESS OF CONCEPTION, IN GREATNESS
AND IN USEFULNESS TO MANKIND THIS BRIDGE
TYPIFIES THE CHARACTER AND CAREER OF
GEORGE WESTINGHOUSE 1846–1914
IN WHOSE HONOR IT WAS DEDICATED ON
SEPTEMBER 10, 1932

Fig. 99. Otto Kuhler, *George Westinghouse Bridge,* 1929. Collection of Westmoreland Museum of American Art, Greensburg, Pennsylvania. Gift of Constance Mellon Bequest, 1985.170.

Fig. 100. Joseph Elliott (photographer), "George Westinghouse Memorial Bridge: Detail of Decorative End Pylon from South," 1997. Shows sculpture: Frank Vittor, *Electricity*, ca. 1930. Library of Congress, Prints and Photographs Division, Historic American Engineering Record, HAER,PA,2-EAPIT,1–10.

Curiously, this inscription, however laudatory, suggests a relationship between bridge and man that is one of analogy rather than memorialization. And the two additional reliefs—representing the early settlers of the Turtle Creek Valley and steel—are not directly associated with Westinghouse at all. It seems, finally, that the prevailing mythology is less a matter of personal giantism and more a matter of broad technological progress. The bridge pylons don't commemorate a George Westinghouse past so much as an industrial present.

For Eugene Levy, the bridge and its pylons "make explicit [a] viewpoint to be taken of the Turtle Creek Valley's past and present," substituting a "morally elevated view of industrialism for the gritty scene that existed on the valley floor." This "idealized mythic view of technology, a view in which numberless, nameless workers toil for the greater benefit of industrial civilization" is, as Levy contends, subject to skeptical evaluation.[61] But it was not only the captains of industry and the bridge-builders who mythologized this place. Monuments emerge from collective perception and experience. From this perspective, the Westinghouse Bridge and its symbolic art ratify the spectator's experience of the technological sublime as embodied in the industrial landscape of the Turtle Creek Valley and the great bridge itself.

Space/Time and the Spectator

Industry interjected new scale and drama into the terrain. The industrial landscape is studded with outsized man-made elements characterized by extreme numbers (miles of track, tons of steel produced, acres of factory floor, height and length of span). It is populated by larger-than-life individuals representing immense economic interests and a host of working men and women. It is a place of shared purpose and a place of conflict; of powerful forces, shifting perceptions, and changing scenes.

The radical topography of the lower Turtle Creek Valley alternately shields and reveals this landscape. It is difficult for the spectator to take in all at once. It requires—and provides—a new way of seeing.

Both the railroad and the highway bridge are more than just technological infrastructure, they are also machines for traversing and viewing the industrial landscape.

The invention of the railroad altered the continuum of time and space. Speed shrank the time between places and simultaneously expanded physical parameters. The spectator as railroad traveler underwent a space/time experience that changed perception. What had been static and pictorial was now a continuous sequence of visual impressions. M. Christine Boyer states, "The landscape through which the train traveler moved was suddenly turned into a vast screen unrolling its fleeting tableaux." Boyer and others have called this effect "panoramic," but it is perhaps better understood as cinematic. As Mitchell Schwarzer observes, "the train turned the built environment into something of a moving picture show, decades before the invention of cinema."[62] At first, explains Wolfgang Schivelbusch, the spectator/traveler felt a loss of control of the senses and a subsequent loss of landscape. The railcar enforced physical detachment from the environment. Visual impressions were intensified and multiplied. Scenery blurred and flew rapidly by. Soon, however, an alternative perception and understanding developed: only with movement and speed was it possible to fully appreciate a broad landscape. The railroad, in this view, created a new way of seeing and enabled the spectator to experience a newfound landscape, rather than a loss of landscape. "The railroad choreographed the landscape. The motion of the train shrank space, and thus displayed in immediate succession objects and pieces of scenery that in their original spatiality belonged to separate realms."[63] This enabled the spectator to take in large objects and networks of objects, and to synthesize a series of perceptions into a whole. Thus the spectator's experience and the nature of a place unfolded as a process of revelation. Glazier's and Embony's descriptions of industrial Pittsburgh emerged from trains entering the city. There were many such spectators and space/time experiences on the trains of the Monongahela and Turtle Creek Valleys.[64]

In 1904, Westinghouse produced a film shot from a moving train as it proceeded past one Westinghouse factory after another in the Turtle Creek Valley.[65] This was an actuality film, capturing everyday scenes as they were commonly seen. A predominant theme is the continuous facades of the buildings, where windows pass by one after the other as if they were the frames of the film itself. The cinematic experience might also be narrative in form. "Like a movie," says Schwarzer, "railroads draw together disparate sights into image narratives."[66] Artist Douglas Cooper has narrated his childhood experience (1953) riding the Pennsy main line as it approached Pittsburgh from the east via the Conemaugh River and Turtle Creek Valleys. Cooper experienced the route as a sequence of contiguous but changing settings, which climaxes at the lower Turtle Creek Valley with the Westinghouse plants, the sudden narrowing of the valley and passage under the Westinghouse Bridge, and release through the mouth of the valley toward the Edgar Thomson Works and then the city. As Cooper recalls the final stretch, after the bridge, "the valley widened, and as the train rounded the bend overlooking Braddock, the smoke and plumes of the Edgar Thomson steelworks rose beside us. It was a layered scene. Rust-brown haze and red heat in the foreground, with dark, stacked profiles behind. Peek-a-boo morning light reflected past the sheds and furnaces from the distant Monongahela River. Gas jets fired overhead. Then, just as quickly, the view closed again as the train turned" to continue on to Pittsburgh proper. The railroad experience gave Cooper "an incremental sense of the city. . . . It was as though the elements that made Pittsburgh's approaching chemistry were laid out for inspection one by one in sequence: first the hills, then the coal, then the valleys, then the water, and finally the fire."[67] Cooper's drawing, *Morning Train Under the Westinghouse Bridge,* pays homage to this sublime cinematic experience (fig. 101). It further distorts the already distorted landscape to provide a more-or-less beginning-to-end depiction of railroad travel through the lower Turtle Creek Valley

As the automobile gradually superseded the train, one cinematic experience superseded another. As Donald Appleyard, Kevin Lynch, and John R. Myer observe, "The sensation of driving a car is primarily one of motion and space, felt in a continuous sequence. . . . The sense of spatial sequence is like that of large-scale architecture; the continuity and insistent temporal flow are akin to music and the cinema." Sigfried Giedion, too, perceived the space/time experience of the automobile, writing in *Space, Time and Architecture* (1941): "The meaning and beauty of the parkway cannot be grasped from a single point of observation, as was possible when from a window of the château of Versailles the whole expanse of nature could be embraced in one view. It can be revealed only by movement, by driving along in a steady flow as the rites of the traffic prescribe. The space-time feeling of our period can seldom be felt so keenly as when driving, the wheel under one's hand, up and down hills, beneath overpasses, up ramps, and over giant bridges."[68]

Levy describes the experience of driving past the sprawling Westinghouse Works, and a short distance further, the Edgar Thomson Works, where "a pall of smoke and grit pressed down on cars." But the Westinghouse Bridge lifted many cars from the valley floor and provided the motoring spectator with an alternative experience of the Turtle Creek Valley (fig. 102). Now the sense of detachment and rapidity of movement that were inherent to both railcar and automobile were compounded by distance and elevation. For some, issues remained unresolved from the first days of the railroad: the bridge (and the highway) meant a loss of landscape. For Levy, "The Westinghouse Bridge, like the interstates that would soon follow, encouraged travelers to avoid intimate contact with the urban-industrial landscape and to pass over, through, or by it as quickly and in as isolated a manner as possible . . . [distancing] us physically and intellectually from many of the elements of . . . the industrial landscape."[69]

Conversely, the Westinghouse Bridge and its highway, soaring high above the valley, can be seen to provide a viewpoint that is alternative rather than disengaged. Dramatic views are inherent to the setting, and were consciously captured as an amenity during the design of the bridge.[70] These views of the industrial landscape are different, to be sure, as the actuality and narrative sequences on the valley floor are

Fig. 101. Douglas Cooper, *Morning Train Under the Westinghouse Bridge,* 1999. Courtesy of Douglas Cooper.

Fig. 102. Dedication of the Westinghouse Bridge, September 10, 1932. Eugene Levy Collection, Carnegie Mellon University Libraries.

replaced by tracking shots, seen from above. But the experience is equally cinematic and equally sublime.

The Westinghouse Bridge is not perceived as a triumphal arch when approached by highway from the east, but it is still a marker of arrival in the Pittsburgh district. Just prior to the bridge the terrain closes in on the motoring spectator. He or she passes between the high earthen embankments of the highway cut, which act as blinders forcing vision straight ahead, and then emerges onto the descending grade of the bridge deck as if coming out of a chute. The bridge itself modulates the space/time experience. The large pylons that flank the roadway frame the view ahead while they synchronize with the terrain to begin and end views from the bridge. The scene opens suddenly, and the spectator must orient him- or herself to expansive light-filled space as a panoramic forward view initially establishes the topographical setting (see fig. 102). The bridge then serves as an elevated viewing platform as views to either side capture the rich complexity and power of the industrial landscape below. The views gradually shift as the spectator travels the length of the bridge deck before reentering the terrain on the opposite bluff, where the scene rapidly closes.

As seen from the train and the automobile, the Turtle Creek Valley has been disclosed as an extreme topographical condition. ET's fire and smoke have been observed as pervasive yet transitory phenomena.The immense trackside and building-top Westinghouse signs have been revealed as billboards that explicitly target the railroad and bridge-borne spectator, and the bridge has been experienced as a locus of mythology and transition.[71]

The space/time sequencing of this sublime industrial landscape has been riveting cinema for more than a century, encompassing scenes of prologue, climax, and denouement. The railroad and the bridge have facilitated acts of arrival *and* departure. Industrial development, which typically reflects exact circumstances of time and place, and is, like cinema, inherently short-lived, has waxed and waned.[72]

Coal barges still ply the Monongahela River and freight trains remain active in the landscape, though their numbers have declined.

Amtrak routes daily passenger trains through the Turtle Creek Valley. With the broad decline of the steel industry, the Edgar Thomson Works is the only major steel mill operating in the Pittsburgh area, though at a much contracted scale.[73] The Westinghouse companies and their signage are gone from East Pittsburgh, and the Westinghouse Works is marketed to all comers as an industrial park. The Westinghouse Bridge carries U.S. Route 30, a secondary highway choked with Wal-Mart traffic, and the bridge pylons now commemorate an industrial past.

The Turtle Creek Valley has been diminished, and demystified; yet it remains largely intact and available to the spectator. Technology and topography continue to set the scene.[74]

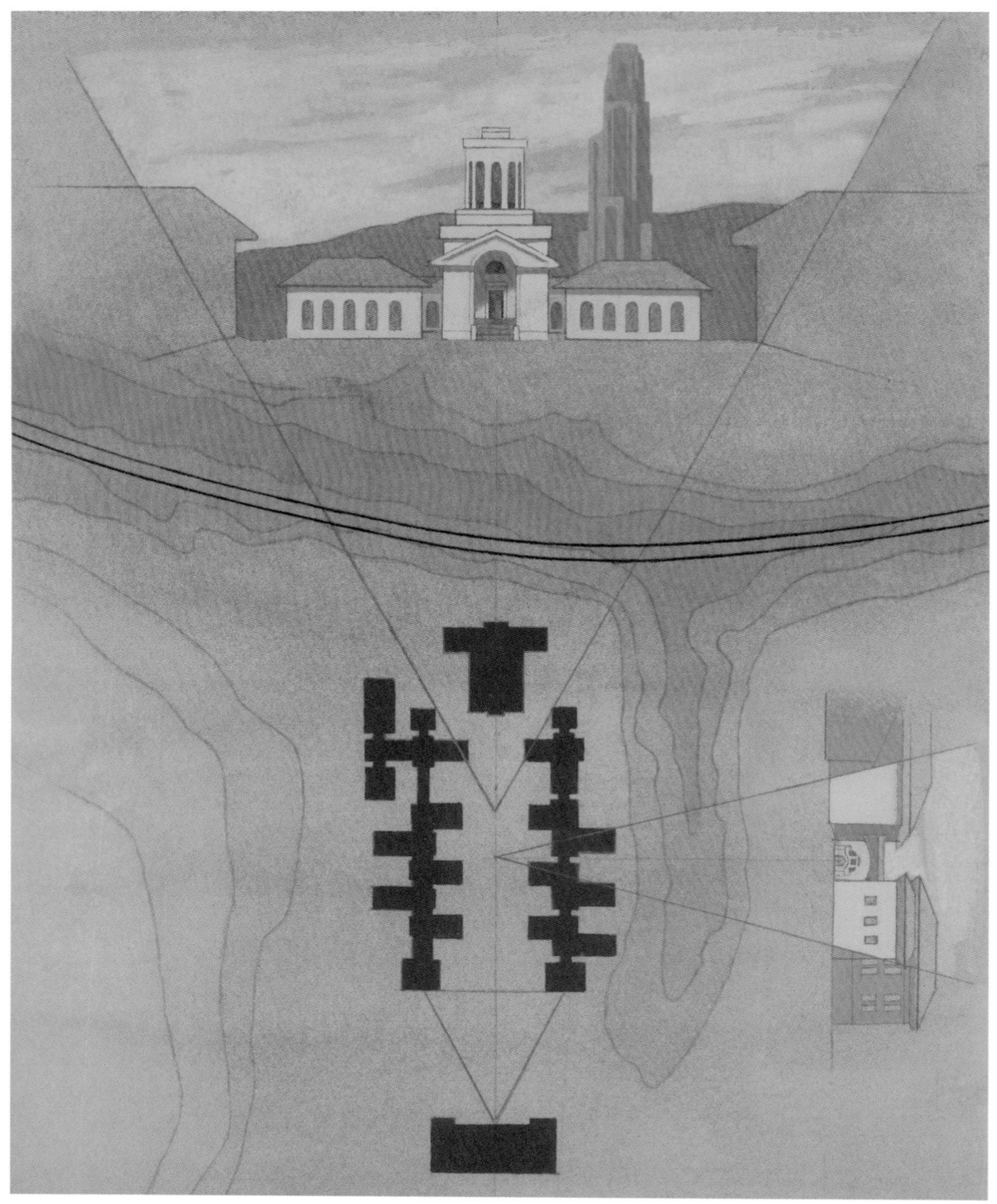

Fig. 103. Clayton Merrell, *The Complex Vista*, 2005. Courtesy of Clayton Merrell.

Oakland and the Complex Vista

Pittsburgh's topographical situation is picturesque but rough and declivitous. The city sits impregnable on seventeen hills, which are divided by steep ravines and often precipitous gulches. To make a "city beautiful" under the circumstances is an Herculean undertaking.

Builder (October 1912)

An American Campus

In 1890, Andrew Carnegie climbed to the top of Herron Hill, looked out over Pittsburgh's Oakland district, and chose a site at the entrance to the new Schenley Park for his gift to the city of a library, museum, and concert hall in one building.[1] Built between 1892 and 1895, and greatly enlarged from 1903 to 1907, the Carnegie Institute put Oakland on the map.

Meanwhile, thirty-two acres of land adjacent to Schenley Park and a mere hollow away from the Carnegie Institute became the chosen site for a second major Carnegie benefaction, the Carnegie Technical Schools (Carnegie Tech) (fig. 103). Founded as a secondary technical school in 1900, Carnegie Tech evolved into a degree-granting institution known as Carnegie Institute of Technology, now Carnegie Mellon University. The proximate location of the two Carnegie institutions was purposeful, for in many respects Carnegie saw them as a single institution. As Franklin Toker suggests, Junction Hollow did not act as a divider but instead as a mirror in which the Carnegie Institute and Carnegie Tech could "admire and congratulate each other."[2]

The Carnegie Tech site sloped more or less steadily downward from east to west and dropped off sharply at its northern and western edges. The shape of the parcel was as irregular as the topography (figs. 104 and 105). As for the land itself: "It was treeless; it was none too fertile ground that ran mainly to cabbages; and it was all either sharp hillside or deep ravine, with scarcely a level square rod of ground."[3] The Carnegie Tech campus would be uniquely shaped by its topographical setting and by developments in American higher education and campus planning.

American democratic ideals have long emphasized the need for an enlightened populace, and colleges and universities were established to further this purpose, beginning in the colonial and early republican periods. Such institutions educated the privileged few, if not the democratic many. In a new land, as new communities unto themselves, American colleges could stand at the edge of a town or even in the wilderness. They created spatial order by grouping collegiate buildings around open green space, and the interplay of landscape and architecture became a key characteristic of the American college and university campus.[4]

The University of Virginia, of which Thomas Jefferson was founder and architect, embodied and extended these early educational and physical ideals. Jefferson sought to produce an educated elite of the best and the brightest, without regard for social and economic distinctions. His campus (1817–1826), near Charlottesville, Virginia, placed "the academic buildings into the landscape as a unified, harmonious merger of architecture with its natural setting." Jefferson called it an "academical village."[5]

According to Paul Venable Turner, "the romantic notion of a college in nature, removed from the corrupting forces of the city, became an American ideal. But in the process, the college had to become even more fully a kind of miniature city. And its design became an experiment in urbanism." This became increasingly true around the turn of the twentieth century as small colleges and universities began to evolve into large, complex, modern institutions, and many new schools were founded in urban settings. The program for an 1899 competition to design the University of California campus charged: "it is a city that is to be created—a City of Learning."[6]

In some cases, wealthy industrialists personally spurred the development of large new institutions from scratch. Leland Stanford at Stanford University, John D. Rockefeller at the University of Chicago, and Andrew Carnegie at Carnegie Tech represented this new breed of patrons. Carnegie Tech embodied Carnegie's educational and philanthropic ideals, as expressed in his Gospel of Wealth: "The main consideration should be to help those who will help themselves; to provide part of the means by which those who desire to improve may do so; to give those who desire to rise the aids by which they may rise; to assist, but rarely or never to do all. . . . [T]he best means of benefiting the community is to place within its reach the ladders upon which the aspiring can rise."[7] Carnegie's offer of means was no more universal than Jefferson's was. But Jefferson's gifted few had become Carnegie's aspiring many. For many were needed to run the industrial society.

If education was one route to betterment, architecture was another. There was a perception, at the turn of the twentieth century, that architecture and urban design could have salubrious effects on the populace and advance social behavior. In Pittsburgh and elsewhere, urban reformers embraced the City Beautiful Movement, which sought to bring order to the chaos of the American industrial city and to civilize and elevate its inhabitants by means of urban planning and beautification. Though prompted by a strong sense of social responsibility, the movement was dominated by an aesthetic point of view that promoted a monumental art integrating architecture, landscape, and the city.[8]

The American campus became a key locus for the implementation of City Beautiful ideals because of its charge to civilize and elevate its

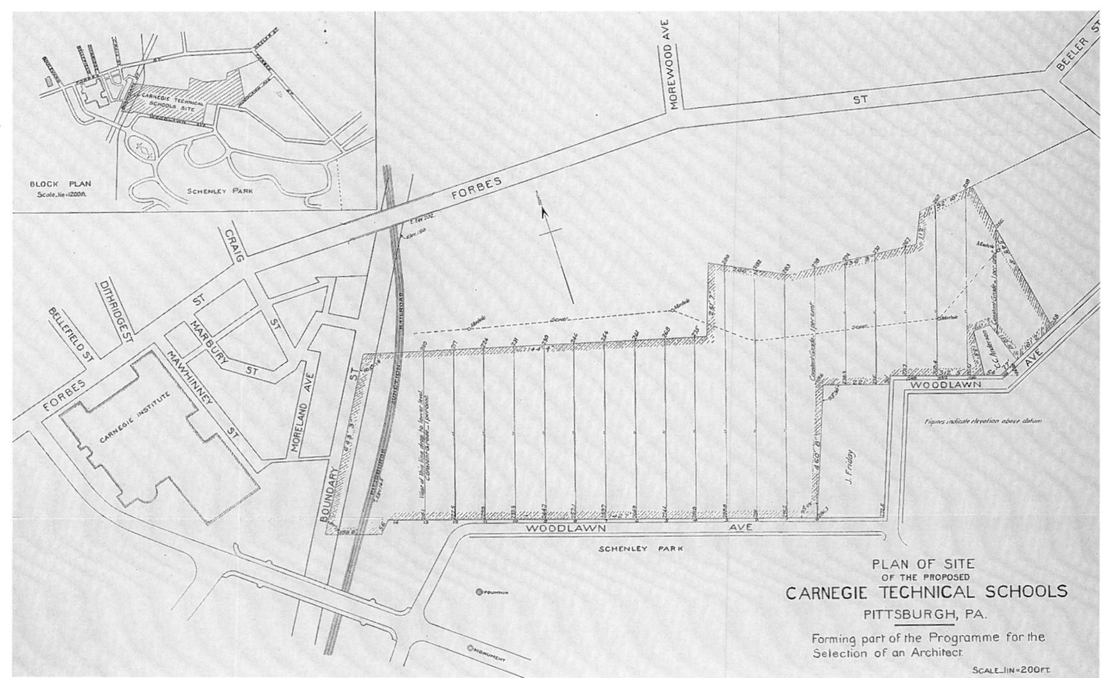

Fig. 104. *Plan of Site of the Proposed Carnegie Technical Schools, Pittsburgh, Pa.* Reprinted from *Programme of a Competition for the Selection of an Architect for the Carnegie Technical Schools in the City of Pittsburgh, Penna.* (Pittsburgh: Murdoch-Kerr Press, 1904), insert. Shows property lines, imposed lines of topography, and location of the Carnegie Institute, whose expanded footprint is on the left. Carnegie Mellon University Architecture Archives.

students, its search for spatial order, its ongoing role as urban experiment, and its centralized planning authority. This new thinking elevated the physical development of the campus to embrace formal site plans and grand architectural schemes, as exemplified by McKim, Mead, and White's 1894 campus plans for New York University and Columbia University. A 1904 competition for the design of the new Carnegie Tech campus attracted entries from numerous architects and firms, including five invited competitors who were among the leading architects of the day: Carrere and Hastings, Frank Miles Day and Brother, Cass Gilbert, Howells and Stokes, and George B. Post. It was the uninvited firm of Palmer and Hornbostel, however, that submitted the winning entry, a quintessential formal site plan and grand architectural scheme (fig. 106).

Fig. 105. Groundbreaking for the Carnegie Technical Schools, ca. 1905. The expanded Carnegie Institute is shown under construction in the background. Carnegie Mellon University Archives.

Henry Hornbostel (1867–1961) was a graduate of Columbia College (later Columbia University), and studied at the École des Beaux-Arts in Paris.[9] Americans had begun to attend the École in the 1850s, and when America's first schools of architecture were founded, beginning with the Massachusetts Institute of Technology in 1865, they closely followed the École's methods of architectural training. Beaux-Arts design principles drew heavily on the so-called Grand Manner, a language of prototypical architectural and spatial elements derived from French Baroque planning. The Grand Manner employed formal compositional rules and devices such as axiality and symmetry, and accommodated a variety of largely classicist styles of architecture. Beaux-Arts design principles dominated the American architectural scene at the turn of the twentieth century and were broadly incorporated into City Beautiful thinking.

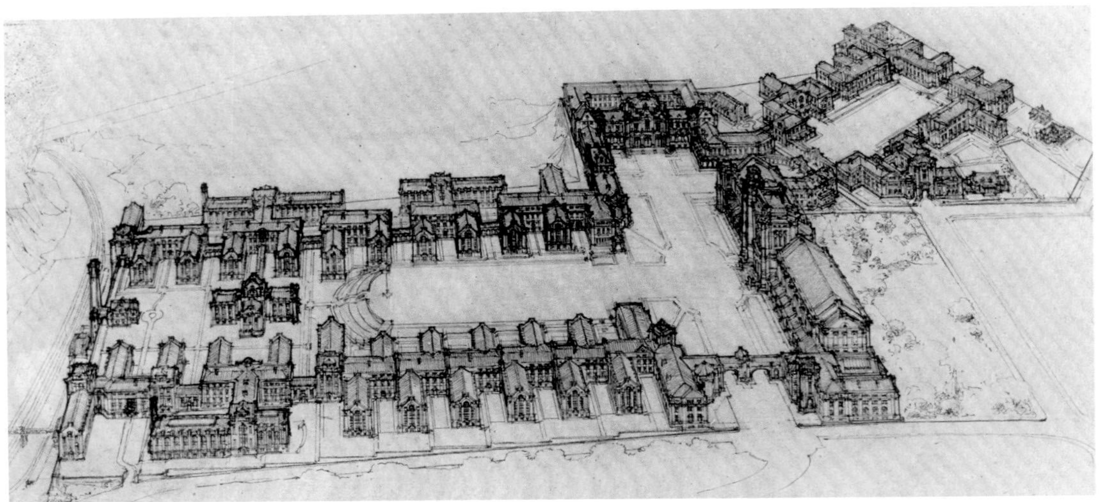

Fig. 106. Palmer and Hornbostel (architects), Carnegie Technical Schools, 1904, competition entry. Carnegie Mellon University Archives.

Hornbostel burst fully upon that architectural scene when his design, entered under the firm name of Howells, Stokes, and Hornbostel, placed second in the University of California competition, which played a key role in promoting formal campus planning in the United States.[10] Subsequently, Hornbostel became the principal design architect at the New York firm of Palmer and Hornbostel, where he established a nationwide practice and reputation that he expanded and enhanced later in firms of his own. He lived and worked in New York until moving to Pittsburgh in the early 1920s, but established a Pittsburgh office in 1904 when he received the commission for Carnegie Tech. Pittsburgh quickly became the primary focus of his professional activities and architectural work. At Carnegie Tech he founded the Department of Architecture; became the first dean of the School of Applied Design; taught for many years as professor, patron, and all-purpose critic and cheerleader; and promoted the school's involvement in the larger academic community of the Beaux-Arts; all while he shaped the development of the campus.

Beginning with Carnegie Tech, Hornbostel developed a penchant for winning architectural competitions. Francis S. Swales wrote in 1926:

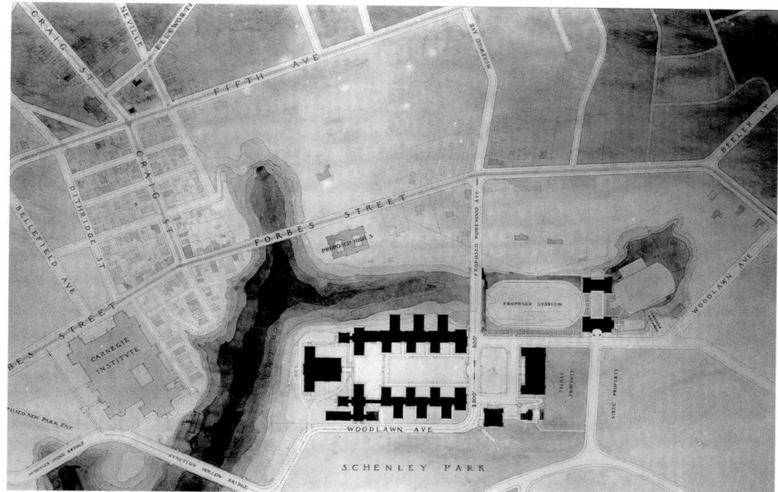

Fig. 107. Henry Hornbostel (architect), Carnegie Technical Schools, 1911, site plan. Shows urban and topographical context. Carnegie Mellon University Archives.

"The number of very important competitions that he has won has brought him a popular reputation such as is achieved by very few. His grasp of 'the big things' of architectural design and his vigorous way of composing them have made him a factor always to be reckoned with in any competition he has entered. This has been true especially in the cases of the very large and complicated problems."[11]

Carnegie Tech was a large and complicated problem, and it seemed that many architects were not quite up to the task. Most of the competition designs appeared as dense urban precincts, cramped by the enormous amount of enclosed square footage required in the program. Numerous entrants tried to introduce an east-west axis through the site at its greatest lateral extent, yet resorted to blocking that axis with buildings or pinching it to the width of a street. Among the known plans in final contention, only Hornbostel's articulated a spatial axis of breadth and definition within the group plan.

Hornbostel worked on the Carnegie Tech campus plan and its buildings from 1904 to 1932. He revised and simplified his campus plan in 1906 and again in 1911 (fig. 107), and largely realized these plans in a series of building campaigns between 1904 and 1919. Hornbostel con-

Fig. 108. Court of Honor, Carnegie Tech, ca. 1919. View toward west from School of Applied Design terrace. Reprinted from the *Thistle* (1919), 25. Carnegie Mellon University Archives.

ceived and built Carnegie Tech in the spirit of both Jefferson and the City Beautiful. In so doing, he brought the campus into a dialog with the land and the city, transformed an awkward parcel into a monumental site, and infused it with a host of formal and associational meanings.[12]

Buildings and Grounds

At Carnegie Tech, Hornbostel utilized Beaux-Arts planning principles to order the unruly land. He manipulated the topography in the interests of building placement and the establishment of open spaces and vistas. His group plan was monumental in scale and rigorous in organization, structured by an axial grid that accommodated a hierarchy of primary and subsidiary elements. The plan and buildings reflected Hornbostel's thorough awareness of artistic and historical precedents, as well as his affinity for practical planning and construction.

Fig. 109. Herman Böÿe, *A Map of the State of Virginia* (detail), 1827. Shows Thomas Jefferson's University of Virginia, view toward Rotunda. Special Collections, University of Virginia Library. Engraving by H. S. Tanner and E. B. Dawson (Richmond, ca. 1827).

Carnegie Tech's essential armature is a major spatial axis flanked by parallel ranges of buildings organized along central spines (fig. 108). This general arrangement has associations with the Greek agora, the Roman forum, and the French *place*, but this specific arrangement is commonly understood to be a variation of Jefferson's plan for the Lawn at the University of Virginia (fig. 109).[13] While various precedents have been cited for Jefferson's campus, including the French Baroque Château de Marly near Paris (begun 1679), both campuses were substantially influenced by a genre of contemporary schools, hospitals, and other large groups of buildings that featured a dominant central building and subsidiary structures arranged symmetrically around a central space.

At the University of Virginia, a central axis extends between two ranges of buildings from the Rotunda—the crowning architectural element—to an open egress.[14] At Carnegie Tech the central axis extends between two ranges of buildings, from the School of Applied Design to Machinery Hall, which is a major architectural element at the downhill

Fig. 110. Palmer and Hornbostel (architects), School of Applied Industries (south range), Carnegie Tech, 1905. Carnegie Mellon University Architecture Archives.

end of the group plan. At both schools, the central space is a grassy lawn with graded terraces and perimeter walkways. Hornbostel's plans for this space at Carnegie Tech were apparent as early as 1914. Final landscaping, however, apparently dates from 1924–1926 and is attributable to noted landscape architect Albert Davis Taylor, who was hired to beautify the campus in the wake of decades of building construction and wartime disruptions.[15]

Carnegie Tech's north and south ranges were planned to house the School of Applied Sciences and the School of Applied Industries, respectively (see fig. 110). These are practical buildings, filled with shops, laboratories, and classrooms, and built of no-nonsense materials like buff and yellow industrial brick and Guastavino tile. Both ranges feature an enfilade arrangement of projecting wings in place of Jefferson's pavilions. The wings provide for natural lighting, ventilation, and programmatic flexibility, and allowed for phased construction. Shaped by Italian Renaissance precedents, these buildings have a common Beaux-Arts vocabulary of tall round-arched windows and low pitched roofs. There is a classical sensibility without the use of classical orders.

When an administration building (now Baker Hall) was built as a head house terminating the south range in 1914, its function and position called for a more elaborate design. The facade integrates two of

Fig. 111. Henry Hornbostel (architect), School of Applied Design, Carnegie Tech, 1912–1916. Carnegie Mellon University Architecture Archives.

the iconic forms of classical architecture—the Greek or Roman temple front and the Roman triumphal arch—combined in the manner of the Basilica of Sant'Andrea (1470–1472) in Mantua, Italy, by architect Leone Battista Alberti.[16]

The School of Applied Design (now the College of Fine Arts) anchors the east end of the through-campus axis (fig. 111). Built in two campaigns in 1912 and 1916, its primary multistory form is C-shaped in plan, and filled with a tall, one-story block. The overall massing is related to buildings such as the Villa Farnesina (1508–1511) in Rome, the *l'enveloppe* of the Château Versailles (1668–1673), and McKim, Mead, and White's Villard Houses (1884) in New York City, the last of which had prompted a wave of Italian Renaissance architecture in the United States. Additionally, Howard Saalman cites the Villa Madama

Fig. 112. Henry Hornbostel (architect), Machinery Hall, Carnegie Tech, 1906–1913. Carnegie Mellon University Archives.

(1516–1517) in Rome as a source for the five large niches on the facade and for major plan elements, including an elliptical theater.[17]

At the opposite end of the through-campus axis is Machinery Hall (now Hamerschlag Hall), which originated as the campus power plant in 1906, and was greatly expanded from 1912 to 1914 (fig. 112). The tripartite massing of a central block and flanking wings is ultimately derived from the works of Andrea Palladio, such as the Villa Barbaro (ca. 1549–1558). Yet the central facade element is also an adaptation of the previously mentioned Alberti facade at Sant'Andrea. A cylindrical tower cloaks the powerhouse's smokestack.[18] Overall, the building's form and austere classicism recall buildings designed by the eighteenth-century French Enlightenment architect Claude-Nicolas Ledoux.[19]

The Machinery Hall tower provides the campus with its sole vertical accent and most striking visual feature. Arthur Wilson Tarbell, Carnegie Tech's first chronicler, calls the tower "the dominating feature

Fig. 113. Carnegie Tech, ca. 1920. View across Junction Hollow from the roof of the Carnegie Institute. Carnegie Mellon University Archives.

of the campus horizon," and notes that "besides cleverly masking the smoke stack of the power plant, [the tower] has generously furnished the decorative motif for numberless drawings and photographs for successive generations of students."[20]

Machinery Hall was designed to be seen by the spectator. It is literally two-faced, with two equally visible facades on the front (east) and rear (west). The rear side is dropped over the edge of Junction Hollow so that multiple stories are exposed. This side has served as a facade for the whole Carnegie Tech group plan from outside of the campus, and has anchored the reciprocal architectural relationship with the Carnegie Institute across Junction Hollow (fig. 113).[21] It also serves as a scenographic element within the topographical setting of greater Oakland (fig. 114). From within the campus, however, Machinery Hall's opposite facade serves as the focal point of a rigorously organized formal landscape (see fig. 108).

Fig. 114. "Schenley Park View of Carnegie Tech, Pittsburgh," ca. 1915. Carnegie Mellon University Archives.

Court of Honor

The City Beautiful Movement was launched by the 1893 World's Columbian Exposition in Chicago, which had been substantially shaped by Beaux-Arts design principles. The centerpiece of the fair was the Court of Honor, a unified architectural ensemble organized around a central open space where a dominant axis, symmetry, and neoclassical styling carefully structured the spectator's visual experience (fig. 115). The perceived beauty and power of this experience introduced a type of architectural sublime into the American urban landscape. Exposition visitors were wowed by the so-called White City; and subsequent expositions in Omaha (1898), Buffalo (1901), and St. Louis (1904) kept this spirit alive.[22]

Fig. 115. C. D. Arnold (photographer), Court of Honor, World's Columbian Exposition, Chicago, 1893. Chicago History Museum. ICHi-13883.

References to Carnegie Tech's Court of Honor appear around 1912, when the school was chartered as a degree-granting institution and the campus reached critical mass. This name, likely generated by Hornbostel himself, affirmed the formal arrangement of the campus' buildings and grounds, and the imposition of explicitly classical aesthetic values on otherwise workmanlike facilities. It also acknowledged the function of the campus as a showplace where spectators could experience a unified and inspiring architectural ensemble. In this way, Horn-

Fig. 116. Carnegie Tech and Experimental Station of the U.S. Bureau of Mines, ca. 1920. This was the essence of Arthur A. Hamerschlag's World's Fair vision. Carnegie Mellon University Archives.

bostel's campus claimed to be a recapitulation of the celebrated World's Columbian Exposition rather than a generic group plan.

Hornbostel had visited the World's Columbian Exposition shortly before leaving for the École des Beaux-Arts.[23] He made drawings for the Paris Exposition of 1900 while he was in France, and for the Buffalo Exposition in 1901 when he was with the firm of Carrere and Hastings.[24] He knew the look of a fair; and others did too. Andrew Carnegie was among the many prominent Pittsburghers who attended the Chicago fair. He subsequently wrote an essay in which he commended the design and grouping of the buildings and acclaimed the fair as the "greatest combination of architectural beauty which man has ever created."[25] In 1915, as Hornbostel designed a new Experimental Station of the U.S. Bureau of Mines complex adjacent to the Carnegie Tech campus, the school's president Arthur A. Hamerschlag remarked of the combined architectural precinct: "It will look like a World's Fair" (fig. 116).[26]

Additional aspects of Carnegie Tech's individual buildings reinforce an association with the era's great public expositions of artistic and industrial progress. The School of Applied Design housed the arts

under one roof—music, drama, painting, sculpture, and architecture. Its great entry hall opened to a large exhibition room, and early accounts referred to the building as a museum.[27] The building's extensive decorative program comprised an encyclopedic history of the arts.[28] The five niches of the exterior were to be carved with architectural and sculptural motifs from different lands and eras (though these were only partially completed for many years). Murals similar in purpose decorated the walls and curtain of the theater. Murals on the ceiling of the grand hall depicted important buildings and sculptures and the portraits of prominent architects, sculptors, composers, and playwrights in what James D. Van Trump calls a "celestial atlas of art history."[29] Plans of prominent buildings were inlaid in the marble flooring in the halls. The School of Applied Design thus joined elements of two building types that were common to public expositions: the Palace of Fine Arts and the international pavilions that represented different nations and cultures.

At the other end of the Court of Honor, as Van Trump notes, "the very name 'Machinery Hall' suggests the great expositions . . . [and]

Fig. 117. *Carnegie Institute of Technology, Annual Exhibition,* n.d., poster. Carnegie Mellon University Archives.

Hornbostel's structure would have been equally at home on any fairground of the time."[30] The Machinery Halls of the expositions displayed the latest in industrial machinery; Hornbostel's Machinery Hall housed the boilers, steam engines, and other machinery of the power plant and mechanical engineering shops. Terra-cotta panels intended for the facade would have depicted contemporary machinery and provided a decorative program of industrial iconography to match the building's mechanical contents.

The exposition theme became explicit on the day of Carnegie Tech's Annual Exhibition. This campus-wide event was part promotional pitch for prospective students and part open house for the city at large. Posters publicizing the event promised demonstrations in the various shops, laboratories, studios, and classrooms, and "a panoramic tour of a modern technical institution" (fig. 117). Crowds of eight and ten thousand visitors were counted by the 1910s.

Like a World's Fair, Carnegie Tech's Annual Exhibition was both education and entertainment, designed to engage the mind and appeal to the imagination. The campus, like the exposition grounds, functioned as a spatial and visual stimulus. Key to the experience, on exhibition day or any day, was a planned arrival sequence. Visitors to the Chicago fair commonly arrived by train or boat, disembarked at strategic locations, and proceeded to staged vantage points at the Court of

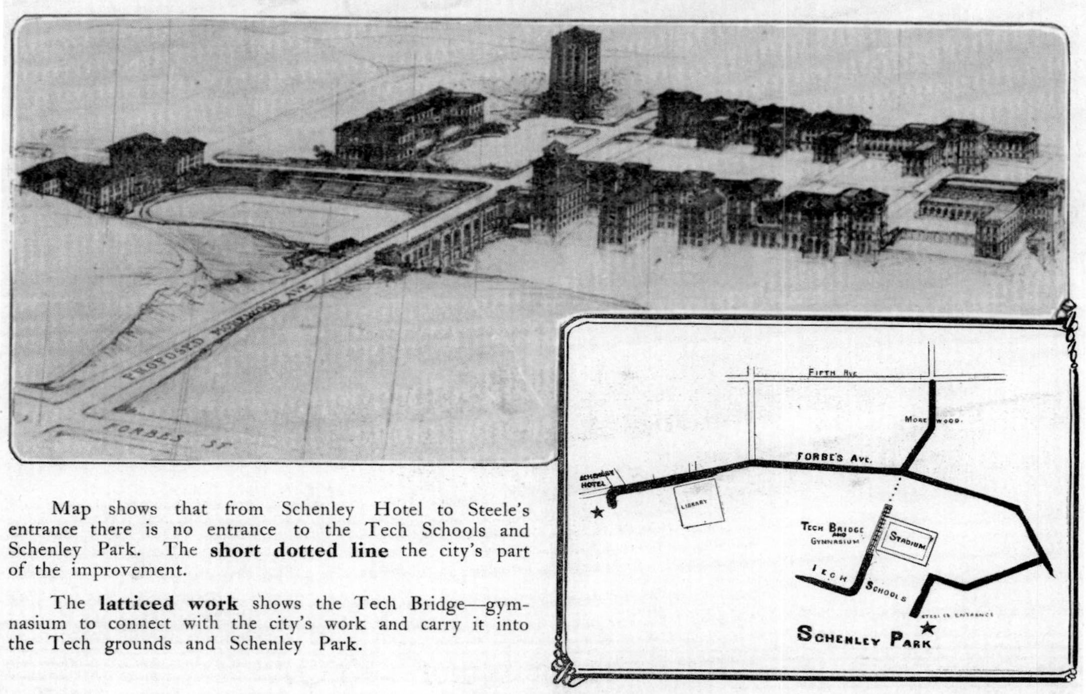

VOTE FOR ITEM No. 11

Proposed Tech Group and Map Showing Morewood Entrance

Map shows that from Schenley Hotel to Steele's entrance there is no entrance to the Tech Schools and Schenley Park. The **short dotted line** the city's part of the improvement.

The **latticed work** shows the Tech Bridge—gymnasium to connect with the city's work and carry it into the Tech grounds and Schenley Park.

Fig. 118. *Proposed Tech Group and Map Showing Morewood Entrance,* 1912. Carnegie Mellon University Archives.

Honor. Visitors to Carnegie Tech arrived by the Forbes Avenue streetcar. Their intended point of access to the campus was clarified in 1912.

Articles published that summer noted that the campus was being graded, and that the school was lobbying for the necessary public approvals to provide access to the campus from the north via a bridge carrying an extension of Morewood Avenue (fig. 118). Press coverage, seemingly scripted by Hornbostel himself, argued that the new point of access would benefit students, who would have better access to campus from the streetcar lines, and the public, which would have better access to Schenley Park though the campus. There was a third potential benefit, as well:

> One of the serious drawbacks to the site of the [Carnegie Tech] buildings is the lack of a proper entrance. As it now stands it is necessary to cross [Schenley] Bridge in order to reach the group. This brings one in at the lower level of the court and, to obtain a view of the group as a whole, it is necessary to pass each building in review, as it were, to gain the upper end of the court and from there to obtain a comprehensive idea of the group in its entirety. . . .
>
> Upon the crossing of the proposed bridge, plans for which are well under way, one would enter the Court of Honor at its upper end, thus obtaining at a glance an impression of the buildings as a group. This will be an impressive sight and one which will not only attract the thousands visiting Pittsburgh annually, but one which will appeal to the imaginations of the citizens of the city.[31]

At the University of Virginia, Jefferson planned for his campus to be entered at its lower end so that the visitor would "view the colonnades and pavilions as they sweep in a triumphal march up to the Rotunda," the primary focal point.[32] From the Rotunda, a return vista extended back along the central axis. Hornbostel, however, wanted his group plan to be entered from its upper end—a point of access that was ultimately achieved, though without the bridge. From the upper part of the campus, the visitor would perceive the entire architectural ensemble laid out in full array and experience the full impact of the architectural sublime.

Hornbostel also had an even more focused intention. From a viewpoint at the terrace of the School of Applied Design he established a planned pictorial vista that extends along the main axis of the campus and beyond, in which the axis is highlighted as a work of art in its own right and made functional as a looking device (see fig. 108).[33] This complex vista showcases Carnegie Tech and Oakland for the spectator.

Perspective and the Theater

The interaction of exhibition and visitor, and of vista and spectator, establishes a dialogue not unlike that between theater and audience. In fact, the city in general, and the City Beautiful in particular, have an analogous relationship with the theater. "In every age," Kostof writes, "urban spaces—streets and squares—have served to stage spectacles in which the citizenry participated as players and audience. Urban life is nothing if not theatrical. . . . What the Grand Manner aspired to achieve was to turn the composition of urban spaces, the spatial experience of moving through streets and squares, itself into a spectacle." From Michelangelo's Campidoglio in Rome to the World's Columbian Exposition, the architectonic forms and scenographic arrangements of the stage have shaped urban space.[34] In this tradition of the urban stage set, Henry Hornbostel's Carnegie Tech plays to an audience.

The tool of linear perspective is key. Perspective was reinvented during the Renaissance—it originated with the Greeks—to depict three-dimensional reality, or rather the appearance of reality, on a picture plane such as a painting. In this way a scene could be represented as if the spectator were actually present at the scene. Perspective presumes a specific viewpoint that is a fixed distance and direction from the picture plane. A cone of vision extends from the viewpoint to the picture plane, which is positioned perpendicular to the axis of sight. From the viewpoint, a spectator sees receding parallel lines converge at a vanishing point, which is commonly located in a distant object or the horizon. In this way, perspective organizes space geometrically, promotes the perception of depth, and "enable[s] an artist to solve mathematically the problem of diminution in size with distance and thereby produce a pictorial space that [is] centrally focused and uniformly scaled."[35]

View of an Ideal City, a late fifteenth-century Italian painting of an idealized urban landscape, exemplifies one-point linear perspective (fig. 119). Two parallel rows of houses and palazzi flank a central space and recede into the distance. Receding perspectival lines converge, not, in this case, on a distant object or horizon, but on a circular temple pulled forward in the center of the picture plane. A pinprick in the door of this building is a literal vanishing point.[36]

Some scholars suggest that *View of an Ideal City* may depict a

Fig. 119. Piero della Francesca [?], *View of an Ideal City*, late 1400s. Galleria Nazionale delle Marche, Urbino, Italy. Photograph by Scala/Art Resource, NY.

stage set. The Renaissance and the Baroque shared a fascination with the theater, and the stage was the scene of much experimentation with perspective.[37] Perspective could be utilized to simulate reality on stage. It could also be manipulated to maximize visual depth within the limited space of the stage. In the sixteenth century, three-dimensional stage scenery and painted backdrops were integrated to form a perspectival and perceptual unity. The seventeenth-century theater invented the *coulisse*—interchangeable screens or walls arranged one behind the other—which made possible an even greater suggestion of spatial depth.

Ultimately, what began in Renaissance painting and theater as a way to depict reality became a tool for organizing objects in space. Catherine M. Howett observes that "The idealized formal order" of a painting or stage set "suggested a model for the design of actual spaces, for buildings, and streets and gardens, even for large rural estates and entire cities."[38] Once the rules were understood, perspective could be used as a tool in the composition of real buildings and landscapes, to shape reality as if it were a picture or a stage. One product of this ap-

Fig. 120. Court of Honor, Carnegie Tech, ca. 1919. Altered by author to demonstrate one-point linear perspective. Base image reprinted from the *Thistle* (1919), 25. Carnegie Mellon University Archives.

proach was the urban vista. As Kostof explains the basic principles: "The primary purpose of a vista is the framing of a distant view, so that it is seen through a composed foreground and is fixed at the opposite end by some worthy marker. . . . Since the foreground brackets and the terminal object play the main role in setting up a vista, the . . . channel in between [must be] straight and [have] enough visual direction to create a strong sense of perspective."[39]

The Carnegie Tech Court of Honor is a textbook urban vista composed with one-point linear perspective (figs. 108 and 120). A cone of vision extends from the viewpoint at the School of Applied Design terrace to encompass the Court of Honor. The cone of vision intersects the picture plane at the eastern end of the two building ranges; and the image captured within the picture plane mirrors Renaissance compositional conventions.[40] The head houses of the two ranges are frontal elements that frame a central space. The ranges themselves recede into the distance. Lines of perspective thrust into space where the ground meets the buildings and the buildings meet the sky. These lines promote the perception of depth, and ultimately converge on Machinery

Fig. 121. Pageant at the laying of the cornerstone of the School of Applied Design, Carnegie Tech, 1912. The buildings in the background are parts of the north range. Reprinted from the *Thistle* (1913), n.p. Carnegie Mellon University Archives.

Hall, the fixed terminal marker of the vista, specifically on the door. This door is raised abnormally within its arched surround, perhaps just for this reason. It is fitting that this vanishing point lies within a facade inspired by Alberti, the architect who wrote the first analysis of one-point linear perspective.

The Carnegie Tech Court of Honor is also a stage set. The head houses of the two ranges act like a proscenium to frame a central space, and the ranges' projecting wings emerge "from the wings" like *coulisses*. Perspective structures the perceived depth of the central space. This space acts as a stage in the context of both the court and the university. Here, students and faculty act out a script dictated by academic program and schedule.

A dramatic persona himself, Hornbostel was a great fan of theater. He reputedly prevailed upon a reluctant Carnegie to include a theater in the School of Applied Design. One telling of the story involves purposely mislabeled floor plans. In any event, Hornbostel not only built a small jewel-box theater in the School of Applied Design, but created an enormous outdoor stage set as well. In 1912, on the occasion of the laying of the cornerstone of the School of Applied Design, Hornbostel staged a grand pageant. Groups of costumed players representing dif-

ferent lands and eras paraded in sequential array in the open space of the unfinished Court of Honor (fig. 121).[41]

Barry Hannegan notes theatrical allusions—and illusions—in the vista at Carnegie Tech:

> The ordered repetition of wings when seen from either end of the mall recalls to mind the arrangement of an eighteenth century French stage setting. As seen . . . from the terrace of the [School of Applied Design] . . . , the vista very forcefully suggests the influence of the theatre. The drop in levels at the lower end is invisible from this vantage point, and the corresponding lowering of the roof line of the wing pavilions gives the illusion of an immense recession of space in just the same manner as the contrived flats of the Baroque stage. Machinery Hall, which is visible only above the level of the last flight of stairs, provides an appropriately scaleless terminal for this closely controlled perspective. One wonders if there was really any deliberate attempt here to revive that device favored by seventeenth century planners—the optical illusion.[42]

Experimentation in painting, theater design, architecture, and landscape had led to the manipulation of perspective for illusory effect.

Might Hornbostel have utilized *trompe l'oeil* to shape the spectator's experience of the Court of Honor?

The Viewpoint of the King

An important legacy of perspective and the Grand Manner was the perception of space as a positive element, rather than just a void. Space could be geometrically structured like architecture and designed like architecture, with a full range of formal characteristics. The Campidoglio showed the way, and the gardens of the Italian villa developed this theme within a larger landscape. It was the seventeenth-century French Baroque garden, however, that first demonstrated concern with the design of space above all else and at the scale of the entire visible environment.[43] As Rob Aben and Saskia de Wit explain: "Thus the garden sought out the landscape and opened up to the horizon. This happened because of the views to be gained, but also to parade [the] taming of nature. To better relate the garden to the landscape . . . the garden became steadily larger, transforming the simple structure of the [enclosed garden] into a complex spatial composition. . . . The distinction between garden and landscape became less and less, until eventually the garden took over the scale of the landscape."[44]

As the French Baroque garden assumed unprecedented scale, many compositional methods and devices were utilized to structure the expansive space. Grading and manipulation of the natural terrain achieved a variety of topographical conditions. Dominant axes (and cross axes and radial axes) geometrically subdivided the space and provided pathways for circulation through the site. The open plots between or within axes became elaborate planted beds known as *parterres*, spacious green lawns known as *tapis verts*, or water elements such as basins and canals. The château from which the garden grew, plus outbuildings, grottos, cascades, fountains, sculpture, trees, and additional plantings provided focal points and visual punctuation.

As a complex designed landscape, the French Baroque garden represented the intersection of nature and human culture. As a demonstration of grand-scale planning, it contained the seeds of the practice of city planning in general and the City Beautiful Movement in particular. It also served as a dramatic new setting for the acting out of aristocratic life and as a real stage for theatrical entertainments. And in the tradition of the theater, it became a place for optical experimentation. Here *trompe l'oeil* became an essential device to both heighten the experience of space and throw that experience into question.

The quintessential French Baroque gardens are Vaux-le-Vicomte, Versailles, and Chantilly. All are near Paris, and all were designed by landscape architect André Le Nôtre, the genius of the French Baroque garden and *trompe l'oeil.* Vaux-le-Vicomte (1656–1661), in particular, is a tour de force of spatial planning, landscape design, and *trompe l'oeil* special effects. Among the many visual effects is an arrangement of descending terraces that visually obscures drops in elevation and major landscape features (including an entire canal) (fig. 122).[45] Hornbostel would have known such gardens from his time in Paris. Significantly, a portrait of Le Nôtre is included among the mural paintings on the ceiling of the grand hall in the School of Applied Design.[46]

The central space of Carnegie Tech's Court of Honor is shaped by the buildings that surround it, but the space is also a positive element that contributes to the ensemble. Viewed as a garden, it suggests a *tapis vert* extending before the château of the School of Applied Design. But the space is also structured by grading and pathways, and geometrically structured by perspective. It harbors illusionary optical effects in the spirit of Le Nôtre and Vaux-le-Vicomte.

The Court of Honor slopes from east to west; yet Hornbostel raised the perceived ground plane by carefully grading the Court of Honor with a series of descending terraces defined by low mounded dips. This arrangement is similar in form to Jefferson's Lawn at the University of Virginia (see fig. 109), and similar in principle to Vaux-le-Vicomte. Hornbostel also raised Machinery Hall high on a podium beyond another more substantial drop in the terrain, where it stands wholly free

Fig. 122. *Queen Maria Leczinska Visiting Vaux in 1728,* n.d. Shows features of André Le Nôtre's garden that are obscured from the ideal viewpoint at the château in the background. Archives, Château Vaux-le-Vicomte. Photograph by Luiz Gonzalez.

of the prevailing ground plane (fig. 123). When seen from the viewpoint at the School of Applied Design terrace, the dips function as ha-has by screening their very existence, and the shifts in the terrain and Machinery Hall's true siting cannot be perceived. The elevation of the lawn appears to be sustained at a higher level than the actual grade that it follows, and Machinery Hall appears to sit comfortably on the grass at the end of a nearly level lawn (see fig. 108).[47]

Machinery Hall's cylindrical tower relates to each of the building's main facades. It is appropriately scaled to carry the large mass of the extra-height rear facade when seen from a distance (see fig. 114). At the same time it is, in a sense, over-scaled for the building's more diminutive front facade (see fig. 112). Because of this discrepancy, the tower pulls forward visually when seen in elevation from the School of Applied Design terrace, and assumes an apparent position in the same visual plane as the building's Alberti facade—which actually occupies a

Fig. 123. Court of Honor, Carnegie Tech, ca. 1925. Carnegie Mellon University Archives.

position 140 feet further east. The facade and tower appear to coalesce into a pavilion that pulls free from the building's wings (see fig. 108).[48]

This illusory effect results in an ambiguity of scale that is heightened by the architectural detailing. Machinery Hall has the only facade to face onto the Court without prominent windows or floor divisions that are clear indicators of scale. The door is set within an outsized surround, and the arch that dominates the facade is enlarged to erode the pediment, yielding greater visual unity within the facade. The pavilion thus evokes the *grande architecture* of the Enlightenment, a neoclassical architecture of large forms with minimal divisions. The resulting scalelessness combats the diminution of scale that is expected of a distant object.

According to John White, "An actual counter-balancing of spatial thrust can be achieved by placing the vanishing point within the confines of an object situated in the foreground. Then the [lines of perspective] . . . also lead the eye back towards the surface of the composition."[49] This effect is made apparent in *View of an Ideal City* (see fig. 119). Hornbostel counters the spatial thrust of linear perspective within the Court of Honor by placing the vanishing point in a scaleless object, which is pulled forward in the picture plane, and is, or appears to be, closer to the spectator than the rest of the perspectival composition would suggest. By introducing depth through linear perspective and countering it in turn, the visual axis functions somewhat like a telescope, with depth projecting toward the spectator.[50]

By employing these illusions in the Court of Honor, Hornbostel facilitated the use of linear perspective to structure a difficult site, created a positive space that appears both expansive and refined, maximized Machinery Hall's impact as the focal point of his vista, and effected false but satisfying compositional relationships in the picture plane for the spectator.

Linear perspective and *trompe l'oeil* imply a specific ideal viewpoint where perspectival effects and illusions effectively resolve. In the theater, this is generally a viewpoint at the center of the auditorium. And in seventeenth-century France, this viewpoint was a seat reserved for the monarch, the so-called viewpoint of the king. In the French Baroque garden, the viewpoint of the king was a terrace at the château with a commanding view of the pictorial vista that was the garden. At Vaux-le-Vicomte and at Versailles, the king was Louis XIV. At Carnegie Tech, this viewpoint is the terrace at the School of Applied Design. Here the king was the Steel King, Andrew Carnegie.

Like the king, Carnegie was frequently invoked though rarely seen. He visited Carnegie Tech occasionally, usually on Founder's Day, an event celebrated by his dual Pittsburgh benefactions, the Carnegie Institute and Carnegie Tech (fig. 124). In 1914, he visited the nearly completed Court of Honor and looked out upon the complex vista from the viewpoint of the king.[51]

Like Vaux-le-Vicomte, Versailles, and the University of Virginia, Carnegie Tech is a site of personal giantism. Nicolas Foucquet ostensi-

Fig. 124. Andrew Carnegie and Henry Hornbostel at Carnegie Tech, 1914 [?]. Carnegie Mellon University Archives.

bly built Vaux-le-Vicomte to honor Louis XIV, but its refined extravagance was all too apparently a portrait of Foucquet's own cultured ambition. So the king jailed Foucquet for his impudence, and hired Le Nôtre to design Versailles in his (the king's) own image. The University of Virginia is a highly personal representation of the educational, architectural, and pastoral ideals of Thomas Jefferson. Carnegie Tech, in turn, was made in the image of Andrew Carnegie.

Technology and Its Temple

Carnegie Tech was conceived with an eye for industry. The program for the 1904 design competition listed a number of technical schools and industrial plants as models for the school's shops and laboratories. Hornbostel described his buildings as industrial architecture, and early campus descriptions refer to them as workshops.[52] Murals in the long hall of the School of Applied Design depict scenes

Fig. 125. Industrial Pittsburgh. Reprinted from "Book of Views," *Bulletin of the Carnegie Institute of Technology* 14, no. 10 (June 1919), n.p. Carnegie Mellon University Archives.

of industrial Pittsburgh.[53] A relief carving planned for the pediment of the administration building featured a heroic figure of Vulcan, posed as a colossus, within an industrial landscape.

The school's industrial orientation was made clear in a 1919 issue of the *Carnegie Bulletin,* which stated:

> Pittsburgh is the greatest industrial center of America. The Carnegie Institute of Technology and the industries of the Pittsburgh District are closely associated:
>
> Through scientific bureaus which are maintained by the Carnegie Institute of Technology in co-operation with some of the great business enterprises.
>
> Through the work of members of its faculties, who are engaged as expert consultants by important industrial organizations.

Fig. 126. Court of Honor at night, Carnegie Tech, ca. 1914. Reprinted from "Book of Views," *Bulletin of the Carnegie Institute of Technology* 14, no. 10 (June 1919), n.p. Carnegie Mellon University Archives.

Through the employment of its graduates in engineering and other technical enterprises.

Through the employment of its undergraduates, both day and night students (many of whom are working their way through college), in the manufacturies.[54]

Side-by-side illustrations accompanied this text (figs. 125 and 126). One is a rendered view of Pittsburgh's industrial landscape, of factories and furnaces and smoke, as viewed through an arched window. The other is an unusual nighttime photograph of the Court of Honor. It is unusual because schools were not commonly pictured at night—mills were. In the darkness, repetitive small-paned windows assume the guise of mill buildings, and the surrounding lights of the campus and city become the nighttime face of Pittsburgh industry.

The Carnegie Tech campus is a landscape that celebrates industry and evokes the technological sublime. Yet it screens out the harsh real-

Élévation d'un des Bâtimens d'Ouvriers qui forment l'enceinte de la grande Cour.

Fig. 127. Claude Ledoux (architect), Blacksmith Building, Saltworks of Chaux, 1770s. © Georges Fessy—Photothèque Institut Claude Nicolas Ledoux.

ities of the industrial workplace. Carnegie Tech speaks of technology shaped by reason, the technology of industrial education and management, of the Carnegie Tech curriculum. Industrial Pittsburgh is seen through the modulating filter of a Carnegie Tech window. In turn, Carnegie Tech is seen through the lens of the Carnegie Steel Company.

Le Nôtre chose the Basin d'Apollon as the focal point of Versailles, and explicitly celebrated the Sun King (Louis XIV) and the sun. Jefferson chose the library as the focal point of the University of Virginia, and spoke of the "march of civilization" passing over Charlottesville "like a cloud of light."[55] Hornbostel chose the power plant as the focal point of his campus to celebrate the Steel King. Machinery Hall filled the sky with black smoke.[56]

Ledoux's Blacksmith Building at the Saltworks of Chaux (1770s) is an early industrial-age precedent for both Machinery Hall and its smoke (fig. 127).[57] Van Trump also sees latter-day iconography at Machinery Hall in "the fantastic rotundity of the tower, with its omnipresent plume of smoke, looking like a giant spool or dynamo." The tower, he says, "is the very apotheosis of the machine, and appropriately crowns the building which somehow suggests early fantasy fiction of

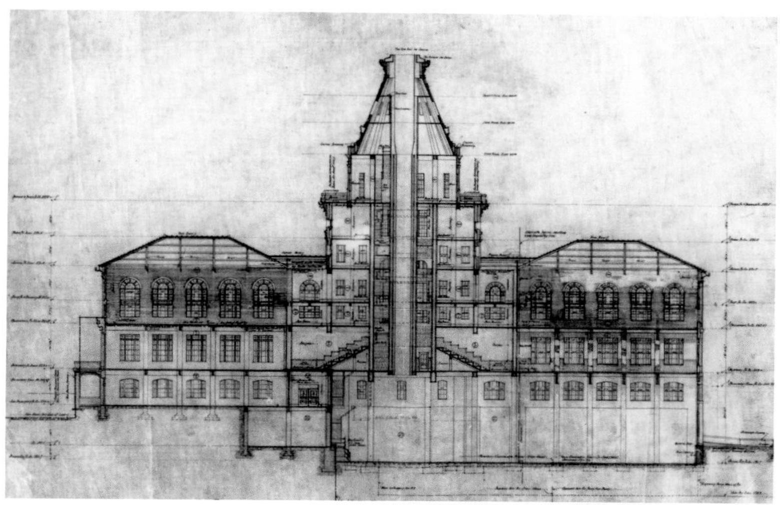

Fig. 128. Henry Hornbostel (architect), Machinery Hall, Carnegie Tech, 1906–1913, longitudinal section drawing. Carnegie Mellon University Architecture Archives.

H. G. Wells." Machinery Hall, the power plant, with its great engines in the basement and its smokestack on the horizon, is a machine in the Jeffersonian garden.[58]

Van Trump also refers to Machinery Hall as Technology's Temple; and the sense that this building houses a vital spirit is reinforced by the architecture as well as the smoke. The form and detailing of the central pavilion evokes the ancient classical tradition of the temple/shrine. The nearly cruciform plan, with a tower at the crossing, is almost ecclesiastical. Lifted on a raised podium, Machinery Hall has the elevated presence of the Meso-American temples that Hornbostel saw and photographed on his 1907 trip to the Yucatan. Like many temples of various time and places, it faces east and receives the dawn through an eastern doorway.

Such temples act as intermediaries between cosmic realms. Machinery Hall's working drawings show the tower in a preliminary form as a volcanic cone, revered in many cultures as a sacred landform (fig. 128).[59] The smokestack provides a literal link between the terrestrial and celestial worlds, and its oculus is an opening to the underworld,

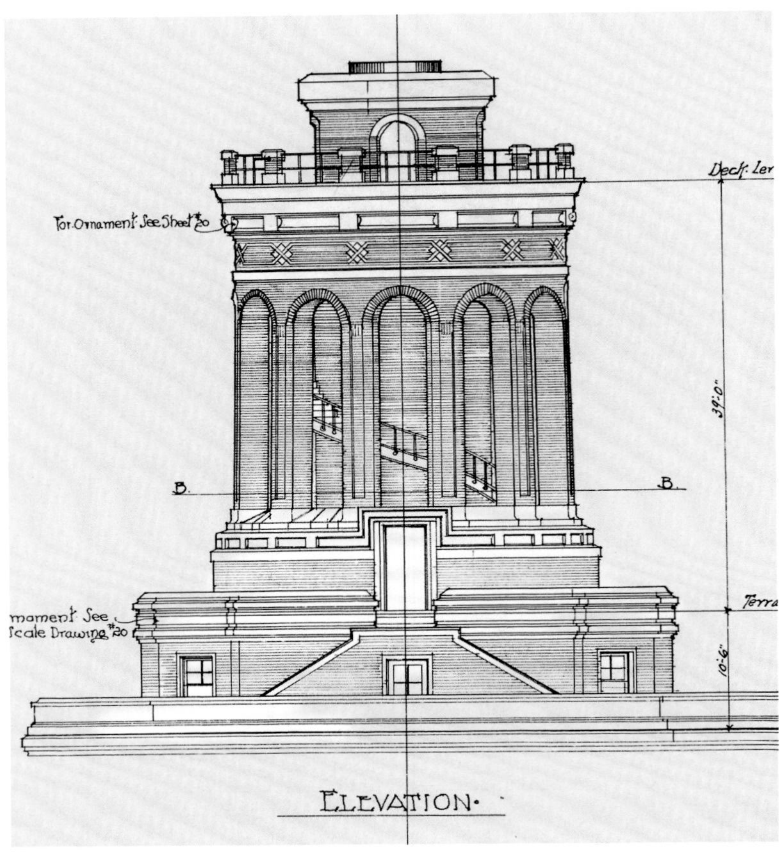

Fig. 129. Henry Hornbostel (architect), Machinery Hall tower, Carnegie Tech, 1906–1913, elevation drawing. Carnegie Mellon University Architecture Archives.

recalling Ledoux's description of his Blacksmith Building as Vulcan's lair, where the smith tames the forces of the underworld.[60] Machinery Hall is the *axis mundi* for the community of Carnegie Tech.

Van Trump also notes temple-like aspects of the tower itself as it was ultimately realized (fig. 129). In its larger context, the tower can be seen as an observatory on the top of a Mesoamerican temple, or a shrine at the top of a Mesopotamian ziggurat. Alone, it recalls the ancient Roman temples at Rome and Tivoli that honored Vesta, the

Roman goddess of fire and the hearth.[61] Hornbostel himself stated that the tower motif "was used in the past as an expression of love," an apparent reference to Marie Antoinette's Temple de l'Amour (1778) in the garden of the Petit Trianon at Versailles. In turn, Van Trump writes that the Machinery Hall tower symbolizes the marrying of Vulcan (the Roman god of fire) and Venus (the Roman goddess of love), of male and female, as a smokestack penetrates the temple of love.[62]

The spectator approaches the temple through the Court of Honor. The complex vista provides connectivity for the eye and the mind, but these connections are fully experienced only by traversing the course of the vista along a path. With architecture and landscape, as opposed to painting or theater, the spectator may literally enter a picture and explore it.[63] From within, the perspectival may become the scenographic. The French Baroque garden, for instance, often features optical effects that can only be experienced from inside of the plan. Progression along an axis can reveal a succession of picture planes and staged vistas; and the same progression, or oblique movements and points of view, can reveal the hidden realities of a *trompe l'oeil* tableau.

Hornbostel, it seems, subscribed to the Baroque ideal of dynamic movement through space. Van Trump notes that the plan and changes of level inside the School of Applied Design assure "a variety of vista and point of view at once Classical and Romantic, ordered and yet oblique and irregular."[64] The spectator has a similar experience in traversing the Court of Honor, with the added pleasure of altered expectations. The featured progression takes the spectator along peripheral pathways at the edges of the Court of Honor. (The central walkway shown in some early photographs was temporary.) Movement through space yields shifts in terrain and oblique views that shatter *trompe l'oeil* illusions. When Machinery Hall is approached off-axis the tower recedes, the facade juts forward, and true compositional relationships become apparent (see fig. 130).

Ultimately, traversing this space reveals that the Court of Honor is more than a formal construct and an optically challenging stage set,

Fig. 130. Henry Hornbostel (architect), Machinery Hall, Carnegie Tech, 1906–1913, postcard. Carnegie Mellon University Archives.

and Machinery Hall is more than a visual confection and the culmination of a group plan. Indeed, the path is a pilgrimage toward a singular goal, which is Technology's Temple.[65]

The final approach to Machinery Hall is a ceremonial sequence of path, bridge, and stair, entailing a return to the central axis, the crossing of a moat of space, and the climbing of steps into a concave opening within the facade. The spectator then enters the building into what should be a sacred space, with the smokestack featured as a totemic column, perhaps, or a sculptural bust of Andrew Carnegie to venerate. But what should be a ceremonial place is in reality just a hallway flanked by classrooms. The smokestack is indistinguishable, and there

Fig. 131. John Kane, *Junction Hollow*, 1932. Note large arched window at rear of Machinery Hall to the right. Another Kane painting, *The Cathedral of Learning,* depicts the view from this window as it appeared in 1930. Whitney Museum of American Art, New York; Gift of B. and Allan Roos in memory of Robert M. Benjamin, 66.57.

is no totem or altar. As a temple, Machinery Hall promises much, but ultimately fails to deliver.

The building's evocation of a triumphal arch and its anticlimatic interior suggest, however, that the path may continue on. The spectator may proceed through the building to a large arched window in the rear facade, which offers an extended westward view across Oakland. *Junction Hollow* (1932), a painting by John Kane, shows this vantage point, and locates Machinery Hall within a larger urban landscape (fig. 131). Might the complex vista extend beyond Machinery Hall, and find its termination beyond the campus?[66]

The Hillside Beyond

In a 1906 discussion of the typologies of the group plan, Alfred Morton Githens cites Carnegie Tech as an exemplar of the closed compositional plan, saying: "The [main axis] starts at [the School of Applied Design], extends down the campus and is closed by the tower . . . at the power house. Both ends of [the axis] are *closed* by buildings of the group; in neither case does the vista along [the] axis extend between the buildings to distant objects." He demonstrates this with a diagram (fig. 132). Indeed, Machinery Hall, as focal point, appears to abruptly close Hornbostel's axial vista to the west. Yet Githens continues, in a hypothetical manner: "The composition would be *open* along [this] axis if for instance the power house and its tower were removed or placed to one side, so that from the [School of Applied Design] at the top of the hill the central vista swept beyond the campus, across the valley with its railroad to the parks or buildings on the hillside beyond and so entirely outside the group."[67]

Githens demonstrates this with another diagram, which shows an unimpeded axis extending westward to points beyond (fig. 133). Jefferson, at the University of Virginia, intended his visual axis to be open in just this way. Save for an arboretum, Jefferson's campus provided a vista to the natural landscape beyond, in affirmation of its designer's pastoral ideals. As described by Vincent Scully: "The first component of the University of Virginia is the landscape, the hill among hills where the buildings are placed. These human works frame the gentle hill slope, crown its summit, and balance, with their climatic Rotunda, the tapestry of hillside that rises southward across the narrow vale. . . . From the Rotunda, the lawn flows out like water over low mill dams, the last one steeper, a real rush which carries the eye across space to the hill beyond."[68]

Toker sees a similar dynamic at Carnegie Tech, and a specific role for the spectator: "Both Jefferson and Hornbostel intended students to look out over a steep slope at the end of the campus: the view for Jefferson was the bucolic Shenandoah Valley [*sic*]; for Hornbostel it was the train tracks of Junction Hollow. Both designers seemed to regard

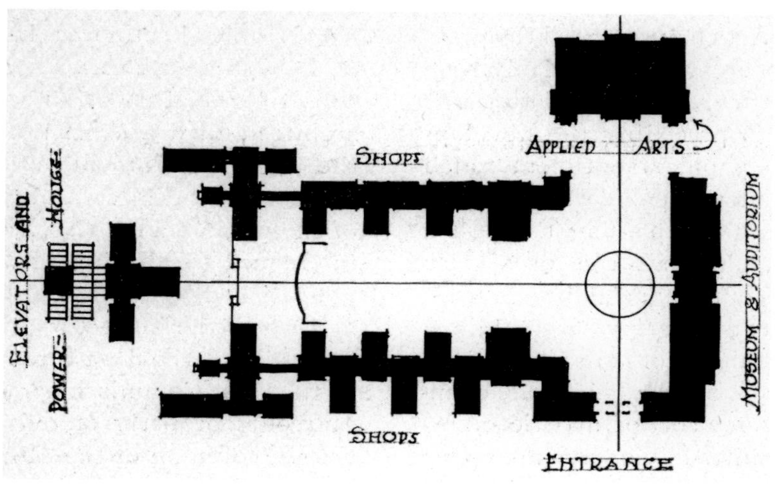

Fig. 132. The closed compositional plan. These diagrams are based on a 1906 version of Hornbostel's campus plan for Carnegie Tech before Machinery Hall and the power house were integrated, and before the School of Applied Design was relocated to the head of the through-campus axis. Reprinted from Alfred Morton Githens, "The Group Plan. I. A Theory of Composition; The Carnegie Technical Schools," *Brickbuilder* 15, no. 7 (July 1906), 134.

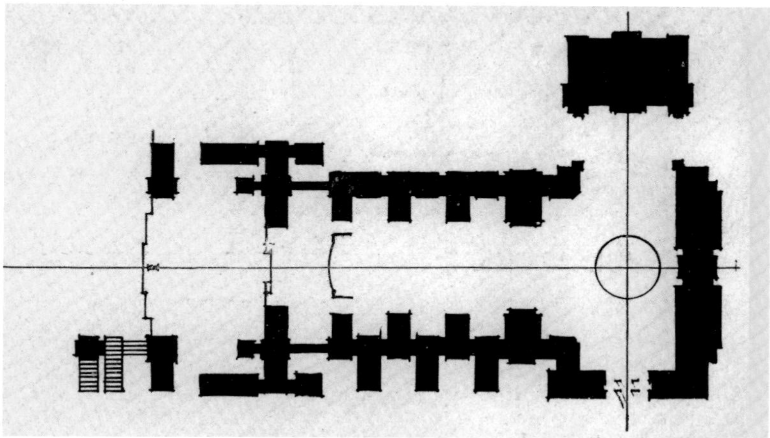

Fig. 133. The open compositional plan. Reprinted from Alfred Morton Githens, "The Group Plan. I. A Theory of Composition; The Carnegie Technical Schools," *Brickbuilder* 15, no. 7 (July 1906), 134.

their end vistas as unfinished business that was left for students at the university to complete: westward expansion in one case, industrial expansion in the other."[69]

Carnegie Tech and the University of Virginia share similar topographical settings. They are both lifted up on sloped sites, and ringed by hills. They were both, it seems, designed to be seen and to see from. Carnegie Tech is perceived to be on high ground when viewed from

Fig. 134. Henry Hornbostel (architect), School of Applied Sciences, Carnegie Tech, 1909. View toward north. Rodef Shalom Synagogue is seen below the bridge. Reprinted from the *Thistle* (1918), 74. Carnegie Mellon University Archives.

other parts of Oakland, and there are view corridors from the campus to the north and to the west.[70] If Hornbostel's compositional plan is closed, might the complex vista nevertheless be open?

The range of buildings on the north edge of the Court of Honor was never fully completed as intended, but Hornbostel's purpose was made clear. The School of Applied Sciences (1907–1908) was designed with periodic gaps in its central spine, and with bridges connecting its sections at an upper-story level.[71] These gaps and bridges break up the architectural massing to visually perforate this side of the Court. The openings under the bridges frame northerly views that extend above an adjacent ravine to hills near and far; views that notably take in Hornbostel's monumental Rodef Shalom Synagogue (1905–1907), whose green tile dome masquerades as a hill (figs. 103 and 134).[72]

More significantly, the westward view from Carnegie Tech extends above and beyond the train tracks of Junction Hollow. It grazes the shoulders of Machinery Hall, skims the roof of the Carnegie Institute, and focuses on Herron Hill, the high terrain on the opposite side of Oakland where Andrew Carnegie stood to survey Oakland, and which Githens called the hillside beyond. At first, this visible flank of Herron

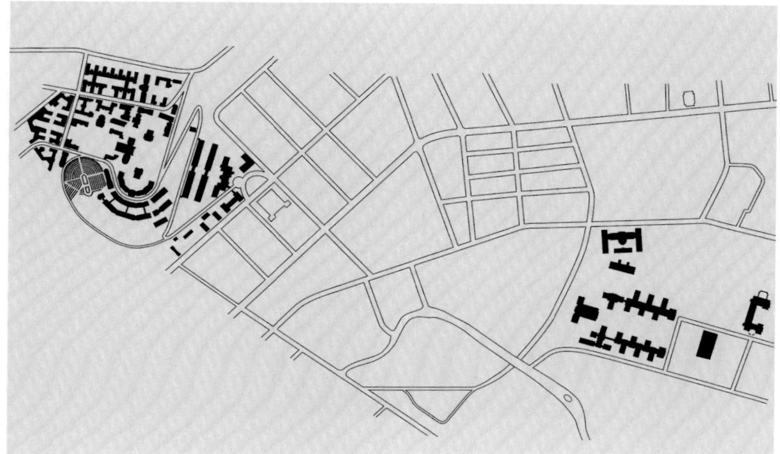

Fig. 135. Composite map of Oakland. Shows relative positions of Carnegie Tech, Western University of Pennsylvania, and other key buildings designed by Henry Hornbostel before World War I. Map by the author. Illustration by David Little.

Hill was not very developed, but in 1908, Palmer and Hornbostel won another competition to design the Western University of Pennsylvania (now the University of Pittsburgh) campus on this hillside.[73] This raised the specter of two full-fledged Hornbostel-designed campuses on raised sites less than a mile apart in full view of one another (fig. 135).

The Western University of Pennsylvania was founded in 1787 by Judge Hugh Henry Brackenridge, and had occupied buildings in the Golden Triangle and in Pittsburgh's twin city of Allegheny before planning a move to Oakland. The ambitious program for the new campus called for an enormous group plan of thirty buildings. Hornbostel's winning design called for upper and lower campuses joined by a sequence of buildings that cascaded down the steep hillside (fig. 136). The buildings took the form of neoclassical temples, prompting the *Pittsburgh Leader* to observe that the full array was reminiscent of the Athenian Acropolis, as "the pillared facades, with their pediments highly adorned, rise above one another, the largest and most majestic being at the summit."[74] The scheme was subsequently known as the Acropolis Plan. In actuality, it reflected a common Beaux-Arts exercise for the design of a group plan on a generic Mediterranean hillside.

Fig. 136. Henry Hornbostel (architect), Western University of Pennsylvania, 1908. This is the so-called Acropolis Plan. University Archives, University of Pittsburgh.

Chancellor Samuel Black McCormick called it "a very remarkable plan which adapts itself to the natural slope and seems to grow out of it."[75]

Hornbostel's elevation rendering belied the complexity of the plan by presenting a unified image of apparent bilateral symmetry organized around a central axis, an effect that was emphasized and framed by two gigantic smokestacks marking the power plant and engineering school.[76] Significantly, the picture plane of this rendering exactly paralleled the picture plane of the vista at Carnegie Tech, and the directional axes of the two campuses were the same, though slightly offset so as to be parallel.[77] When seen from Carnegie Tech, the "largest and most majestic" building at Hornbostel's Western University of Pennsylvania would appear over the right shoulder of Machinery Hall. Thus, Carnegie Tech's axis was an open axis, and the complex vista was an open vista that purposefully integrated two campuses and their specific topographical settings into a single pictorial composition for the spectator.

Classical City

There was also a view back toward Carnegie Tech from the Western University of Pennsylvania campus on Herron Hill.[78] When the hillside campus was fully built up, buildings and smokestacks would frame this

Fig. 137. R. W. Johnston Studios (photographer), view of Oakland from the Western University of Pennsylvania, 1909. Soldiers and Sailors Memorial Hall is right of center. Rodef Shalom Synagogue is left of center. Carnegie Tech lies between, beyond the Carnegie Institute. Courtesy of Gary Thomas, Photography and Graphic Services at Mellon Institute, Carnegie Mellon University.

Fig. 138. *Pittsburgh's Fifty Million Dollar Beauty Center*, 1916, postcard. Carnegie Mellon University Architecture Archives.

view for the spectator. Hornbostel's own Soldiers and Sailors Memorial Hall (1907–1911) stood prominently at the foot of the campus, and Carnegie Tech and its flagship Machinery Hall could be seen nearly on axis across the intervening upland.[79] But this panoramic view was inherently less controlled than the view from Carnegie Tech, encompassing a multiplicity and reciprocity of visual linkages rather than a perspectival axial vista. The view from Herron Hill took in key buildings throughout Oakland (figs. 137 and 138).

The City Beautiful Movement introduced the architectural and planning principles of the World's Columbian Exposition into real American cities, and Oakland had become a City Beautiful sort of place, even apart from its monumental campuses. The November 1910 issue of Pittsburgh's the *Builder* exulted, "The City Beautiful! Well might that splendid section of the city of Pittsburgh, known as Schenley Farms [Oakland], be described."[80] Schenley Park and the Carnegie Institute had signaled the beginning of this development. A combined public and private initiative that shaped the district during the 1890s was more or less explicitly inspired by the World's Columbian Exposition, well before Hornbostel evoked the fair at Carnegie Tech.[81] Momentum accelerated after 1905, when developer Franklin F. Nicola implemented his own expansive vision for Oakland and convinced numerous clubs, churches, and other public and private institutions to build there. Thus Oakland assumed the character of a civic center, which in City Beautiful parlance was a monumental grouping of public buildings adjoining public space.

The Oakland civic center was more a matter of cumulative effect than of rigorous planning. Nevertheless, as early as 1911, Montgomery Schuyler described Oakland as "a real civic center" as opposed to the merely aspiring.[82] The October 1912 issue of the *Builder* stated: "Few will dispute, after seeing it, that one of the finest Civic Centers possessed by any city in the country, of the world, for that matter, is to be found in Pittsburgh. At no time since the Columbian Exposition at Chicago in 1893 has there been brought together such an imposing grouping of architectural art. The Columbian Exposition was temporary; Pittsburgh's is permanent."[83]

For Nicola, it was but a small conceptual step from exposition and civic center to new city. He saw Oakland as a new Pittsburgh, apart from and safely above the industry, smoke, floods, and crowded conditions of downtown Pittsburgh and the river valleys. His goal was "to make of this piece of property an example which will be known all over the country as a model city." Consequently, he planned civic, cultural, educational, and residential sectors; and he thought big, explaining: "It seemed an opportunity to create a civic center that would be big in all of its phases. The thought was dominant to develop in Pittsburgh a grouping of buildings similar to those found in Athens, Rome, Munich, Paris and Washington. Pittsburgh, great in all things, should not be less in architecture and monumental expression than the capitals of the world."[84]

Nicola's Oakland, it seems, was the classical city. From ancient Athens and imperial Rome to the ideal city of Renaissance art, from Second Empire Paris and Washington, D.C., to the World's Columbian Exposition, the classical city has been a recurring phenomenon and urban ideal. The classical city embodies rational rules of organization, incorporates an established repertoire of building forms and spaces, and displays a classical vocabulary of design and ornamentation. It is vested with the architectural sublime. It aspires to greatness.

Hornbostel, too, worked to realize the classical city in the Oakland civic center. The planning, architecture, and aspirations of his university campuses made each a classical city. Yet they were also part of a larger whole, and Hornbostel's urban intentions encompassed that whole. "The artistic development of buildings in the Oakland district," he remarked in 1908, "has progressed to a very definite state and should be kept up. To continue along the lines that have been adopted in the [recent] past would eventually make the Oakland district one of the most gorgeous of any city in the world." For Hornbostel, Oakland's "beautiful possibilities" were tied to its development as a classical city.[85]

Like Jefferson before him, Hornbostel was something of a Francophile. France, in turn, was habitually Roman-centric under both kings and emperors, and Rome was the wellspring of the French Beaux-Arts. While Jefferson was antiurban, Hornbostel embraced the breadth and scale of the classical city. Hornbostel had visited Rome while on grand tour. He knew its temples, villas, and churches, and absorbed the lessons of its topography, architecture, and urbanism. In his eyes and in his hands, Oakland's hills became Roman hills.[86]

Hornbostel gave Rome primacy in the decorative program of Carnegie Tech's School of Applied Design. The central sculptural niche of the facade is Roman. The proscenium curtain in the theater was em-

Fig. 139. Theater curtain, School of Applied Design, Carnegie Tech. Reprinted from Samuel Howe, "Academic Theatre, Carnegie Institute, Pittsburgh," *International Studio* 55 (March–June 1915), supplement, xcvi.

bellished with a scenographic montage of the monuments of Rome (fig. 139).[87] A painting of St. Peter's in Rome has central placement in the murals on the ceiling of the grand hall, and a plan of St. Peter's is laid into the floor directly below.[88]

Hornbostel also set a Roman tone for the classical city in his consistent choice of building materials and colors.[89] His buff and yellow brick surfaces were not just industrial construction or an inexpensive substitute for stone. They recalled warm Roman walls of Roman brick or stucco. White terra-cotta and concrete stood in for Roman travertine in architectural elements and trim. Terra-cotta tile roofs and Guastavino tile vaulting added texture and color to the earthy Roman palette (fig. 140).[90]

When Hornbostel opened the complex vista to the north and to the west and extended views to the surrounding hills, he integrated the topographical horizon into his group plan. Whereas the French Baroque garden was typically self-contained, and extended to an artificial horizon within the limits of its own plan, the Italian Renaissance

Fig. 140. R. R. Rutili, montage of Hornbostel buildings at Carnegie Tech, with the look and feel of Rome. Reprinted from the *Thistle* (1925), frontispiece. Carnegie Mellon University Archives.

villa was projected against its topographical setting. As Edith Wharton wrote in her seminal book, *Italian Villas and Their Gardens*: "One day the architect looked forth from the terrace of his villa, and saw that, in his survey of the garden, the enclosing landscape was naturally included: the two formed a part of the same composition."[91] Steenbergen and Reh explain further: "This natural landscape was integrated into the panorama of the villa; it is the setting to which the villa, in the foreground, had to be linked. . . . Framed by a loggia, an arcade or a portico, or disconnected by means of foreground terraces, the panorama became a decorative and controllable part of the villa architecture. . . . It is not the perimeter of the estate which was portrayed as the boundary of optical space, but the natural horizon far beyond it."[92]

The Italian Renaissance villa commonly occupied a sloping suburban or exurban site. It generally comprised a villa proper, in a classical style; a formal garden with ornamental sculpture and plantings; and

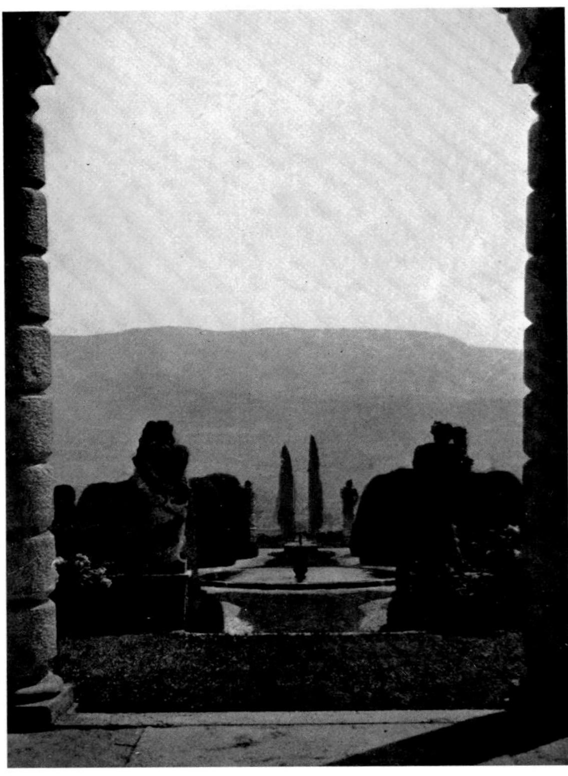

Fig. 141. Villa Arvedi a Cuzzano. Reprinted from J. C. Shepherd and G. A. Jellicoe, *Italian Gardens of the Renaissance* (London: E. Benn, 1925), plate 70.

views of the surrounding landscape—all carefully structured by axes and perspective (fig. 141). The villa plan can be seen as the *integrazione scenica* of the villa into the larger landscape.[93]

The villas of ancient Rome and the Renaissance have served as analogs for the University of Virginia in particular, and for the American university campus in general. William Mullen says that the American university as a type "is in many respects an extension of [the] ancient concept of the villa as a loose assembly of buildings in the open country."[94] At Carnegie Tech, the School of Applied Design can be seen as a villa proper, and the campus as its terraced garden. In this context, Machinery Hall is a sculptural object to be seen from the villa against the landscape beyond, more classical artifice or folly than industrial generator or temple.

The villa, like the university, lies apart from—but in association with—the so-called real world. When Alberti prescribed the ideal location of a villa, he recommended a site from which there was a view of the distant landscape of hills and of the town. For "one withdrew from the town, but not to turn one's back on it, and even less as a form of criticism. . . . The villa embodied the enjoyment of rural life, which was undertaken in an urban manner."[95] The Roman *villa suburbana*, in particular, embodied this dual separation and dependence. Despite its private role as a place apart, it was linked to the public domain.

Renaissance Rome was a city composed of churches and monuments on the Tiber River plain, and villas ranged around the famous Roman hills. The villas featured views of the surrounding terrain, but, in this context, views of nature deferred to views from villa to villa and

Fig. 142. Gaspar van Wittel, *Veduta Panoramica con Villa Medici*, 1683. Galleria Nazionale d'Arte Antica, Rome.

from villa to church or monument.[96] Sight lines knit the villas to each other and to key sites below in a web of visibility across the city (fig. 142). According to Steenbergen and Reh: "In this elevated position above the low-lying city the villas were in each other's field of vision . . . balanced on the edge of free space. . . . In the bowl shape (two or three kilometers in diameter) formed by the geomorphological conditions, the town is the stage for the villas nestled on the balconies of this gigantic open-air theatre. The residents of the villas could look down on the ecclesiastical and political centre of the world."[97]

Sight lines linked Carnegie Tech to the Western University of Pennsylvania on Herron Hill, and to Hornbostel's Rodef Shalom Synagogue in town.[98] The return view from Herron Hill took in the numerous monumental buildings of the classical city as well as Carnegie Tech. Campuses and buildings assumed the metaphorical roles of villas and churches and monuments, visually interconnected across the open bowl of Oakland's topographical space.

Sites of Giantism

More often than not, the classical city has been the product of a singular visionary—a Caesar or a pope in Rome, Baron Haussmann in Paris, Daniel H. Burnham in Chicago. As Reyner Banham bluntly states it, "In architecture, classicism . . . and grandomania persistently go together."[99]

Henry Hornbostel was an ambitious man with a healthy ego "who never faltered in his faith of his own pre-eminence."[100] He had a commanding vision of Oakland and the commissions to make it real, and his work quickly achieved critical mass. The scope of Hornbostel's achievement did not go unnoticed. Aymar Embury II wrote of the Oakland civic center:

> This assemblage is interesting not only because of the size and character of the buildings, but also because so many of the buildings were done by a single firm, Palmer, Hornbostel & Jones. . . . [T]his is still more interesting when one recalls the fact that they won [most of them] in open competitions which included many of the most distinguished architects of America. It must be exceedingly gratifying to this firm to have assembled so many notable examples of their work, and to feel that their assemblage is due not to personal interest and friendship, but to their ability in design.[101]

Carnegie and others were the founders, Nicola was Oakland's master developer, and there were other architects who contributed major buildings to the civic center.[102] Still, Embury's impression was real—Oakland was a Hornbostel showcase. His two extensive university campuses, Rodef Shalom Synagogue, Soldiers and Sailors Memorial Hall, and the Experimental Station of the U.S. Bureau of Mines were all monumental in scale and significance and were unified in their distinctive styling and their palette of building materials and colors. Together, these sites and buildings dominated the urban landscape, established evocative relationships, and embodied Hornbostel's grandiose vision of Oakland.[103] In an act of personal giantism, Hornbostel left his imprint at the scale of the urban landscape.

Full realization of Hornbostel's Oakland ultimately foundered, however, on a failure to complete the Western University of Pennsylvania campus. The university's aspirations exceeded its resources from day one, and World War I blunted any momentum. The university ultimately rescinded Hornbostel's commission for the Acropolis Plan campus after only a few buildings had been built. What was built was too diffuse to make a whole. The lack of progress was compounded, it seems, by inherent problems with Hornbostel's design and the elevation rendering that promoted it (see fig. 136). The symmetry of the elevation was more impressionistic than real, and the total effect broke down quickly from any viewpoint other than the ideal. What's more, the ideal viewpoint lay considerably outside of the group plan, and was, in fact, in an unattainable position for the spectator. Embury had written as early as 1915, "The scheme so excellent on paper, can not be appreciated in reality . . . and it seems unlikely that its full force and logic will ever become apparent."[104] The impressive paper image may have won Hornbostel the commission, but when reality fell short of image, it may have contributed to his downfall as well.

Subsequently, the university left Herron Hill for a level site in the heart of the civic center, rejected the group plan for a singular architectural gesture, and traded the classical for the Gothic by erecting the so-called Cathedral of Learning (1926–1937) and related buildings by architect Charles Z. Klauder—a bold architectural vision and act of grandomania in its own right (fig. 143). In this case, however, the grandomania characterized the client more than the architect. Hornbostel's Oakland was superseded by what Toker has called Chancellor Bowman's Oakland.[105]

Chancellor John G. Bowman assumed leadership of the University of Pittsburgh in 1921 when it was crowded, debt-ridden, and forlorn.

Fig. 143. Charles Z. Klauder (architect), Cathedral of Learning, 1927. Carnegie Mellon University Architecture Archives.

His mission was to reinvigorate the school, and his self-assigned task was to build thirteen million additional cubic feet of space. He chose to put all of this space and all of his energy into a single project, for which he acquired a parcel of flat undeveloped land at the core of the civic center. Here he created an extraordinary site: a skyscraper campus.[106]

There was no need to build high on this large property. The practicality of an academic skyscraper was always doubtful at best, though lip service was frequently paid to flexibility and economy. But Bowman had a vision; and according to Thomas A. P. van Leeuwen, Bowman made the case for the Cathedral of Learning by "exciting patriotic and religious sentiments—just as in medieval practice—to complete [the Cathedral] to its proper splendour."[107] Such spiritual purpose was, of course, inherent in the building's name, a popular moniker that Bowman adopted as a symbol of aspiration.

Bowman enunciated three aims for the new building, revealing a strong belief in the power of architecture and a canny instinct for fund-raising: first, to "express the meaning of the University"; second, "to interpret the spirit of Pittsburgh both to itself and to the world"; and third, to build on a heritage of pioneers and immigrants in order to "memorialize in a lasting, dignified and appropriate way those men and women who brought . . . hope here and who achieved." To realize these aims, according to Bowman, the building had to be tall. "To catch the spiritual, driving, courageous stuff that made Pittsburgh," he wrote, "the designer of the Cathedral of Learning had to use architecture which expresses such stuff. Such effects can not be attained in low buildings. They can be attained in high buildings. . . ." The sense of height would be amplified by "the unmeasurable quality of its lift, buttress after buttress rising but never arriving at a spire," and lines that are "parallel, and project themselves into infinite space."[108]

"The effect," said Bowman, "is to dumbfound our comprehension. Not measured, not visible, greatness rises before us. Men seem dwarfed beside the structure." But then, "the imagination starts. A rush of self-expansion comes and a feeling that we can go beyond our own limits."[109] Thus the Cathedral of Learning would evoke the architectural

Fig. 144. Cathedral of Learning. Reprinted from the *Owl* (1942), frontispiece. University of Pittsburgh Libraries.

sublime and elicit awe and wonder in the spectator (fig. 144). Such sensations, Bowman asserted, would promote personal advancement and call forth civic and spiritual virtues. "Steel of the city's steel, summit in a people's struggle, voice of architecture, [the Cathedral of Learning] speaks of achievement in Pittsburgh, not done and ended, but going on and up."[110]

Ultimately, Bowman wore everybody down with the height of his rhetoric, and his skyscraper campus was financed by the Mellons and other wealthy donors and a vast confederation of common citizens including 97,000 children (at a dime each).[111] All, Bowman had assured them, had a stake in the Cathedral of Leaning. Both the rhetoric and the architecture grew a bit stale as completion was forestalled by funding gaps and the Depression, but the building was finally finished more than ten years after it was begun.[112]

Bowman found the Gothic style to be essential to his task. Klauder was hired because of his extensive experience with academic buildings and his skill with the collegiate Gothic. Bowman and Klauder reportedly found inspiration for the design by listening to Richard Wagner's Fire Music from *Die Walküre*. Musical climax after musical climax begot architectural buttress after architectural buttress.[113] This story, however fantastic, may be true, but the building emerged equally out of precedents such as the Harkness Tower at Yale University (Klauder had assisted in its design) and the Woolworth Building in New York (known as the Cathedral of Commerce).

Klauder designed the Cathedral of Learning and the nearby Heinz Chapel (1934–1938) and Stephen Foster Memorial (1935–1937) in the same Gothic style, and all three buildings reached completion more or less simultaneously. This new concentration of the Gothic, when combined with St. Paul's Cathedral, which already stood at the periphery of the classical city, opened Oakland to a different set of visual and cultural meanings. John Kane's *Pietà* (1933) depicted the post-crucifixion scene on an imaginary Oakland hilltop, with a northern Gothic backdrop provided by St. Paul's Cathedral and the Cathedral of Learning (fig. 145).[114]

Though originally conceived at fifty-two stories, the Cathedral of Learning topped out at forty-two. Like other skyscrapers, it offered a new elevated viewpoint. There are views of Oakland all around, of Carnegie Tech to the east, and of the Golden Triangle in the distance to the west.[115] More significantly, the building draws the spectator's attention to itself. Its sheer mass and height are magnified because it stands nearly alone on a grassy plot, not on a city sidewalk among skyscraper peers. It acts as a terminal marker on Forbes Avenue and other Oakland streets, and was purposefully designed in the round to be seen from all directions.[116]

Klauder remarked that the Cathedral of Learning was "unhampered by its surroundings" and depicted it that way (see fig. 143).[117] At the same time, the building greatly impacted those surroundings as it immediately dominated all views of Oakland. At 535 feet on a 900-foot site, it tops the terrain like the U.S. Steel Building and other skyscrapers in downtown Pittsburgh, and is visible from great distances above the horizon.[118] Like the U.S. Steel Building, it is a central reference

Fig. 145. John Kane, *Pietà*, 1933. Carnegie Museum of Art, Pittsburgh; Purchase: Bequest of Paul J. Winschel in memory of Jean Mertz Winschel.

point for the spectator within its topographical setting, and in the larger terrain as well. This ubiquity has been observed and recorded by photographer Duane Michal in his photograph series *Six Views of the Cathedral of Learning in the Manner of Hiroshige* (1982), and by artist Felix de la Concha in his painting series *One A Day: 365 Views of the Cathedral of Learning* (1999) (fig. 146).[119]

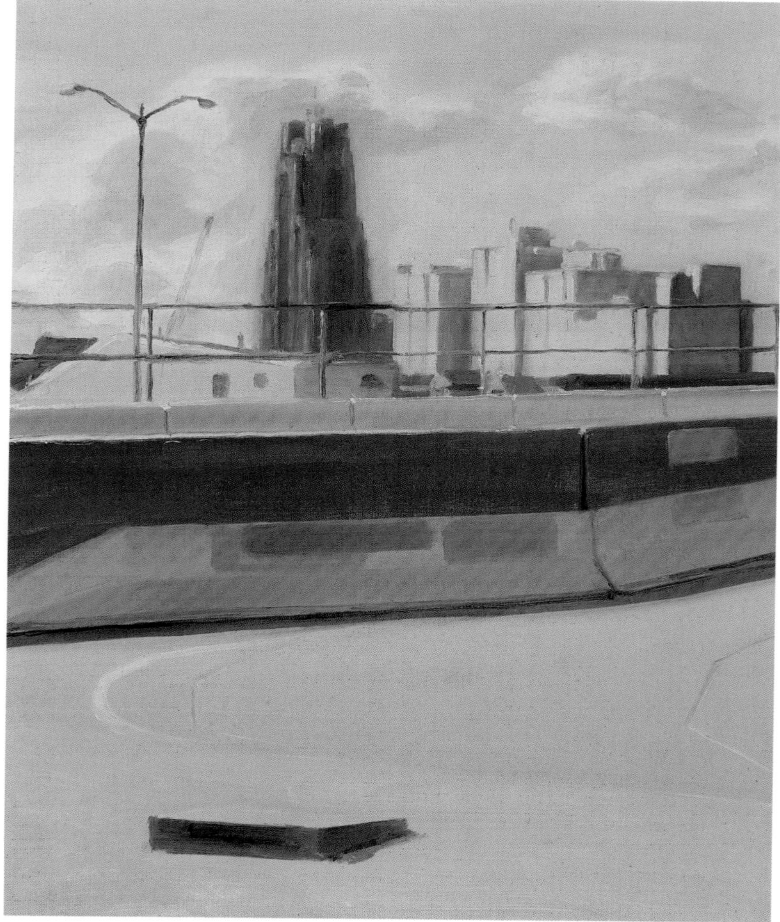

Fig. 146. Felix de la Concha, *April 5*, ca. 1998. © 2006 Felix de la Concha/Artists Rights Society (ARS), New York. Courtesy of University of Pittsburgh.

As the Cathedral of Learning drew attention to itself, it wreaked havoc on the classical city and the vista seen from Carnegie Tech (fig. 147). It introduced height in the midst of breadth, and hung heavily over Machinery Hall's right shoulder where classical temples should have been. As a singular monument, it inexorably pulls the complex vista and all sight lines across Oakland to itself. Hornbostel designed numerous monuments in Oakland, but not *the* monument.[120]

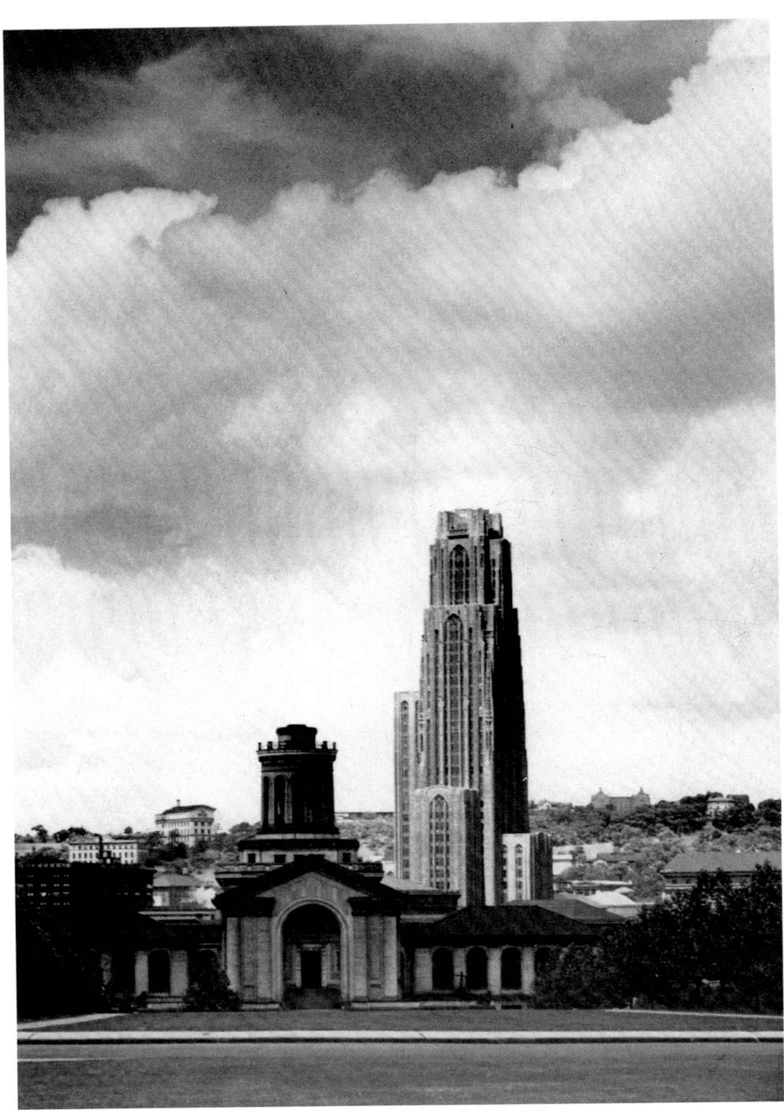

Fig. 147. Cathedral of Learning as seen from Carnegie Tech, ca. 1935. Note an Acropolis Plan building (now demolished) to the left of the Machinery Hall tower. Carnegie Mellon University Architecture Archives.

Whose image, then, lies within the site(s) of giantism? Andrew Carnegie left his imprint on Oakland through his two large-scale benefactions, and Hornbostel created Carnegie Tech in Carnegie's image, yet Hornbostel's own image was at play throughout Oakland. Some see Carnegie embodied in Carnegie Tech's Machinery Hall and Hornbostel in the School of Applied Design, facing off across the Court of Honor. Then Chancellor Bowman altered the balance with his own statement of personal giantism. Heinz Chapel and the Stephen Foster Memorial had other names attached to them, but the Cathedral of Learning personified Bowman himself. Carnegie Tech, Oakland, and the complex vista accommodated multiple sites of giantism.

Each Spectator in Turn

Vistas imply ideal viewpoints. Ideal viewpoints imply spectators. What seventeenth-century Europe thought of as the viewpoint of the king, however, is, in modern America, what Howett calls the "I/eye," a viewpoint and identity that may be assumed by various individuals in succession.[121] As Allen Weiss explains, in a discussion of perspective: "This unique viewpoint thus implies the existence of an individual ego, the one looking at the scene; but this self is fully replaceable by other selves. The system of linear perspective is thus a social and historical system of exchange by means of articulating diverse subjects as potential viewers, interchangeable and identical before a given scene."[122] Spectators are interchangeable—yet not so identical—at the ideal viewpoint of the complex vista.

When the spectator is Andrew Carnegie, the complex vista is seen as a product of industry and philanthropy made in Carnegie's own image. He sees the workshops of Carnegie Tech and the smoking tower of Machinery Hall as symbols of his own identity and wealth; he sees the City Beautiful campus as the physical embodiment of his cultural philanthropy; he experiences the paternal satisfaction of the institutional founder; more pragmatically, he sees Carnegie Tech as a producer of trained workers and educated citizens for the industrial society. In imagery that embodies the social ideals of Carnegie's Gospel of Wealth, an illustration from a student yearbook shows the student/citizen being welcomed to Carnegie Tech by a friendly genie (fig. 148).[123] Carnegie sees himself, it seems, as the benevolent genie, writ large, sprung from the smokestack of Machinery Hall, conferring success on those who aspire.

When the spectator is Henry Hornbostel, the complex vista is seen as ordered pictorial space shaped by Beaux-Arts planning principles and overlaid with Renaissance geometry, Baroque spatial effects, and neoclassical architecture. He sees space that opens from the perspectival to the scenographic. A man more cosmopolitan than Carnegie, he sees the classical city. He also sees Hornbostel's Oakland, a personal act of design and self-portraiture. When the stone niches of the School of Applied Design were belatedly carved with architectural motifs in the 1990s, a bust of Hornbostel himself was carved on a keystone in the central niche. The scenario recalls Thomas Cole's painting, *The Architect's Dream* (1840) (fig. 149).[124] From here, the ideal viewpoint, Hornbostel is a perpetual spectator, looking out on the complex vista of his making.

When the spectator is Chancellor Bowman, the viewpoint is not really ideal. He finds himself on the opposing campus, and the complex vista urges him to admire Machinery Hall and to imagine Hornbostel's Acropolis Plan campus on Herron Hill. Yet his eye is forcibly drawn off axis to the Cathedral of Learning, which appears daring, forceful, and sublime. He sees the Cathedral of Learning as an expressive embodiment of the University of Pittsburgh, the city of Pittsburgh, and the peoples of the region, and as a monument to his own efforts and achievement. He admires and is uplifted by its height, and gratefully observes its dominance of the environs.

When the spectator is the student or citizen, aspects of the technological and architectural sublime and the giantism in the landscape may threaten to overwhelm, but the complex vista is (ideally) seen as

Fig. 148. Donald M. Shafer, Carnegie Tech beckons. Reprinted from the *Thistle* (1929), 67. Carnegie Mellon University Archives.

Fig. 149. Thomas Cole, *The Architect's Dream*, 1840. Note the figure of the architect on the column in the foreground. Toledo Museum of Art. Purchased with funds from the Florence Scott Libbey Bequest in memory of her father, Maurice A. Scott, 1949.162.

affirmation, opportunity, and inspiration. The vista is affirmation of an identity grounded in Western civilization.[125] It is opportunity for individual betterment and success for those who aspire. It is inspiration for those who would discover and explore its formal and associational meanings (fig. 150).

For each spectator in turn, the complex vista reveals that the land and the city and art and industry are the foundations of life itself.

Fig. 150. Jill Watson, study drawing of the complex vista, 1996. Carnegie Mellon University Architecture Archives.

Postscript

If the topographical city reveals, it may also conceal. Land and architecture frequently mirror themselves (not the sky), and a hill or building may loom as much as it may mirror. Changes of level can block views and make the in-between spaces seem small and finite indeed. Terrestrial rooms, sunken among the hills, are invisible to one another.

Topographical space yields to singular space only in Pittsburgh's highest terrain—a sometimes surreal landscape where the city's second datum line becomes its second skyline, and its singular sky line. Here, the rootless masses and disembodied crests of skyscrapers surmount the terrain. They make the terrestrial rooms below visible by implication and link them one to another. Views that encompass the skyscrapers of the Golden Triangle and the Cathedral of Learning take the city's measure, and anchor it in place amid the swirling terrain.

Civic infrastructures populate a technological horizon and utilize the topography for operational advantage. Water towers are the zenith points of a system that moves water from river to hilltop and back again. Transmission towers broadcast and relay signals above the terrain. They are the technological totems of our time, filling the air with an invisible matrix of electronic communications more pervasive than smoke.

Earthbound buildings cling to the heights for their own unearthly reasons and celebrate their own celestial points-of-view. St. Paul of the Cross Monastery is a pinnacle of architecture and faith. The Allegheny Observatory sits high above the city's smoke and light. Its ocular domes mimic both hills and heavens and provide sight lines to the stars.

Hilltop cemeteries and golf courses bristle with obelisks and pinflags. Ball fields raise nighttime lights against the sky, and pop flies visibly leave the planet. Grassy parks and new-growth forests blanket the summits.

The land itself forms the overarching plateau. Hills set against hills scribe a continuous line at the base of a hemispherical sky. Here, finally, the spectator may lengthen his or her gaze toward a true and visible horizon, where the topographical city ends and the sky begins, as far as the eye can see.

Notes

PREFACE

1. Florence Lipsky, *San Francisco: la grille sur les collines = The Grid Meets the Hills* (Marseille: Parenthèses, 1999), 17.

2. James Parton wrote as early as 1868, "[The] hills, once so beautifully rounded and in such harmony with the scene, have been cut down, sliced off, pierced, slanted, zig-zagged, built upon, built under, until almost every trace of their former outline has been obliterated. . . ." James Parton, "Pittsburg," *Atlantic Monthly* 21, no. 123 (January 1868), 18. On the other hand, Walter C. Kidney has recently written, in counterpoint to Parton, "For nearly two-and-a-half centuries, man has scraped and scratched at this primitive terrain, building roads on its slopes, bridging its voids, tunneling its hills, filling in its shallower depressions. But despite all of this activity the nature of the terrain is largely unchanged." *Pittsburgh's Landmark Architecture: The Historic Buildings of Pittsburgh and Allegheny County* (Pittsburgh: Pittsburgh History and Landmarks Foundation, 1997), 5.

3. Spiro Kostof, *The City Shaped: Urban Patterns and Meanings Through History* (Boston: Little, Brown and Co., 1991), 53.

4. The field of cultural landscape studies provides an exception to this generalization. In addition, the intersection of architecture and landscape is increasingly a subject of design investigation and theoretical discourse in the twenty-first century. See, for example, Catherine Spellman, ed., *Re-envisioning Landscape/Architecture* (Barcelona: Actar, 2003).

5. William Rees Morrish, *Civilizing Terrains: Mountains, Mounds and Mesas* (San Francisco: William Stout Publishers, 1996), i.

6. See, for instance, the activities of the Riverlife Task Force at: Riverlife Task Force, "Riverlife Task Force, Pittsburgh Pennsylvania," http://www.pittsburghriverlife.org/.

7. Gina Crandell, *Nature Pictorialized: The "View" in Landscape History* (Baltimore: The Johns Hopkins University Press, 1993), 30.

8. Ibid, 1–14, 27.

9. M. Christine Boyer, *The City of Collective Memory: Its Historical Imagery and Architectural Entertainments* (Cambridge, Mass.: MIT Press, 1994), 302.

PERCEIVING THE TOPOGRAPHICAL CITY

1. Walter C. Kidney, "Pittsburgh: A Study in Urban Identity," *Progressive Architecture* 49, no. 3 (March 1968), 119. When Benjamin H. Latrobe, among the region's and America's first and most important architects, came to Pittsburgh in 1813–1814, he instinctively realized that the best way to describe the terrain to a distant friend was by way of a section drawing. Benjamin H. Latrobe to James Eakin, Esq., December 18, 1813, Pittsburgh History and Landmarks Foundation.

2. See Edward K. Muller and Joel A. Tarr, "The Interaction of Natural and Built Environments in the Pittsburgh Landscape," in *Devastation and Renewal: Perspectives on the Environmental History of Pittsburgh and Its Region*, ed. Joel A. Tarr (Pittsburgh: University of Pittsburgh Press, 2003), 25–33; Walter C. Kidney, *Pittsburgh's Bridges: Architecture and Engineering* (Pittsburgh: Pittsburgh History and Landmarks Foundation, 1999); Bruce S. Cridlebaugh, "Bridges and Tunnels of Allegheny County and Pittsburgh, Pennsylvania," http://pghbridges.com/; and Bob Regan, *The Steps of Pittsburgh: Portrait of a City* (Pittsburgh: Local History Co., 2004).

3. Bruce Lindsey, "Topographic Memory," in *Re-envisioning Landscape/Architecture*, ed. Catherine Spellman (Barcelona: Actar, 2003), 48.

4. Patrick Horsbrugh, *Pittsburgh Perceived; A Critical Review of Form, Features and Feasibilities of the Prodigious City* (Pittsburgh: Department of City Planning, 1963), 42; Kidney, "Pittsburgh: A Study in Urban Identity," 119; Clyde Hare, *Clyde Hare's Pittsburgh* (Pittsburgh: Pittsburgh History and Landmarks Foundation, 1984), 42.

5. Morrish, *Civilizing Terrains,* drawing 4.

6. Raymond E. Murphy and Marion Murphy, *Penn-*

sylvania: A Regional Geography (Harrisburg, Pa.: Pennsylvania Book Service, 1937), 37.

7. Horsbrugh, *Pittsburgh Perceived,* 41.

8. Parton, "Pittsburg," 21, 18.

9. Michael Chabon, *The Mysteries of Pittsburgh* (New York: HarperCollins, 1989), 49. A descent into Pittsburgh is observable from routes that cross the plateau before dropping into the river valleys. This effect may be most apparent to the average motorist at Greentree Hill on the Parkway West, the point where the Parkway East leaves the Squirrel Hill Tunnel and dips below the Greenfield Bridge, and where the Parkway North descends toward the city via the East Street Valley.

10. Kidney used Henry Koerner's painting *Oh Fearful Wonder of Man* (fig. 7) to illustrate his article, "Pittsburgh: A Study in Urban Identity." Kidney described the painting as a "fantasy on Pittsburgh phenomena" and quoted Koerner regarding Pittsburgh: "It is for me what Rome is for Fellini. Most everything that I want to say about contemporary existence I can find visually realized here—or better, its visual realizations spark my imagination again and again. . . . The mixture and diversity of buildings, houses and bridges on hills and valleys and over rivers, nature and industries, races and religions, are forever forming changing mutations of motif-possibilities. As if in a dream, but with your eyes wide open" (116–17). For additional discussion of this painting see Gail Stavitsky, "Oh Fearful Wonder of Man," *Carnegie Magazine* 56, no. 8 (May/June 1983), 14–15.

11. Frederick Law Olmsted Jr., *Pittsburgh Main Thoroughfares and the Down Town District; Improvements Necessary to Meet the City's Present and Future Needs* (Pittsburgh: Pittsburgh Civic Commission, 1911), 15–17.

12. Horsbrugh, *Pittsburgh Perceived,* 88.

In View of a Golden Triangle

1. Morrish, *Civilizing Terrains,* drawing 17.

2. Charles W. Moore, William J. Mitchell, and William Turnbull Jr., *Poetics of Gardens* (Cambridge, Mass.: MIT Press, 1988), 2.

3. See John A. Harper, "Precambrian Fractures and Pleistocene Reversals: A History of Drainage in Western Pennsylvania," in *A Geographic Perspective of Pittsburgh and the Alleghenies: From Precambrian to Post-Industrial,* ed. Kevin J. Patrick and Joseph L. Scarpaci (Washington, D.C.: Association of American Geographers, 2000), 97–103.

4. Mircea Eliade, *The Sacred and the Profane: The Nature of Religion* (New York: Harcourt Brace Jovanovich, 1959), 22.

5. The sacred mountain is found in Mesopotamian, Egyptian, Mesoamerican, and many other cultures. See Vincent Scully, *Architecture: The Natural and the Manmade* (New York: St. Martin's Press, 1991), 1–37. Examples of the *omphalos,* which is often embodied in a stone, include Apollo's Temple at Delphi, the Kaaba at Mecca, the Oneida stone of the Oneida Indian Nation (the "people of the upright stone"), and Plymouth Rock. Pittsburgh's Point is not a stone, but it is a promontory.

6. River tributaries that drain the surrounding landscape are commonly named for their distance from the Point and called runs, e.g., Nine Mile Run.

7. Eliade, *Sacred and the Profane,* 50.

8. Roger G. Kennedy, *Hidden Cities: The Discovery and Loss of Ancient North American Civilization* (New York: Free Press, 1994), 7–22.

9. William N. Morgan, *Precolumbian Architecture in Eastern North America* (Gainesville: University Press of Florida, 1999); Morrish, *Civilizing Terrains,* drawings 11, 31.

10. Kennedy, *Hidden Cities,* 5–6.

11. Neither mound survives today. For additional mounds in the Pittsburgh area, see Edmund S. Carpenter, "Tumuli in Southwestern Pennsylvania," *American Antiquity* 16, no. 4 (April 1951), 329–46. Carpenter fails, however, to mention the mound at the Forks of the Ohio.

12. Hugh Henry Brackenridge, *Pittsburgh Gazette,* July 29, 1786, quoted in James D. Van Trump, *Majesty of the Law: The Court Houses of Allegheny County* (Pittsburgh: Pittsburgh History and Landmarks Foundation, 1988), 12.

13. Kennedy, *Hidden Cities,* 177–89.

14. John Palmer, quoted in Van Trump, *Majesty of the Law,* 12.

15. George Washington, *The Journal of Major George Washington* (Ann Arbor: University Microfilms, 1966), 4.

16. Native Americans built both fortifications and formal gardens elsewhere in North America. For fortifications, see David E. Jones, *Native North American Armor, Shields, and Fortifications* (Austin: University of Texas Press, 2004). For gardens, see William Emery Doolittle, *Cultivated Landscapes of North America* (Oxford: Oxford University Press, 2000), 82–117, 199–201.

17. Charles Morse Stotz, "The King's Gardens," *Carnegie Magazine* 35, no. 1 (January 1961), 11–15; Charles Morse Stotz, *Outposts of the War for Empire: The French and English in Western Pennsylvania: Their Armies, Their Forts, Their People, 1749–1764* (Pittsburgh: Historical Society of Western Pennsylvania, 1985), 80–87, 126–40; Kidney, *Pittsburgh's Landmark Architecture,* 21–22.

18. Union Savings Bank of Pittsburgh, *Grant's Hill: Center of the Pittsburgh Drama* (Pittsburgh: Union Savings Bank, 1939), 3.

19. Ralph E. Griswold, "From Fort Pitt to Point Park: A Turning Point in the Physical Planning of Pittsburgh," *Landscape Architecture* 46, no. 4 (July 1956), 194. Griswold here describes a *patte d'oie*, or goose foot, a device of French Baroque city planning that is a three-pronged set of radial streets.

20. For the role of the grid in urban development see Kostof, *City Shaped,* 95–157. Woods and Vickroy struggled a bit with the details. Their surveyor's chain was allegedly one inch too long every ten feet.

21. Kidney, *Pittsburgh's Landmark Architecture,* 22.

22. The visual effects of Pittsburgh's grids were not always viewed as salubrious. John Melish wrote in the early nineteenth century: "The plan was meant to accommodate the town to both rivers, but it is by no means so well designed as it might have been. The streets are generally too narrow, and they cross one another at acute angles, which is both hurtful to the eye and injurious to the buildings." *Travels Through the United States of America in the Years 1806–1807* (Philadelphia: T. and G. Palmer, 1812), 54.

23. Quoted in Van Trump, *Majesty of the Law,* 8.

24. Van Trump, *Majesty of the Law,* 14.

25. National Archives and Records Service, *Washington, Design of the Federal City* (Washington, D.C.: Acropolis Books, 1981), 10.

26. Henry Marie Brackenridge, *Recollections of Persons and Places in the West* (Pittsburgh: John I. Kay, 1834), quoted in Van Trump, *Majesty of the Law,* 13.

27. Van Trump, *Majesty of the Law,* 11.

28. Quote from Sarah Hutchins Killikelly, *The History of Pittsburgh, Its Rise and Progress* (Pittsburgh: B. C. and Gordon Montgomery Co., 1906), 176. For a discussion of this combination of temple form, dome, and wings in American public buildings see Vincent Scully, *American Architecture and Urbanism,* rev. ed. (New York: Henry Holt and Company, 1988), 68–69. In 1843, Chislett began to plan Allegheny Cemetery, the first of many cemeteries that he designed in western Pennsylvania and beyond. His Indianapolis cemetery is Crown Hill Cemetery. Chislett knew his way around the landscape, and he knew how to crown a hill.

29. Eliade, *Sacred and the Profane,* 39.

30. Morrish, *Civilizing Terrains,* drawing 15.

31. Van Trump, *Majesty of the Law,* 20.

32. Morrish, *Civilizing Terrains,* drawing 2.

33. Olmsted, *Pittsburgh Main Thoroughfares,* 128; Leland D. Baldwin, *Pittsburgh: The Story of a City, 1750–1865* (Pittsburgh: University of Pittsburgh Press, 1937), 232.

34. Morrish, *Civilizing Terrains,* drawing 6.

35. Van Trump, *Majesty of the Law,* 20.

36. Wayne Attoe, *Skylines: Understanding and Molding Urban Silhouettes* (New York: Wiley, 1981), xii.

37. Kostof, *City Shaped,* 290.

38. Paul Spreiregen, *Urban Design: The Architecture of Towns and Cities* (New York: McGraw-Hill, 1965), 220.

39. In this, Richardson's buildings are a reflection of a nineteenth-century American preoccupation with geology as a means of establishing history and identity. See Rebecca Bedell, *The Anatomy of Nature: Geology and American Landscape Painting, 1825–1875* (Princeton: Princeton University Press, 2001), 3–15.

40. Thomas C. Hubka, "The Picturesque in the Design Method of H. H. Richardson: Memorial Hall, North Easton," in *H. H. Richardson: The Architect, His Peers, and Their Era*, ed. Maureen Meister (Cambridge, Mass.: MIT Press, 1999), 25. Hubka relates Richardson's work in a picturesque vein to ideas of the natural sublime (26).

41. Henry Hobson Richardson, quoted in Margaret Henderson Floyd, *Henry Hobson Richardson: A Genius for Architecture* (New York: Monacelli Press, 1997), 110.

42. Henry Russell Hitchcock, *The Architecture of H. H. Richardson and His Times*, rev. ed. (Hamden, Conn.: Arcon Books, 1961), 259.

43. Floyd, *Henry Hobson Richardson,* 110.

44. See Montgomery Schuyler, "The Building of Pittsburgh," *Architectural Record* 30, no. 3 (September 1911), 226; James D. Van Trump, "The Romanesque Revival in Pittsburgh," *Journal of the Society of Architectural Historians* 16, no. 3 (October 1957), 22–29.

45. Richardson, quoted in Floyd, *Henry Hobson Richardson,* 110.

46. Floyd, *Henry Hobson Richardson,* 125.

47. Horsbrugh, *Pittsburgh Perceived,* 117; J. W. F. White, quoted in Van Trump, *Majesty of the Law,* 93–94.

48. Walter C. Kidney, *H. H. Richardson's Allegheny County Courthouse and Jail* (Pittsburgh: Allegheny County Bureau of Cultural Programs, 1981), n.p.

49. Franklin Toker, *Pittsburgh: An Urban Portrait* (University Park: Pennsylvania State University Press, 1986), 76.

50. Richardson, quoted in Mariana Griswold Van Rensselaer, *Henry Hobson Richardson and His Works* (1888; reprint, Park Forest, Ill.: Prairie School Press, 1967), 36. Richardson, who died in 1886, did not live to see "Pittsburgh finished."

51. Valerie Sue Grash, "The Commercial Skyscrapers of Pittsburgh: Industrialists and Financiers, 1885–1932" (PhD diss., Pennsylvania State University, 1998), 70. Two additional stories were added to the Carnegie Building in 1905. It was demolished in 1952 when U.S. Steel moved its headquarters across the street.

52. Named buildings perpetuate the memories of those whose names they carry. See James D. Van Trump, "The Skyscraper as Monument: A Field of Commemorative Buildings in Pittsburgh," *Charette* 43, no. 4 (April 1963), 10–13, 21. For a discussion of gigantism in the landscape, see Martin Warnke, *Political Landscape: The Art History of Nature* (Cambridge, Mass.: Harvard University Press, 1995), 89–113.

53. Martha Frick Symington Sanger, *Henry Clay Frick: An Intimate Portrait* (New York: Abbeville Press Publishers, 1998), 273–311.

54. Ibid., 288; Van Trump, "Skyscraper as Monument," 13.

55. Kidney, *H. H. Richardson's Allegheny County Courthouse and Jail,* n.p.; Van Trump, *Majesty of the Law,* 128. There is no reason to think that Frick sought to overshadow the courthouse; it was merely a casualty in his competition with Carnegie.

56. Frick also bought and developed the site of the Third Presbyterian Church. The relocation of these congregations followed a trend in residential growth toward the east, so Frick's actions were not necessarily hostile. Grash, "Commercial Skyscrapers of Pittsburgh," 90. Frick planned the Union Arcade and the William Penn Hotel as early as 1905, but awaited further cutting

of the hump before proceeding with their construction between 1914 and 1917. "Frick Plans Magnificent Building," *Construction* 11, no. 2 (July 5, 1905), 27.

57. Toker, *Pittsburgh,* 21; Van Trump, "Skyscraper as Monument," 10.

58. Van Trump, "Skyscraper as Monument," 13, 21.

59. Ibid., 10.

60. *Union Arcade Building* (Pittsburgh: Union Arcade Building, 1916), n.p.

61. Gail Fenske and Derek Holdsworth, "Corporate Identity and the New York Office Building: 1895–1915," in *The Landscape of Modernity: Essays on New York City, 1900–1940,* ed. David Ward and Oliver Zunz (New York: Russell Sage Foundation, 1992), 131.

62. Ibid., 154.

63. The most intriguing story to explain this moniker states that Mayor William J. Howard, when confronted by the devastation from Pittsburgh's Great Fire of 1845, proclaimed: "We shall make of this triangle of blackened ruins a golden triangle whose fame will endure as a priceless heritage." Ann Oakley, *Our Pennsylvania: Keys to the Keystone State* (Indianapolis: Bobbs-Merrill, 1950), 389. The term was not much used until the early twentieth century, however, at which time it seemingly referenced the wealth of downtown banks and corporations and the thriving commercial climate.

64. From the *Bulletin* (Pittsburgh), quoted in Roy Stryker and Mel Seidenberg, *A Pittsburgh Album, 1758–1958: Two Hundred Years of Memories in Pictures and Text* (Pittsburgh: Pittsburgh Post-Gazette, 1959), 50.

65. Schuyler, "Building of Pittsburgh," 218.

66. The 1927 amendment to the zoning code echoed Schuyler's argument for density, stating "It is reasonable to believe that for years to come the business of Pittsburgh will be constricted within the Golden Triangle, and to meet this situation some laxity is almost mandatory regarding height restrictions. Land within this section is so costly that every foot of it must be utilized to the last possible degree." "The Change in the Zoning Law—Being a Study of Tall Building Heights in Pittsburgh," *Charette* 7, no. 9 (September 1927), 11–12.

67. Diane Agrest, "Architectural Anagrams: The Symbolic Performance of Skyscrapers," in *Architecture from Without: Theoretical Framings for a Critical Practice* (Cambridge, Mass.: MIT Press, 1991), 83, 88–91. See also Attoe, *Skylines,* 108.

68. The Keenan Building specifically emulated the World Building (1890) in New York, and the Spreckels-Call Building (1896) in San Francisco. See Grash, "Commercial Skyscrapers of Pittsburgh," 153.

69. Schuyler, "Building of Pittsburgh," 218; Kidney, *Pittsburgh's Landmark Architecture,* 232.

70. "New Skyscraper, Seventeen-Story Structure to be Erected on Seventh Street," *Pittsburgh Press,* March 24, 1907, 40.

71. See James D. Van Trump, "The Skyscraper Style in Pittsburgh: Deco Form and Ornament (1920–1940)," *Carnegie Magazine* 51, no. 5 (May 1977), 198–219.

72. The Grant Building explicitly—if somewhat dubiously—commemorated Major James Grant. A promotional flyer for the building stated that Grant "led the British Forces against the French and Indians on the site of the building," and remarked that Grant's "sterling qualities are typified by the first-class materials used in the construction of the Grant Building." It also asserted (and exaggerated) the building's primacy and centrality. See Walter C. Kidney, *Henry Hornbostel: An Architect's Master Touch* (Pittsburgh: Pittsburgh History and Landmarks Foundation, 2002), 168.

73. Toker, *Pittsburgh,* 77.

74. Since both the Koppers Corporation and Gulf Oil were controlled by Mellon family interests, E. P. Mellon was the associate architect for both buildings.

75. The Gulf Building has close stylistic parallels with Trowbridge and Livingston's Bankers' Trust Building (1914) in New York, and with Graham, Anderson, Probst, and White's S. W. Straus and Company Building (1924) in Chicago.

76. See Dietrich Neumann, *Architecture of the Night: The Illuminated Building* (New York: Prestel, 2002).

77. Rem Koolhaas, *Delirious New York: A Retroactive Manifesto for Manhattan* (New York: Oxford University Press, 1978), 77. This was also the time of the celebrated Christopher Columbus Monumental Lighthouse Competition (1928–1930) for Santo Domingo, Dominican Republic. A. Marshall Bell and Edward B. Lee (1930) and Robert Moses (1939) each proposed tall illuminated "lighthouses" at Pittsburgh's Point.

78. The Grant Building beacon outclassed the Lindbergh-tribute beacon at the top of the Palmolive Building in Chicago. For a detailed description of the beacon and its accompanying directional projector see "Grant Building, Pittsburgh, Pa.," *Architecture and Building* 61 (April 1929), 131.

79. Charles F. Danver, "Pittsburghesque: The Lights of the Skyscraper Roof," *Pittsburgh Post-Gazette,* May 10, 1930, 6.

80. The weather signals are: steady orange = fair and rising temperatures; flashing orange = fair and falling temperatures; steady blue = rain or snow and rising temperatures; flashing blue = rain or snow and falling temperatures. In 2001 the Gulf Tower's lighting began to signal home runs and wins for the Pittsburgh Pirates baseball team, to capitalize on the building's visibility from the new PNC Park.

81. Agrest, "Architectural Anagrams," 89; Horsbrugh, *Pittsburgh Perceived*, 112.

82. Koolhaas, *Delirious New York,* 130; Montgomery Schuyler, "The Sky-line of New York, 1881–1897," *Harper's Weekly,* March 20, 1897, 295.

83. James D. Van Trump and Arthur P. Ziegler Jr., *Landmark Architecture of Allegheny County, Pennsylvania* (Pittsburgh: Pittsburgh History and Landmarks Foundation, 1967), 56.

84. Pittsburgh's current downtown plan promotes skyscrapers with "distinctively designed tops which serve as identifying features and contribute to the high quality of the city skyline." *The Pittsburgh Downtown Plan: A Blueprint for the 21st Century: Urban Design Guidelines* (Pittsburgh: Department of City Planning, 1998), n.p.

85. The following toast was made to W. J. Strassburger at the beacon's dedication dinner: "A TOAST to our city of Iron and Steel. / A City of animation. / And here's to the Nymph to whom we kneel. / The Goddess of Aviation. / Here's to the pilot alone on his flight. / Winging across the Nation. / Here's to the Beacon that guides him right. / Safe to his destination. / So here's to the man that placed the light. / A true and loyal Pittsburgher. / And pays for the juice night after night. / W. J. Strassburger." From "World's Largest Air Beacon," *Greater Pittsburgh,* March 23, 1929, 5.

86. Adnan Morshed, "A Tale of Two Symbols," *Thresholds* 23 (Fall 2001), 8. The unified power of these two modernist symbols was initially challenged by the Hindenburg disaster of 1937, which dashed hopes for a city of flying machines; and was perhaps extinguished by the terrorist attack on New York's World Trade Center using airplanes on September 11, 2001 (6–10).

87. Agrest, "Architectural Anagrams," 91.

88. Gulf's 360-degree view has been captured in Douglas Cooper's panoramic drawing *Turning Gulf* (2000), located in the Gulf Tower offices of Urban Design Associates.

89. Charles Waldheim, "Aerial Representation and the Recovery of Landscape," in *Recovering Landscape: Essays in Contemporary Landscape Architecture,* ed. James Corner (New York: Princeton Architectural Press, 1999), 122.

90. Henry Hornbostel, "Your County Parks Today and Tomorrow," in *Labor Day Program: Fourth Annual Allegheny County Fair* (Board of County Commissioners, 1936), 9–10. Architect Henry Hornbostel had taken Depression-era employment as director of the Allegheny County Department of Parks and Aviation. Horn-

bostel proposed developing airport land as parkland with shelters, camps, dance pavilions, and lodges to accommodate the public interest.

91. Raymond M. Marlier, "Architecture and Aeronautics," *Charette* 7, no. 8 (August 1927), 1, 7.

92. Le Corbusier, *The Four Routes* (London: D. Dobson, 1947), 97; *The City of To-morrow and Its Planning* (New York: Payson and Clarke, 1929), 280; Le Corbusier, *Aircraft* (London: The Studio Ltd.; New York: The Studio Publications, 1935), 11.

93. Le Corbusier, *Aircraft,* 12; Le Corbusier, *City of To-morrow and Its Planning,* 220.

94. Boyer, *City of Collective Memory,* 43.

95. Le Corbusier, *Four Routes,* 110.

96. See Boyer, *City of Collective Memory,* 46; Le Corbusier, *City of To-morrow and Its Planning.* Le Corbusier decried the competitive and promotional impulse of the skyline and the crowning of the skyscraper with what he called an academic cupola or stopper. "America," he exclaimed, "*bristles* with [skyscrapers]. Is it good, is it wise, to be *bristling* with anything? Is it beautiful to bristle?" *The Radiant City* (New York: Orion Press, 1967), 127–28.

97. Waldheim, "Aerial Representation," 121.

98. See Stefan Lorant, *Pittsburgh: The Story of an American City* (Garden City, N.Y.: Doubleday and Company, Inc., 1964), 364–65, 374–75.

99. Mitchell and Ritchey, *Pittsburgh in Progress* (Pittsburgh: Kaufmann's, 1947), n.p. The study was reported and acclaimed in "Pittsburgh in Progress: Towards a Master Plan," *Progressive Architecture [Pencil Points]* 28, no. 6 (June 1947), 14, 67–72.

100. See Richard Louis Cleary, "Edgar J. Kaufmann, Frank Lloyd Wright and the 'Pittsburgh Point Park Coney Island in Automobile Scale,'" *Journal of the Society of Architectural Historians* 52, no. 2 (June 1993), 139–58. Mitchell and Ritchey and its successor firms designed and realized a number of large-scale projects derived from *Pittsburgh in Progress,* including the Civic Arena (1947–1961) and Allegheny Center (1959–1967).

101. Mitchell and Ritchey, *Pittsburgh in Progress,* n.p. The Pittsburgh Survey was a study of life and labor in the Pittsburgh area that documented "an exploited labor force, a degraded physical environment, and corrupt civic institutions." See Maurine W. Greenwald and Margo Anderson, eds., *Pittsburgh Surveyed: Social Science and Social Reform in the Early Twentieth Century* (Pittsburgh: University of Pittsburgh Press, 1996), 1.

102. Mitchell and Ritchey, *Pittsburgh in Progress,* n.p.

103. Many of Margaret Bourke-White's photographs were published in the photographic essay: "Mellon's Miracle: The Head of Pittsburgh's First Family Leads His City into a Renaissance," *Life* 40, no. 20 (May 14, 1956), 151–59.

104. Caroline Constant, "From the Virgilian Dream to Chandigarh: Le Corbusier and the Modern Landscape," in *Denatured Visions: Landscape and Culture in the Twentieth Century,* ed. Stuart Wrede and William Howard Adams (New York: Museum of Modern Art, 1991), 80.

105. Mitchell and Ritchey, *Pittsburgh in Progress,* n.p.

106. Griswold, "From Fort Pitt to Point Park," 195–97.

107. Like many urban renewal projects, Gateway Center precipitated some displacement of building occupants. See Rachel Balliet Colker, "Gaining Gateway Center: Eminent Domain, Redevelopment, and Resistance," *Pittsburgh History* 78, no. 3 (1995), 134–44.

108. *Pittsburgh Post-Gazette,* ca. Sept. 15, 1952, quoted in Robert C. Alberts, *The Shaping of the Point: Pittsburgh's Renaissance Park* (Pittsburgh: University of Pittsburgh Press, 1980), 127.

109. Griswold, "From Fort Pitt to Point Park," 200.

110. Even the park's principles of natural and historical reconstruction and evocation are modern principles.

111. See Alberts, *Shaping of the Point,* 154–62; Griswold, "From Fort Pitt to Point Park," 200.

112. Alberts, *Shaping of the Point,* 86. These buildings were first conceived as apartment buildings, but

the developers ultimately opted for office towers as better suited for the location. Architects Otto Eggers and Daniel Higgins, with Irwin Clavan, were brought to the project unusually late in the process, after many decisions—including the cruciform footprint—had already been made by the developers.

113. Together with subsequent buildings, the towers of Gateway Center introduced a new and lighter pallete of materials and colors to the city, replacing brick and stone with metals and concrete; and replacing reds, ochres, and dark grays with whites, blues, and light grays, and metallic silvers and gold. Kidney, "Pittsburgh: A Study in Urban Identity," 122.

114. Douglas Haskell, "Architecture: Stepchild or Fashioner of Cities?" *Architectural Forum* 99 (December 1953), 117. Later buildings at Gateway Center were built to different designs. Some were highly praised in the contemporary architectural press.

115. Designed by Clarke and Rapuano, the landscape plan was, like the office towers, much criticized. It was described as "stiffly traditional" and "weak Versaillaise." See "Office Towers in a Park," *Architectural Forum* 99, no. 6 (December 1953), 114; Haskell, "Architecture: Stepchild or Fashioner of Cities?" 117. In contrast, Simonds and Simonds designed an exemplary modern garden for a later phase of Gateway Center. See John O. Simonds, "Equitable Plaza, Pittsburgh," *Landscape Architecture* 53, no. 1 (October 1962), 19–20.

116. "Office Towers in a Park," 113.

117. Alberts, *Shaping of the Point*, 122. Mitchell Schwarzer observes that "from the sky . . . architecture becomes graphic and geographic." *Zoomscape: Architecture in Motion and Media* (New York: Princeton Architectural Press, 2004), 125.

118. The buildings are no closer than 80 feet at their corners, and all parallel exterior walls are at least 150 feet apart. No desk was to be more than 24 feet from a window. The windows are 6 feet tall. "Office Towers in a Park," 114–16.

119. Griswold, "From Fort Pitt to Point Park," 200.

120. Alberts, *Shaping of the Point*, 8.

121. Paul Shepheard, *The Cultivated Wilderness, or, What is Landscape?* (Cambridge, Mass.: MIT Press, 1997), 168–70.

122. Mitchell and Ritchey were associated architects for the Alcoa Building.

123. See "Two New Skyscrapers of Smart, Clean Design Will Flank a New Mid-City Park," *Architectural Forum* 91, no. 5 (November 1949), 66; Attoe, *Skylines*, 108, 37–38. Attoe notes that whole skylines can reflect a predominant local industry, e.g., insurance in Hartford and oil in Texas. Later buildings for U.S. Steel and PPG (Pittsburgh Plate Glass) added to Pittsburgh's material skyline.

124. John Ormsbee Simonds wrote, "It was evident that the park space should function as a focal point for these and the existing structures which would surround it on four sides. It must relate structures and space into one harmonious unity. It must also serve, for each building seen from within the park, as an appropriate foreground." "Mellon Square: An Oasis in an Asphalt Desert," *Landscape Architecture* 48, no. 4 (July 1958), 211. The Alcoa Building includes a light, airy entrance pavilion at ground level that has been called a birdcage. It is a captured breath of air, and a transitional connection to the open space of the square.

125. Frederick Gutheim, "Projects Without Plans," *Architectural Forum* 106, no. 2 (February 1957), 150.

126. John Mauro, "Magnificent Square in the Golden Triangle," *Charette* 35, no. 12 (December 1955), 15.

127. Mitchell and Ritchey had recently completed *Pittsburgh in Progress*. John Ormsbee Simonds attended Harvard University, where landscape design was taught in terms of pattern and abstraction with an emphasis on plan geometry. See Anthony Alofsin, *The Struggle for Modernism: Architecture, Landscape Architecture, and City Planning at Harvard* (New York: W. W. Norton and Co., 2002), 168–69.

128. Rob Aben and Saskia de Wit, *The Enclosed Garden: History and Development of the Hortus Con-*

clusus and Its Reintroduction into the Present-Day Urban Landscape (Rotterdam: 010 Publishers, 1999), 129, 137.

129. One article described the cars in the parking garage below the square as "twentieth-century beetles burrowing under a twentieth-century garden," a metaphor derived from the viewpoint of the skyscraper. "An Open Place in the Heart of the City," *Architectural Record* 121, no. 2 (February 1957), 195.

130. Simonds, "Mellon Square," 211.

131. Ibid., 208, 212.

132. Aben and de Wit, *Enclosed Garden,* 22–26, 210.

133. Environmental Planning and Design, *Mellon Square Improvements* (Pittsburgh: Environmental Planning and Design, n.d.), 10.

134. Aben and de Wit, *Enclosed Garden,* 110, 37.

135. "Open Place in the Heart of the City," 195.

136. Gutheim, "Projects Without Plans," 150.

137. "New York Firm Suggests Model Plan for Pittsburg," *Pittsburg Leader,* September 27, 1908.

138. *American Architect and Building News* 91, no. 1635 (April 27, 1907), 153; 91, no. 1637 (May 11, 1907), 190.

139. Shepheard, *Cultivated Wilderness,* 162–92.

140. Van Trump, "Skyscraper Style in Pittsburgh," 198. In Greek and Roman myth, some of the giant one-eyed Cyclopes were assistants to Vulcan, god of fire and blacksmith to the gods. Agrest says that "skyscrapers are in effect columns supporting the sky." See "Architectural Anagrams," 82. The steel spike metaphor appears in John Morris Dixon, "Big Steel Spike: U.S. Steel Building," *Architectural Forum* 135, no. 5 (December 1971), 24–29.

141. Leon Battista Alberti, *Della pittura* (1435), quoted in Scully, *Architecture: The Natural and the Manmade,* 184.

142. U.S. Steel, *The Steel Triangle in the Golden Triangle* (Pittsburgh: United States Steel, 1970).

143. Raymond Hood was New York's premier skyscraper architect of the time. In 1929 he proposed a series of mountain-like skyscrapers to be spread across Manhattan like a discontinuous mountain range. In the same year, Hugh Ferriss, an influential image-maker for the skyscraper, prefaced his *Metropolis of Tomorrow* with a drawing entitled *Buildings Like Mountains*; and the setback skyscrapers shown in other drawings explicitly recalled mountain-form Mayan temples. See Raymond Hood, "Three Visions of New York: Raymond Hood," *Creative Art* 9, no. 2 (August 1931), 160–61; Hugh Ferriss, *Metropolis of Tomorrow* (New York: I. Washburn, 1929); Koolhaas, *Delirious New York,* 174–77; Scully, *Architecture: The Natural and the Manmade,* 3–4, 16–18; and Morrish, *Civilizing Terrains,* drawing 29. Curiously, Hood had worked for Henry Hornbostel in 1907, when Hornbostel proposed his addition to the Allegheny County Courthouse and embarked on an expedition to explore the ancient Mayan ruins of the Yucatan. See Francis S. Swales, "Master Draftsmen: XVII Henry Hornbostel," *Pencil Points* 8, no. 2 (February 1926), 78, 83.

144. Kenneth Frampton, "*Megaforma Come Paesaggio Urbano* / Megaform as Urban Landscape," *Ottagono* 37, no. 153 (September 2002), 79. Frampton begins with architecture, not with the land; otherwise, his concept of the "megaform" is not far removed from Morrish's "site."

145. This tendency is now affirmed by the current Pittsburgh Urban Zoning Code (1999), which enforces lower building heights along the Golden Triangle's river frontages. Kevin J. Patrick makes the case that Pittsburgh's physical and economic development can be modeled as a series of concentric triangles. "Pittsburgh as a Concentric Triangle," in Patrick and Scarpaci, *Geographic Perspective of Pittsburgh,* 62–70.

146. Rafael Viñoly, "Rafael Viñoly Architects," http://www.rvapc.com (accessed 2002; Web site content now changed).

147. Conversely, Bruce Lindsey suggests that it is the Y of the river valleys (negative space) rather than the Golden Triangle (positive space) that lingers in memory. "Topographic Memory," 48.

148. Kostof, *City Shaped,* 283.

149. Ibid., 284. Spectators entering Pittsburgh from the airport by car pass through Mount Washington, via the Fort Pitt Tunnel, and exit onto an elevated bridge. The bridge crosses the Monongahela River and connects directly to the Golden Triangle. The exit portal of the tunnel yields a stunning view of the city that is much remarked by visitors and locals alike, but it is fleeting and difficult to capture. See Paul Goldberger, "A Tempered Skyline Strengthens a City of Steel," *New York Times,* January 3, 1988, H28.

150. See Joseph Warin, "Plan of the Town of Pittsburg," 1826. Engraving by Antoine Francois Tardieu. Catherine R. Miller Collection, Chatham College.

151. For the story of two early panoramic lithographs of the city—both depicting the view from Mount Washington—see Rina C. Youngner, "A Tale of Two City Views," *Pittsburgh History* 76, no. 2 (Summer 1993), 92–96. In 2003, *USA Weekend* magazine named the nighttime view of Pittsburgh from Mount Washington as the second most beautiful place in America. "The 10 Most Beautiful Places in America," *USA Weekend,* May 18, 2003.

152. Peter B. Hales, *Silver Cities: The Photography of American Urbanization, 1839–1915* (Philadelphia: Temple University Press, 1984), 70.

153. James D. Van Trump, "An Antiphon of Stones: Some Random Native Notes to a Visiting Architectural Critic in Pittsburgh," *Charette* 43, no. 7 (July 1963), 11.

154. See Griswold, Winters, and Swain, *Mount Washington, Duquesne Heights, Pittsburgh, Pennsylvania: A Study for the Department of Parks and Recreation* (Pittsburgh: Griswold, Winters, and Swain, 1970).

Scenes from the Turtle Creek Valley

1. For the patterns of industrial development in the Pittsburgh region see Kenneth Warren, *The American Steel Industry, 1850–1970: A Geographical Interpretation* (Oxford: Clarendon Press, 1973), 134–38; Edward K. Muller, "Industrial Suburbs and the Growth of Metropolitan Pittsburgh, 1870–1920," *Journal of Historical Geography* 27, no. 1 (2001), 58–73.

2. Edward K. Muller, "Pittsburgh's Many Landscapes," *Western Pennsylvania History* 85, no. 1 (Spring 2002), 20; Greenwald and Anderson, *Pittsburgh Surveyed.*

3. Williard Glazier, "The Great Furnace of America," in *Peculiarities of American Cities* (Philadelphia: Hubbard Brothers, 1883), 332.

4. "The A. H. Gorson Memorial Show at Gillespie's," *Pittsburgh Post-Gazette,* March 19, 1934, 17; Rina Youngner, *The Power and the Glory: Pittsburgh Landscapes by Aaron Harry Gorson, 1872–1933* (New York: Spanierman Gallery, 1989), n.p.; Aaron Gorson, quoted in David G. Wilkins, *Paintings and Sculpture of the Duquesne Club* (Pittsburgh: Duquesne Club, 1986), 55. Gorson's Pittsburgh paintings were sometimes compared to the work of James McNeill Whistler and John Singer Sargent.

5. David E. Nye, *American Technological Sublime* (Cambridge, Mass.: MIT Press, 1994), xvi, 15; Leo Marx, *The Machine in the Garden: Technology and the Pastoral Ideal in America* (New York: Oxford University Press, 1964), 195.

6. John R. Stilgoe discusses an industrial aesthetic derived from the dynamic forms and atmosphere of the industrial landscape. See *Metropolitan Corridor: Railroads and the American Scene* (New Haven: Yale University Press, 1983), 73–103.

7. See Muller and Tarr, "Interaction of Natural and Built Environments," 22–23.

8. Muller, "Industrial Suburbs and the Growth of Metropolitan Pittsburgh," 62.

9. Nye, *American Technological Sublime,* 126, 55.

10. Ibid., 86.

11. Ibid., xiii–xiv.

12. See, for example, *The Illustrated Guide and Handbook of Pittsburgh and Allegheny, Describing and Locating the Principal Places of Interest in and about the*

Two Cities . . . (Pittsburgh: Fisher and Stewart, 1887), 31–86.

13. Parton, "Pittsburg," 21. Laurie Graham's book in praise of industrial Pittsburgh includes a chapter on the sublime. Laurie Graham, *Singing the City: The Bonds of Home in an Industrial Landscape* (Pittsburgh: University of Pittsburgh Press, 1998), 154–66.

14. George Washington reportedly boarded with Frazier on trips through the region.

15. Hugh P. Meese, "Survey of Industrial Braddock," in *The Unwritten History of Braddock's Field,* ed. George Harris Lamb (Pittsburgh: Nicholson Printing Co., 1917), 84.

16. Meese, "Survey of Industrial Braddock," 84.

17. See Joseph Pennell, *Joseph Pennell's Pictures of the Wonders of Work: Reproductions of a Series of Drawings, Etchings, Lithographs, Made by Him Around the World, 1881–1915* (Philadelphia: J. B. Lippincott Company, 1916), XII. Pennell's Pittsburgh-area etchings were part of his worldwide Wonders of Work series.

18. Meese, "Survey of Industrial Braddock," 121. The dam was rebuilt at a slightly different location in 1906, and again in 2004.

19. Ken Kobus and Jack Consoli, *The Pennsy in the Steel City: 150 Years of the Pennsylvania Railroad in Pittsburgh* (Upper Darby: Pennsylvania Railroad Technical and Historical Society, 1996), 4; Citizens Committee on the City Plan of Pittsburgh, *Railroads—A Part of the Pittsburgh Plan* (Pittsburgh: Citizens Committee, 1923), 41.

20. Carnegie had served for a time as superintendent of the Pennsylvania Railroad's western division.

21. Dan Cupper, *Crossroads of Commerce: The Pennsylvania Railroad Calendar Art of Grif Teller* (Mechanicsburg, Pa.: Stackpole Books, 2003), 82.

22. Aymar Embury II, "Impressions of Three Cities: Pittsburgh," *Architecture* 31, no. 4 (April 1915), 105.

23. Thomas Bell, *Out of This Furnace* (Boston: Little, Brown and Co., 1941), 122.

24. Joel Sabadasz, "The Mon Valley: Discovering the Genesis of the Modern American Steel Industry," *Cultural Resource Management* 16, no. 3 (1993), 27.

25. John N. Ingham, *Making Iron and Steel: Independent Mills in Pittsburgh, 1820–1920* (Columbus: Ohio State University Press, 1991), 48.

26. Jeanne McHugh, *Alexander Holley and the Makers of Steel* (Baltimore: The Johns Hopkins University Press, 1980), 253.

27. Sabadasz, "The Mon Valley," 27.

28. See Mark M. Brown, "The Architecture of Steel: Site Planning and Building Type in the Nineteenth-Century American Bessemer Steel Industry" (PhD diss., University of Pittsburgh, 1995), 85–90.

29. Stilgoe, *Metropolitan Corridor,* 81; Ingham, *Making Iron and Steel,* 48.

30. A blast furnace emitted flames from the top when it was charged with fuel, prior to the invention of the double-bell-and-hopper top mechanism. A pour of molten iron lights up the cast house. But the actual smelting of the iron is internal and essentially invisible.

31. For grain elevators see Lisa Mahar-Keplinger, *Grain Elevators* (New York: Princeton Architectural Press, 1993). Photographers Bernd and Hilla Becher observe: "The blast furnace's distinctive appearance makes it both the symbol of the steel industry and the landmark of certain steel-producing regions. The cityscapes of Pittsburgh, Birmingham, Charleroi, Longwy, and Duisburg are dominated by their blast furnace structures just as are medieval cities by their ecclesiastical buildings." *Blast Furnaces* (Cambridge, Mass.: MIT Press, 1990), 15.

32. See Le Corbusier, *Towards a New Architecture* (London: J. Rodker, 1931), 21–31; and Reyner Banham, *A Concrete Atlantis: U.S. Industrial Building and European Modern Architecture, 1900–1925* (Cambridge, Mass.: MIT Press, 1986). A few artists from outside of Pittsburgh found compelling qualities in the steel mills and their machines. Noted precisionist artist Charles Sheel-

er completed a series of paintings based on photographs taken at a U.S. Steel plant in Pittsburgh, most notably *Ore Into Iron* (1953). See Carol Troyen and Erica E. Hirshler, *Charles Sheeler: Paintings and Drawings* (Boston: Little, Brown, 1987), 204. Joseph Stella and the precisionists Elsie Driggs and Louis Lozowick also painted Pittsburgh mills and blast furnaces.

33. The Bechers suggest that unlike other large industrial structures that might display some degree of aesthetic treatment, the blast furnace is all about function. Thus the blast furnace has not been broadly accepted as an architectonic structure, and "has not established itself as a generic form in human consciousness." *Blast Furnaces,* 15.

34. The Bechers write: "The blast furnace is like a body without skin. Its insides are visible from the outside; organs, arteries, and skeleton create its form." *Blast Furnaces,* 15.

35. Edgar Thomson was always more of a name than a presence. Carnegie was heavily involved in the mill's affairs in the early years, but his residency in New York and his union-busting ways made him a largely absent adversary for the steelworkers. For Carnegie and his complex relationship with the Edgar Thomson Works and Braddock, see Paul L. Krause, "Patronage and Philanthropy in Industrial America: Andrew Carnegie and the Free Library in Braddock, Pa.," *Western Pennsylvania Historical Magazine* 71, no. 2 (April 1988), 127–45.

36. Owen Francis, "The Saga of Joe Magarac: Steelman," *Scribner's* 90, no. 5 (November 1931), 505–11; Janet Marstine, "William Gropper's 'Joe Magarac' Icon of American Industry," in *The Gimbel Pennsylvania Art Collection: From the Collection of the University of Pittsburgh* (Greensburg: Westmoreland Museum of Art, 1986), n.p. In about 1950, sculptor Frank Vittor proposed the erection of a one-hundred-foot stainless steel statue of Magarac—a true colossus—at Pittsburgh's Point. See Kidney, *Pittsburgh's Landmark Architecture,* 146–47. For the story of an actual colossus born of the American iron and steel industry, see Matthew A. Kierstead, "Vulcan: Birmingham's Industrial Colossus," *IA: The Journal of the Society for Industrial Archeology* 28, no. 1 (2002), 59–74.

37. See Barry Brummett, *Rhetoric of Machine Aesthetics* (Westport, Conn.: Praeger, 1999), 43–47; and Steven Slavishak, "Bodies of Work: Industrial Workers' Bodies in Pittsburgh, 1880–1915" (PhD diss., The University of North Carolina at Chapel Hill, 2002), 5, 160–65. The imagery of industrial workers' bodies assumed both heroic and non-heroic forms.

38. James McIntyre Camp and C. B. Farnacis, *The Making, Shaping and Treating of Steel,* 4th ed. (Pittsburgh: Carnegie Steel Company, 1925), 191.

39. James Oppenheim, *The Olympian: A Story of the City* (New York: Harper and Brothers, 1912), 359; Graham, *Singing the City,* 40, 159. Graham describes her own arousal in an imaginary encounter with molten steel.

40. Graham, *Singing the City,* 159–60.

41. Otto Kuhler, *My Iron Journey: An Autobiography of a Life With Steam and Steel* (Denver: Intermountain Chapter, National Railway Historical Society, 1967), 210.

42. *The Story of Pittsburgh and Vicinity: Illustrated* (Pittsburgh: Pittsburgh Gazette Times, 1908), 213.

43. Betsy Hunter Bradley, *The Works: The Industrial Architecture of the United States* (New York: Oxford University Press, 1999), 38–39, 207–13. Bradley attributes the term "production shed" to Banham, *Concrete Atlantis,* 61.

44. See *Works of the Westinghouse Electric and Manufacturing Company: Their Industrial and Sociological Aspect* (Pittsburgh: The Company, 1904).

45. Bradley, *The Works,* 98–101, 146–47; *The Pittsburgh Electrical Hand-Book* (Pittsburgh: The American Institute of Electrical Engineers, 1904), 60.

46. Bradley, *The Works,* 98.

47. Lindy Biggs, *The Rational Factory: Architecture, Technology, and Work in America's Age of Mass Production* (Baltimore: The Johns Hopkins University Press,

1996), 2–3. Both Biggs and Bradley make reference to the master machine concept. Biggs attributes it to early twentieth-century trade literature.

48. Bradley, *The Works,* ix, 83.

49. Biggs, *Rational Factory,* 48. The industrial engineers were trained in business management and engineering at schools like Carnegie Tech in Pittsburgh (42).

50. The Westinghouse companies facilitated the electrification of key processes at the Edgar Thomson Works.

51. Nye, *American Technological Sublime,* 60.

52. As an entrepreneur, Westinghouse founded sixty-one companies. *Scenes From a Great Life: George Westinghouse Centennial, 1846–1946* (Westinghouse Electric Corporation, 1945), n.p. George Westinghouse lost control of the Westinghouse East Pittsburgh Works in 1907, and died in 1914, but he continued to loom large.

53. Though primarily implemented in prisons, the panopticon was devised with an eye toward industrial applications. For a brief discussion of the panopticon in an industrial context see Gillian Darley, *Factory* (London: Reaktion, 2003), 48, 52–54, 95.

54. See Brian Butko, *Pennsylvania Traveler's Guide: The Lincoln Highway* (Mechanicsburg, Pa.: Stackpole Books, 1996).

55. V. R. Covell, "Concrete Bridge Makes New Record," *Scientific American* 147, no. 5 (November 1932), 276. Covell stated that the overall project resembled "first-class railroad construction" in its complex manipulation of the terrain through cuts, embankments, and the bridging of the landscape.

56. George S. Richardson, "The Design of Concrete Arches in Allegheny County, Pennsylvania," *Journal of the American Concrete Institute* 3, no. 10 (June 1932), 638.

57. John E. Sweetman, *The Artist and the Bridge* (Brookfield, Vt.: Ashgate, 1999), 1; Kidney, *Pittsburgh's Bridges,* 10. Grif Teller painted several potential calendar views of trains in the Turtle Creek Valley passing beneath the Westinghouse Bridge in which he responded to the inherent pictorial qualities of the topography and the bridge. None of these views were accepted for the PRR calendars, however—perhaps because they incorporated a highway bridge that was emblematic of a competing system of transportation. See Cupper, *Crossroads of Commerce,* 68, 110, 151, 152.

58. "Remarks by Mr. A. W. Robertson" on the dedication of the George Westinghouse Bridge, September 10, 1932, quoted in Eugene Levy, "High Bridge, Low Bridge," *Places* 8, no. 4 (Summer 1993), 13.

59. "Building America's Longest Concrete-Arch Bridge," *Engineering News Record* 109, no. 3 (July 21, 1932), 67.

60. Curiously, Vittor had aspirations to execute a true sculptural colossus. See previous note on Joe Magarac; see also Vernon Gay and Marilyn Evert, *Discovering Pittsburgh's Sculpture* (Pittsburgh: University of Pittsburgh Press, 1983), 182–83.

61. Levy, "High Bridge, Low Bridge," 14, 18. For scenes of industrial life in the valley see David Demarest and Eugene Levy, "Visualizing the Industrial Landscape: The Photographers of Pittsburgh's Westinghouse Air Brake Company, 1900–1960," *Pittsburgh History* 77, no. 1 (1994), 4–21.

62. Boyer, *City of Collective Memory,* 41; Stilgoe, *Metropolitan Corridor,* 252; Schwarzer, *Zoomscape,* 32.

63. Wolfgang Schivelbusch, *The Railway Journey: The Industrialization of Space and Time in the 19th Century* (Berkeley: University of California Press, 1986), 53–57. See also Stilgoe, *Metropolitan Corridor,* 249–57.

64. H. L. Mencken composed a famous anti-appreciation of the Pittsburgh region upon riding through the Turtle Creek Valley from west to east, but he mainly shared his impressions of more outlying locales. See H. L. Mencken, "The Libido for the Ugly," in *Prejudices: Sixth Series* (New York: A. A. Knopf, 1927), 187–93. Some of Mencken's observations have been identified as true prejudices. See John W. Larner, "'The Libido for the

Ugly': H. L. Mencken versus Western Pennsylvania," *Western Pennsylvania Historical Magazine* 71, no. 1 (January 1988), 84–94.

65. *Panorama Exterior Westinghouse Works* (American Mutoscope and Biograph Company, 1904). This film can be viewed online at: Library of Congress, "American Memory: Inside an American Factory: Films of the Westinghouse Works, 1904," http://memory.loc.gov/ammem/papr/west/westhome .html. This film, and others showing the plant interiors and operations, represented Westinghouse interests at the Louisiana Purchase Exposition in St. Louis.

66. Schwarzer, *Zoomscape,* 58.

67. Douglas Cooper, *Steel Shadows: Murals and Drawings of Pittsburgh* (Pittsburgh: University of Pittsburgh Press, 2000), 4, 3.

68. Donald Appleyard, Kevin Lynch, and John R. Myer, *The View from the Road* (Cambridge, Mass.: MIT Press, 1964), 4; Sigfried Giedion, *Space, Time and Architecture: The Growth of a New Tradition* (Cambridge, Mass.: Harvard University Press, 1941), 554.

69. Levy, "High Bridge, Low Bridge," 13–14, 18–19.

70. Covell, "Concrete Bridge Makes New Record," 276.

71. Alternative space/time experiences of the Turtle Creek Valley have been obtainable from boats on the Monongahela River and from roller coasters and other rides at the Kennywood amusement park, a short distance upriver. At Kennywood, the culture of amusement adds another layer of disengagement from the industrial landscape.

72. Darley, *Factory,* 9. Steel towns and their residents may also be creatures of a specific time and place, and cinematic in scope and character. Noted independent filmmaker Tony Buba has filmed a number of documentary and feature films in the town of Braddock, including *The Braddock Chronicles* (1972–1985), *Voices from a Steeltown* (1983), and *Lighting Over Braddock: A Rustbowl Fantasy* (1988).

73. ET has two remaining blast furnace plants with one active blast furnace each. Steel is now made with the basic oxygen process and fabricated with a continuous caster installed in 1992.

74. The proposed Mon-Fayette Expressway may provide the motoring spectator with an additional space/time experience, and conclusively transform the Turtle Creek Valley into an automobile landscape.

Oakland and the Complex Vista

1. "A Growing City," *Pittsburgh Post,* May 9, 1890, 1; John F. Bauman and Edward K. Muller, *Before Renaissance: Planning in Pittsburgh, 1889–1943* (Pittsburgh: University of Pittsburgh Press, 2006), chap. 2.

2. Toker, *Pittsburgh,* 94–96.

3. Arthur Wilson Tarbell, *The Story of Carnegie Tech; Being a History of Carnegie Institute of Technology from 1900 to 1935* (Pittsburgh: Carnegie Institute of Technology, 1937), 129.

4. Paul Venable Turner, *Campus: An American Planning Tradition* (Cambridge, Mass.: MIT Press, 1984), 3–6.

5. Patricia C. Sherwood and Joseph Michael Lasala, "Education and Architecture, The Evolution of the University of Virginia's Academical Village," in *Thomas Jefferson's Academical Village: The Creation of an Architectural Masterpiece,* ed. Richard Guy Wilson (Charlottesville: University Press of Virginia, 1993), 10; Frederick D. Nichols and Ralph E. Griswold; *Thomas Jefferson, Landscape Architect* (Charlottesville: University of Virginia, 1978), 148.

6. Turner, *Campus,* 4; *The International Competition for the Phoebe A. Hearst Architectural Plan for the University of California* (San Francisco: Trustees of the Phoebe A. Hearst Architectural Plan, 1900), 8.

7. Joseph Frazier Wall, ed., *The Andrew Carnegie Reader* (Pittsburgh: University of Pittsburgh Press, 1992), 139–40.

8. Richard Guy Wilson, "Architecture, Landscape, and City Planning," in *The American Renaissance, 1876–1917* (Brooklyn: The Brooklyn Museum, 1979), 75.

9. For Hornbostel, see: Kidney, *Henry Hornbostel*; James D. Van Trump, "Henry Hornbostel (1867–1961): A Retrospective and a Tribute," *Charette* 42, no. 2 (February 1962), 16–17; and Swales, "Master Draftsmen: XVII Henry Hornbostel," 73–92. Charles Rosenblum is preparing a PhD dissertation on Hornbostel.

10. *The International Competition for the Phoebe A. Hearst Architectural Plan for the University of California*; Turner, 180–82. The staging of high-profile architectural competitions was itself a reflection of the Beaux-Arts method.

11. Swales, "Master Draftsmen: XVII Henry Hornbostel," 75.

12. Previous studies of Carnegie Tech include: James D. Van Trump and Barry Hannegan, "The Stones of Carnegie Tech: Of Temples and Technology: The Drama of Henry Hornbostel's Buildings at Carnegie Institute of Technology," *Charette* 38, no. 9 (September 1958), 23–27 and 38, no. 11 (November 1958), 26–29, 35, revised and reprinted as Barry Hannegan, "Henry Hornbostel and His Campus," *Carnegie Alumnus* 45, no. 3 (December 1959), 4–7; James D. Van Trump, "Technology's Temple," *Carnegie Alumnus* 45, no. 5 (April 1960), 2–7; James D. Van Trump, "Henry Hornbostel: The New Brutalism," *Charette* 46, no. 5 (May 1966), 8–11. See also Rives Trau Taylor, "The American College and Its Architecture: An Institutional Imperative" (master's thesis, MIT, 1988). See also Kidney, *Henry Hornbostel,* 70–109. Hornbostel designed another major Beaux-Arts campus on another topographically challenging site at Emory University in Atlanta in 1915–1916. See Clark V. Poling, *Henry Hornbostel, Michael Graves: An Exhibition of Architectural Drawings, Photographs and Models* (Atlanta: Emory University Museum of Art and Archaeology, 1985).

13. Jefferson's University of Virginia campus also influenced Hornbostel's University of California competition scheme.

14. The open egress was closed in 1898 with the construction of McKim, Mead, and White's Cabell, Rouse, and Cocke Halls.

15. See "Beautifying the Campus," *Carnegie Alumnus* 11, no. 2 (December 1924), 15; "Beautifying the Campus," *Carnegie Alumnus* 11, no. 5 (May 1925), 9; and *Carnegie Alumnus* 12, nos. 4–5 (May 1926), 11. Taylor and Hornbostel likely cooperated in this work, as they were concurrently working together on the Warren G. Harding Memorial in Marion, Ohio.

16. Toker, *Pittsburgh,* 106.

17. Howard Saalman, "College of Fine Arts Building Description" (Department of Architecture, Carnegie Mellon University, photocopy), 4. The Villa Madama, though never fully completed, had become an important architectural touchstone. Hornbostel had visited while on grand tour. An early scheme for the School of Applied Design building had a three-bay entrance loggia that was directly derived from the villa. The building's executed scheme of a facade with five niches may have been derived from the villa's garden wall.

18. A 1912 magazine article discussed the problem of cloaking the power plant's chimney stack in a suitable manner. "An Interesting Chimney Problem," *Architecture and Building* (August 1912), 345–46. In the course of the design process, the tower evolved from a cone to a slender cylinder to a thick cylinder on an octagonal drum.

19. For Ledoux see Anthony Vidler, *Claude-Nicolas Ledoux: Architecture and Social Reform at the End of the Ancien Régime* (Cambridge, Mass.: MIT Press, 1990). A specific source for Hornbostel's tower may be Ledoux's Barriére [toll house] de Reuilly (1786) outside Paris. See Michel Gallet, *Claude-Nicolas Ledoux 1736–1806* (Paris: Picard, 1980), 185. Hornbostel claimed no knowledge of Ledoux, though he must have seen Ledoux's buildings around Paris. James D. Van Trump to Henry Hornbostel, July 15, 1957, annotated and returned on July 31, 1957, Pittsburgh History and Landmarks Foundation. Jefferson knew Ledoux's work, and may have been in-

fluenced by Etienne Louis Boullee, another prominent architect of the French Enlightenment, in his design for the Rotunda at the University of Virginia.

20. Tarbell, *Story of Carnegie Tech,* 141. Artists such as John Kane and Henry Koerner have also painted Machinery Hall and its tower. Architect Philip Johnson reportedly called it "the most beautiful smokestack in the world." David Lewis, "Designing the Carnegie Mellon Campus," *Carnegie Magazine* 59, no. 1 (January/February 1988), 16.

21. Carnegie Mellon's Roberts Hall (1993–1996) now partially obscures Machinery Hall's rear elevation and compromises its command of the landscape. See Raul A. Barreneche, "Campus Interloper: Carnegie Mellon's Newest Building Destroys the Formal Finesse of the University's Original Plan," *Architecture* 86, no. 6 (June 1997), 81.

22. The Beaux-Arts borrowed the terminology and concept of the *cour d'honneur* from the French *hôtel.* Pittsburgh never hosted a major exposition, but instead sponsored an ongoing local exposition near the Point beginning in 1889. The site was tightly constrained, and the grounds could little reflect City Beautiful planning principles. Yet Daniel H. Burnham, who had been the leading architect of the World's Columbian Exposition, designed some of the buildings. With ongoing exhibits, concerts, and amusements, the exposition buildings were the hub of Pittsburgh's social and cultural life for many years. Alberts, *Shaping of the Point,* 36–37. An even earlier exposition grounds occupied a site on the north shore of the Allegheny River from 1875 to 1883 in what was then the City of Allegheny.

23. Notes by Henry Hornbostel, n.d., Henry Hornbostel Collection, Carnegie Mellon University Architecture Archives.

24. Van Trump and Hannegan, "Stones of Carnegie Tech," *Charette* 38, no. 9, 24; *Charette* 38, no. 11, 29.

25. Andrew Carnegie, "Value of the World's Fair to the American People," *Engineering Magazine* 6, no. 4 (January 1894), 417–22. For Carnegie and the World's Columbian Exposition see Bauman and Muller, chap. 2.

26. "New Building for Bureau of Mines," *Tartan* 9, no. 28 (April 22, 1915), 2.

27. "The New Buildings," *Tartan* 6, no. 16 (February 1, 1912), 4.

28. Thomas Jefferson had a similar rationale in choosing different architectural styles for the pavilions along the Lawn at the University of Virginia.

29. Van Trump and Hannegan, "Stones of Carnegie Tech," *Charette* 38, no. 11, 27.

30. Ibid., 29. Van Trump adds that "Hornbostel's tower is more original than much contemporary exposition architecture, say the Tower of Jewels at the Panama-Pacific Exposition of 1915 in San Francisco."

31. Transcriptions of unidentified newspaper articles, Physical Plant Collection, Carnegie Mellon University Archives.

32. Richard Guy Wilson, "Jefferson's Lawn: Perceptions, Interpretations, Meanings," in *Thomas Jefferson's Academical Village,* 47.

33. Clemens Steenbergen and Wouter Reh, *Architecture and Landscape: The Design Experiment of the Great European Gardens and Landscapes* (New York: Prestel, 1996), 9.

34. Kostof, *City Shaped,* 222; Boyer, *City of Collective Memory,* 74.

35. Boyer, *City of Collective Memory,* 79; John White, *The Birth and Rebirth of Pictorial Space,* 2nd ed. (Boston: Boston Book and Art Shop, 1967).

36. See Hubert Damisch, "The Ideal City," in *The Renaissance from Brunelleschi to Michelangelo: The Representation of Architecture,* ed. Henry A. Millon and Vittorio Magnago Lampugnani (New York: Rizzoli, 1994), 538–39.

37. This phenomenon was exemplified by Sebastiano Serlio's Comic Stage Scenery and Tragic Stage Scenery as published in his sixteenth-century text *Tutte l'opere d'architettura et prospectiva.*

38. Catherine M. Howett, "Where the One-Eyed Man Is King: The Tyranny of Visual and Formalist Values in Evaluating Landscapes," in *Understanding Ordinary Landscapes*, ed. Paul Groth and Todd W. Bressi (New Haven: Yale University Press, 1997), 87.

39. Kostof, *City Shaped*, 263.

40. The width of the picture plane and its distance from the viewpoint are approximately equal, which is a normative relationship for one-point linear perspective. White, *Birth and Rebirth of Pictorial Space*, 194–95.

41. Ultimately the players assumed the respective positions of the five niches of the future School of Applied Design, foreshadowing that building's encyclopedic intent. "The Laying of the Design School Corner Stone," *Tartan* 6, no. 28 (May 2, 1912), 1, 6.

42. Van Trump and Hannegan, "Stones of Carnegie Tech," *Charette* 38, no. 9, 25.

43. Scully, *Architecture: The Natural and the Manmade*, 221.

44. Aben and de Wit, *Enclosed Garden*, 70.

45. See F. Hamilton Hazelhurst, *Gardens of Illusion: The Genius of André Le Nostre* (Nashville: Vanderbilt University Press, 1980); Allen S. Weiss, *Mirrors of Infinity: The French Formal Garden and 17th Century Metaphysics* (New York: Princeton Architectural Press, 1995).

46. When Robert Schmertz visited Hornbostel's retirement home in Connecticut, he reported, only partly in jest, that Hornbostel "insisted that we go on a personally conducted tour of his gardens. The approach to the *Grand Allee* or *Tapis Vert* is flanked by two outsized terra-cotta *vases de Nuit*. . . . The main axis of the garden terminates at a viewing point which overlooks a valley and on either side are the vegetable plots lush and orderly with every rutabaga in its proper place. Le Notre couldn't have done any better." Robert Schmertz, "Hornbostel Hits Eighty-One," *Charette* 28, no. 10 (October 1948), 6.

47. Jefferson also employed illusion at the University of Virginia. He spaced his pavilions farther and farther apart as they extend from east to west in order to make them appear equally spaced when seen from the Rotunda. Nichols and Griswold, *Thomas Jefferson, Landscape Architect*, 162.

48. This effect is strengthened by the building's current night-lighting scheme.

49. White, *Birth and Rebirth of Pictorial Space*, 191.

50. Steenbergen and Reh, *Architecture and Landscape*, 179.

51. "Carnegie Visits the Schools," *Tartan* 8, no.30 (May 7, 1914), 1, 3.

52. A persistent campus myth claims that the buildings were designed to be convertible into a factory, should the school fail. The south range has a very long sloping hallway that suggests the efficiencies of a factory, but would have been equally useful for students moving equipment from workshop to workshop.

53. These murals are by George W. Sotter. Murals at the opposite end of the hall by Arthur Watson Sparks depict the buildings of Carnegie Tech not as pristine classical monuments but as built objects in the throes of construction, enveloped in retaining walls, scaffolding, and machinery.

54. "Book of Views," *Bulletin of the Carnegie Institute of Technology* 14, no. 10 (June 1919), n.p.

55. Quoted in Walter L. Creese, *The Crowning of the American Landscape: Eight Great Spaces and Their Buildings* (Princeton: Princeton University Press, 1985), 37. For the moral and political implications of the iconography of heavenly bodies and atmospheric conditions, see Warnke, *Political Landscape*, 115–44.

56. Machinery Hall no longer serves as a power plant, and the drama that its smoke added to the campus is now lacking. The Bellefield Boiler Plant, which currently provides power to Carnegie Mellon and other Oakland institutions, stands nearby in Junction Hollow. It has two tall smokestacks, and its steam emissions sometimes waft onto campus. This facility plays a leading role in Michael Chabon's *Mysteries of Pittsburgh*, in

which it is known as the Cloud Factory.

57. A related building was Benjamin H. Latrobe's Philadelphia Waterworks Engine House (1799).

58. Van Trump and Hannegan, "Stones of Carnegie Tech," *Charette* 38, no. 9, 29; Toker aptly writes: "A viewer reads the [Carnegie Tech] campus simultaneously as Jefferson's academic village and as the rolling mills and blast furnaces of Carnegie Steel." *Pittsburgh,* 106.

59. Morrish, *Civilizing Terrains,* drawing 34.

60. Richard A. Etlin, *Symbolic Space: French Enlightenment Architecture and Its Legacy* (Chicago: University of Chicago Press, 1994), 113.

61. The mural paintings on the ceiling of the grand hall in the School of Applied Design include a depiction of the Temple of Vesta at Tivoli, and the proscenium curtain in the theater included an image of the Temple of Vesta at Rome.

62. Van Trump and Hannegan, "Stones of Carnegie Tech, *Charette* 38, no. 11, 29, 35. Van Trump notes that the tower motive "is also to be noted in the landscape background of French Classical painting from Poussin to Hubert Robert." This reading is supported by certain views of Machinery Hall from Schenley Park in which the building appears as if in a romantic Arcadian landscape reminiscent of, for example, Claude Lorrain's *Landscape with the Nymph Egeria Mourning Over Numa* (1669) (see fig. 114).

63. Weiss, *Mirrors of Infinity,* 39.

64. Van Trump and Hannegan, "Stones of Carnegie Tech," *Charette* 38, no. 11, 28.

65. See Anthony Lawlor, *The Temple in the House: Finding the Sacred in Everyday Architecture* (New York: G. P. Putnam's Sons, 1994), 15–47.

66. Kane takes some liberties in composing his urban landscape. An early Hornbostel scheme for Machinery Hall seemingly launched a bridge across the hollow to the Carnegie Institute and Oakland, literally extending the campus axis.

67. Alfred Morton Githens, "The Group Plan: I. A Theory of Composition; The Carnegie Technical Schools," *Brickbuilder* 15, no. 7 (July 1906), 135.

68. Scully, *American Architecture and Urbanism,* 57. For Jefferson's perceptions of the landscape around Charlottesville as a context for his buildings see Creese, *Crowning of the American Landscape,* 11–14. Richard Guy Wilson notes that in a famous 1856 engraving, Jefferson's Rotunda is exaggerated in size and itself becomes "a topographic feature competing with the nearby mountains." "Jefferson's Lawn," 49.

69. Toker, *Pittsburgh,* 106.

70. The sense of this is now somewhat diminished due to alterations of the terrain and dense building development.

71. The head house for the north range (Doherty Hall) was not built until 1949–1950, and the western end of the range was filled in by Wean Hall in 1968–1971. Thus only one of the north-range bridges was actually built; but Wean Hall includes a bridge-like link to the Hornbostel sections of the range. The bridges in Hornbostel's design were seemingly inspired by the so-called Bridge of Sighs at Richardson's Allegheny County Courthouse, a device that Hornbostel also borrowed for his 1907 proposal to expand the courthouse (see figs. 19 and 58).

72. This major commission was also won in competition. See Henry Hornbostel, "Rodef Shalom Synagogue, Pittsburg," *Architecture* 19, no. 1 (January 15, 1909), 2–3.

73. Hornbostel's scheme and other competition entries were published in *American Competitions,* vol. 2 (New York: E. Helburn, 1908), 40–64.

74. *Pittsburgh Leader,* October 18, 1908, quoted in Robert C. Alberts, *Pitt: The Story of the University of Pittsburgh, 1787–1987* (Pittsburgh: University of Pittsburgh Press, 1986), 60.

75. Samuel Black McCormick to Benjamin Thaw, April 14, 1908, University Archives, University of Pittsburgh. Hornbostel's competition drawings showed an underground moving platform for navigating the slope along the central axis of the group plan.

76. Like their counterpart at Carnegie Tech, the smokestacks were transformed by their architectural context. Here, noted the *Pittsburgh Post,* April 14, 1908, the smokestacks masqueraded as obelisks. Alberts, *Pitt,* 61.

77. This offset was seemingly dictated by the nature of the terrain at the Western University of Pennsylvania site, where a continuation of the Carnegie Tech axis would have prevented the implementation of bilateral symmetry.

78. Herron Hill is one of the highest points in Pittsburgh. A reservoir at the summit was a favorite excursion spot at the turn of the twentieth century. Here was a 360-degree panoramic view, "a cyclorama of the works of God and man." "On the Heights," *Pittsburgh Post,* May 19, 1890, 1.

79. Soldiers and Sailors Memorial Hall was yet another major Hornbostel commission won in competition. See *American Competitions,* vol. 1 (New York: W. Helburn, 1907), 1–6. It was modeled after the ancient Greek Mausoleum of Halicarnassus, but Hornbostel called it "Greek Architecture Done in the Roman style." Henry Hornbostel, "Architecture," in *Allegheny County: A Sesqui-Centennial Review, 1788–1938,* ed. George E. Kelly (Pittsburgh: Allegheny County Sesqui-Centennial Committee, 1938), 254.

80. "The City Beautiful," *Builder* (Pittsburgh) 28, no. 7 (November 1910), 13.

81. For the history of the development of Oakland and the influences of the World's Columbian Exposition see Bauman and Muller, *Before Renaissance,* chap. 2.

82. Schuyler, "Building of Pittsburgh," 229–43. Governmental civic centers were twice proposed for downtown Pittsburgh but were not built.

83. "Pittsburgh's Civic Center," *Builder* (Pittsburgh) 30, no. 6 (October 1912), 36. Additionally, the January 1912 issue of the *Builder* published a photograph of the center of Oakland captioned "Court of Honor." *Builder* 29, no. 9 (January 1912), supplement.

84. *Schenley Farms* (Pittsburgh: Schenley Farms Company), n.p; Franklin F. Nicola, quoted in "Oakland Civic District Nomination Report," (Historic Review Commission, City of Pittsburgh, photocopy), 20.

85. "New York Firm Suggests Model Plan for Pittsburg," *Pittsburg Leader,* September 27, 1908.

86. Oakland's documentary record includes references to the Athenian Acropolis, the sacred Greek mountain of Parnassus, and the Hellenistic city of Pergamon. But Hornbostel's sensibilities and urbanism were more of Rome than of Greece, and even the Acropolis Plan was as Roman as it was Greek. Toker refers to the upper part of Hornbostel's group plan for the Western University of Pennsylvania as "a full-scale reproduction of the Forum of Trajan in Rome." *Pittsburgh,* 93.

87. Murals that flanked the stage represented Greece, Assyria, and Egypt on the left, and the Byzantine, Pointed Gothic, and Renaissance periods on the right. A contemporary commentary states, "The selection of Rome for the center and largest panel is due not merely to its chronological position, but especially to its significance as forming the connecting link between ancient and modern art." The curtain and murals are now gone. "Design Theatre is Dedicated," *Tartan* 8, no. 29 (April 29, 1914), 3.

88. Students have built physical models of St. Peter's over this plan. All of this suggests a layer of analogy within the complex vista in which buildings and topographical features play specific Roman roles. In this scenario, the School of Applied Design signifies St. Peter's, and Machinery Hall signifies the cylindrical Hadrian's Tomb (Castel Sant'Angelo). Junction Hollow serves as the Tiber River. The Western University of Pennsylvania plays the role of the Villa Quirinale, built on Rome's highest hill, with a view back toward the Vatican.

89. McKim, Mead, and White and other architects had recently introduced a light Beaux-Arts palette into the predominantly dark-hued American city through the use of Roman brick and stone. See David Lowe,

Stanford White's New York (New York: Doubleday, 1992). Hornbostel's use of bands of polychrome terracotta ornamentation on his Carnegie Tech buildings specifically recalls McKim, Mead, and White's celebrated and controversial Madison Square Presbyterian Church (1903–1906), which combined buff brick surfaces and polychrome terra cotta ornamentation in a way that was unprecedented in American architecture. See Leland M. Roth, *McKim, Mead & White, Architects* (New York: Harper and Row, 1983), 276–77. The trim at Carnegie Tech may also reflect Hornbostel's lifelong love of colorful neckwear. Swales, "Master Draftsmen: XVII Henry Hornbostel," 73.

90. See Bente Lange, *The Colours of Rome* (Copenhagen: Danish Architectural Press and The Royal Danish Academy of Fine Arts, School of Architecture, 1995). This palette was reestablished in the late nineteenth century, when modern Rome took on the predominant ochre hues that Hornbostel knew and that endure today.

91. Edith Wharton, *Italian Villas and Their Gardens* (New York: The Century Co., 1904), 7. Wharton's book and Charles A. Platt's *Italian Gardens* (New York: Harper and Brothers, 1894) first introduced the Italian villa to a large American audience. Platt called for the revival of the Italian villa as a type and for its application to the often similar landscape of the United States (154). Poling reports that Hornbostel's choice of the Italian Renaissance style for buildings at Emory University "was prompted at least in part by his reaction to the natural landscape of the Atlanta region, which he felt had characteristics similar to Northern Italy." *Henry Hornbostel, Michael Graves,* 7.

92. Steenbergen and Reh, *Architecture and Landscape,* 43–45.

93. Ibid., 15.

94. William Mullen, "Roses for the Rotunda" *Modulus* 16 (1983), 36. The University of Virginia has often been compared to Cicero's villa of ancient Rome, and was equally shaped by Palladio's Renaissance-era villas. See Wilson, "Jefferson's Lawn," 68. Jefferson might well have called his campus the academical villa instead of the academical village.

95. Steenbergen and Reh, *Architecture and Landscape,* 35.

96. Nearly every villa had a view of the dome of St. Peter's, and such views were especially featured at the Villa Quirinale and the Villa dei Cavalieri. Paul van der Ree, Gerrit Smienk, and Clemens Steenbergen, *Italian Villas and Gardens: A corso di disegno* (Munich: Prestel, 1992), 88.

97. Steenbergen and Reh, *Architecture and Landscape,* 17, 88–91. In Rome, the bowl-shaped topographical space measures 2.5 kilometers east to west, 3 kilometers north to south, and 50 meters high. In Oakland, it measures approximately 0.85 mile (less than 1.5 kilometers) across, and 250–275 feet high. Similarly, in the Arno Valley of sixteenth-century Florence, Medici family villas were frequently sited with views of each other and a view of the town, the center of their power (18, 47).

98. In an analogous manner, Monticello and the University of Virginia were in eyeshot of each other, and Jefferson reportedly oversaw the construction of the University by telescope while at Monticello. Nichols and Griswold, *Thomas Jefferson, Landscape Architect,* 161–62.

99. Reyner Banham, "Marbled Perspectives," *New Society* 51, no. 907 (February 21, 1980), 400–401. Banham's point of departure was Thomas Cole's painting *The Architect's Dream* (fig. 149).

100. Hornbostel also displayed "a memorable personality [and] a gift for self-promotion." Carlton G. Ketchum, "Some Interesting Pittsburghers, 1911–14: Part Two," *Western Pennsylvania Historical Magazine* 65, no. 2 (April 1982), 103. Hornbostel's own Hell Gate Bridge (1907–1914) in New York City is immodestly included among the monuments of all time that are depicted in the didactic murals inside the School of Applied Design.

101. Embury, "Impressions of Three Cities: Pittsburgh," 107.

102. Of other architects who contributed to the civic center, the most notable is Benno Janssen (1874–1964). See Donald Miller, *The Architecture of Benno Janssen* (Pittsburgh: Donald Miller, 1997).

103. More Hornbostel projects were built in Oakland after World War I, including: an apartment building complex for Nicola, where both Nicola and Hornbostel became residents; a hotel; a theater; a club; and a house for Carnegie Tech's president Hamerschlag. These buildings were less monumental in form and siting.

104. Embury, "Impressions of Three Cities: Pittsburgh," 107–8. Perhaps the best view of the group plan would have been obtainable from the bridge that Hornbostel proposed at Carnegie Tech.

105. Toker, *Pittsburgh,* 83.

106. Alberts, *Pitt,* 85–92.

107. Thomas A. P. van Leeuwen, *The Skyward Trend of Thought: The Metaphysics of the American Skyscraper* (Cambridge, Mass.: MIT Press, 1988), 70.

108. John G. Bowman, *Inside the Cathedral* (Pittsburgh: University of Pittsburgh, 1925), 19.

109. John G. Bowman, *The Cathedral of Learning of the University of Pittsburgh* (Pittsburgh: Eddy Press Corp., 1925), 9.

110. Bowman, *Inside the Cathedral,* 30.

111. Alberts, *Pitt,* 105.

112. Many commentators have critiqued the Cathedral of Learning on both aesthetic and functional grounds. Le Corbusier, who ridiculed American skyscrapers in general, and their emblematic crests in particular, took special notice of the Cathedral of Learning, which he illustrated in *The Radiant City* paired with a medieval Gothic tower (Tour St. Jacques, Paris). The caption reads: "An American university (can you believe it?). What childishness!" See Le Corbusier, *Radiant City,* 129.

113. Mark M. Brown, *The Cathedral of Learning: Concept, Design, Construction* (Pittsburgh: University of Pittsburgh, 1987), 6–7.

114. Kane's painting was closely modeled after the *Pietà of Avignon* (ca. 1455). See Diana J. Strazdes, *American Paintings and Sculpture to 1945 in the Carnegie Museum of Art* (New York: Hudson Hills Press, 1992), 292–93.

115. *Life* magazine photographer George Silk used the Cathedral of Learning as a vantage point to shoot a famous photograph of nearby Forbes Field during the 1960 World Series between the New York Yankees and the Pittsburgh Pirates. See "The Bucs Heist Series and the Lid Blows Off," *Life* 49, no. 17 (October 24, 1960), 31–32.

116. See Wyatt Hibbs, "Charles Z. Klauder, FAIA, Architect, 1872–1938: His Office Practice and My University of Pittsburgh Experience, 1926–1935," 5, Charles Z. Klauder Collection, Carnegie Mellon University Architecture Archives.

117. Alberts, *Pitt,* 108.

118. Two other buildings in Oakland feature towers that purposefully top the terrain (if barely): the Presbyterian-University Hospital (1938), and Raymond Marlier's Western State Psychiatric Hospital (1942). This phenomenon is now obscured by newer buildings on the hills.

119. Japanese artist Hiroshige repeatedly depicted the omnipresent Mount Fuji in his work. Michal's work was exhibited at Pittsburgh's Carnegie Museum of Art in 1997 in *Pittsburgh Revealed: Photographs Since 1850.* De la Concha's work was exhibited at the same museum in 1999, and is now on permanent display in the University of Pittsburgh's Alumni Hall. See "Duane Michals: Sechs Ansichten «der Lern-Kathedrale» (Universität) von Pittsburgh, 1982," *Du* 2 (1983), 38–41; and Mark Francis, *Felix de la Concha* (Pittsburgh: Carnegie Museum of Art, 1999).

120. Remarkably, Hornbostel had proposed a twelve- to twenty-five-story skyscraper for Carnegie Tech between 1911 and 1916 (see fig. 118 for one itera-

tion). The tower, it was said, "will be [the] only one of its kind in any college." See "Plans Finished for Administration Building," *Tartan* 7, no. 22 (March 13, 1913), 4; "Future Extension Plans," *Tartan* 10, no. 2 (September 29, 1915), 3; "$250,000 for New Entrance," *Tartan* 10, no. 13 (December 15, 1915), 1, 8; "New Prospectus for Our Group," *Tartan* 10, no. 15 (January 12, 1916), 1, 6.

121. Howett, "Where the One-Eyed Man Is King," 86.

122. Weiss, *Mirrors of Infinity,* 62.

123. A more didactic version of this dynamic appears at the George Westinghouse Memorial in Schenley Park, a short distance from Carnegie Tech. Here, a freestanding sculptural figure by Daniel Chester French, entitled *The Spirit of American Youth,* gazes for inspiration at an exedra that depicts George Westinghouse and his industrial achievements. Hornbostel did the site planning and designed the exedra (1926–1930). See Gay and Evert, *Discovering Pittsburgh's Sculpture,* 193–95, 247–49.

124. See Banham, "Marbled Perspectives." A montage drawing from the Grant Building's promotional brochure suggests the full scope of Hornbostel's architectural ambition. It depicts Pittsburgh's Golden Triangle from the Point to Grant Street, with Hornbostel's Grant Building—greatly exaggerated in scale—as the central reference point, and all of Hornbostel's other major Pittsburgh-area commissions assembled and clustered at its base. Here they substitute for, and assume the guise of, the city. See W. J. Strassburger and Henry Hornbostel, *Grant Building* (Pittsburgh: Grant Building Incorporated, 1928), 3; and Kidney, *Henry Hornbostel,* 167.

125. Notable parallels to this scene and its archetypal elements in twentieth-century art and architecture include Giorgio de Chirico's *Piazza d'Italia* paintings (mid-1920s to early 1970s), and Aldo Rossi's Town Hall for Borgoricco (1983–1988).

Index